# CRITICAL READING IN HIGHER EDUCATION

p. 44

"students were asked to practice integrating quotations in a paragraph ... "

Select specific ~~quotes~~ statements from source that they agree or disagree with and say why.

What ? So What ? Now WHAT ?

Identify
&
Summarize
Key Parts
Of
Text

SCHOLARSHIP OF TEACHING AND LEARNING

*Editors*
Jennifer Meta Robinson
Whitney M. Schlegel
Mary Taylor Huber
Pat Hutchings

# CRITICAL READING IN HIGHER EDUCATION

## Academic Goals and Social Engagement

Karen Manarin, Miriam Carey,
Melanie Rathburn, and Glen Ryland

Foreword by Pat Hutchings

Indiana University Press

Bloomington and Indianapolis

This book is a publication of

Indiana University Press
Office of Scholarly Publishing
Herman B Wells Library 350
1320 East 10th Street
Bloomington, Indiana 47405 USA

iupress.indiana.edu

*Manufactured in the United States of America*

*Cataloging information is available from the Library of Congress*

ISBN 978-0-253-01883-0 (cloth)
ISBN 978-0-253-01892-2 (paperback)
ISBN 978-0-253-01898-4 (ebook)

1 2 3 4 5   20 19 18 17 16 15

# Contents

Foreword by Pat Hutchings     *vii*

Preface     *xi*

Acknowledgments     *xv*

Introduction     *1*

1  Different Courses, Common Concern     *15*

2  Can Students Read?     *29*

3  Critical Reading for Academic Purposes     *47*

4  Critical Reading for Social Engagement     *65*

5  So Now What?     *86*

Introduction to the Appendixes     *105*

Appendix 1: Rubrics and Worksheets     *107*

Appendix 2: Taxonomy of Absence Regarding Social Engagement     *121*

Appendix 3: Coda on Collaboration     *123*

Notes     *129*

Bibliography     *143*

Index     *155*

# Foreword

THIS BOOK OFFERS a pair of welcome gifts. The first, as promised by its title, is a sustained examination of the character of that mostly invisible, often taken for granted but essential capacity that the authors call "critical reading." As teachers who care about that capacity from quite different disciplinary perspectives, Karen Manarin (English), Miriam Carey (political science), Melanie Rathburn (biology), and Glen Ryland (history) have much to tell us about how higher education can improve our students' reading skills in ways that advance not only academic success but also the ability to engage with the social world in consequential ways. Their findings reflect the authors' in-depth exploration of these issues in their own classrooms at Mount Royal University as well as their journey through the wider research literature about reading and how we learn to do it well. What they bring us is, as they say, "good news, not-so-good news, and bad news," and a wonderfully detailed account of their own practices as teachers striving to foster effective reading in their students; reflections on how those practices have been changed by this study; and a plea, finally, for a radically more intentional, collaborative approach to the development of critical reading as a cornerstone of effective undergraduate liberal education.

The second gift, which follows from this collaborative vision, is a powerful model for undertaking the scholarship of teaching and learning. The work reported in this book began as part of a Mount Royal University campus program in which faculty were invited to work together on what Richard Gale (who directed the program in its early days) has described as "collaborative investigation and collective scholarship" (2008). The idea, as I understand it, was to create a space for individual faculty to explore questions they were individually passionate about but to do so in ways that led to shared insights and findings that are thus more likely to deliver on the scholarship of teaching and learning's promise to create new knowledge that others can build on. This vision, this possibility, has recently been championed by others as especially promising. In a session at the 2014 International Society for the Scholarship of Teaching and Learning (SOTL), for instance, Peter Felton, Arshad Ahmad, and Joelle Fanghanel argued for what they call "translational research in SOTL," work that is iterative and collaborative in ways that can make a difference beyond the individual classroom. In this they were building on conceptions of the scholarship of teaching and learning put forward by

Lee Shulman (2013) and, as noted earlier, by Richard Gale, among others. Indeed my co-authors, Mary Taylor Huber and Anthony Ciccone, and I write about the value of harnessing the practices of the scholarship of teaching and learning to larger, shared institutional goals (and it's hard to imagine a more important one than developing critical readers) in our 2011 volume, *The Scholarship of Teaching and Learning Reconsidered: Institutional Integration and Impact.* The Mount Royal authors deliver on this transformational vision as they move back and forth from the particulars of their own classrooms—visiting and revisiting and making sense of the extensive evidence they have gathered from their students—to uncovering the implications for higher education more broadly.

It is perhaps useful to back up a few steps here. *Critical Reading in Higher Education: Academic Goals and Social Engagement* represents several years of study and writing by Manarin and her co-authors, each teaching a foundational (first-year) course in the institution's then newly designed general education program. Manarin, coming from the field of English, focuses her work on a course called Critical Writing and Reading. Carey, with her background in political science, focuses on Communities and Societies. Rathbun, the biologist, gathers data in her course Controversies in Science. And the historian in the group, Ryland, explores students' practices as readers in Texts and Ideas—Genocide. Looking across these diverse course contexts, and drawing on work by scholars from a wide range of traditions, they identify common elements that comprise critical reading, including comprehension, analysis, interpretation, and evaluation. But, unsurprisingly, one circumstance that becomes clear early on in their work—one of the features that must have made their collaboration particularly irresistible, though perhaps challenging as well—is that reading does not look the same in their four fields. Thus, part of what these scholars are doing is exploring the impact of different disciplinary contexts on the learning and teaching of critical reading, which, as has been recognized in the case of critical thinking, does not really exist in the abstract. One must think or read *about* something.

In fact, the importance of context turns out to be a key theme throughout the volume, and not only around issues of disciplinary identity. Expert readers are different from novices in that they recognize that a newspaper article must be read differently from a poem; a scholarly scientific article from a personal essay. Some things must be read slowly; others can be gone through more glancingly. Some invite, even require, emotional engagement; some ask that the reader maintain a sense of distance. But readers are not born making these distinctions, and as teachers we must interrogate our own reading practices in order to make them visible and available to students. That's a huge step forward, and one we learn a lot about from Manarin, Carey, Rathburn, and Ryland, whose work can be seen in the tradition of what a group of faculty at Indiana University Bloomington has called "decoding the disciplines."

But here's the thing. While Manarin and her colleagues propose, illustrate, and analyze the evidence from a wide range of strategies designed to help students engage in critical reading in different contexts, they cast a cold eye on easy answers. They note, for example (this in a set of bullets at the end of chapter 2), that "students can be coached to display particular traits in writing about their reading." That is, reading behaviors can be improved with the right scaffolding and explicit prompts. But they come back in the next bullet to say, "Prompted levels of engagement did not remain when the prompts were removed." Even more, they tell us after analyzing hundreds of student reading logs and other artifacts, and tracing the development of critical reading over time in each of their courses, they found "no developmental pattern in reading over the semester despite our assumptions that we were helping students read critically." There was simply "no evidence that students had improved" in any of the categories of reading proficiency they explored. And, as they tell us in chapter 4, it is especially hard to get students to engage socially—to read not only the words but also (as they say, invoking Paulo Freire) "the world." Teaching students to read in sophisticated ways, to make meaning, is hard going, and this is a courageous book in facing up to just how challenging that task is.

It is this recognition that brings the authors, and us as readers, to the most powerful injunctions in the book, which are not about the need to use this or that particular strategy for teaching reading (although readers who are interested in strategies will find lots of them), but about a rethinking of what it will take to advance students' proficiency with the highly complex set of practices called critical reading. Their answer is that this work invites—nay, requires—joining forces as teachers and as scholars. Critical reading is not something that can be mastered in a single course; it requires an intentional, collaborative approach in which faculty work together based on shared understandings and goals. It requires an approach that is in this sense "across the curriculum" and thus engages faculty who have likely not thought of themselves as being in the business of teaching reading. This in turn takes an institutional commitment and support as well as hard work by individual faculty.

Finally, I would add that this vision requires the scholarship of teaching and learning—the kind of systematic, collaborative, and collective inquiry exemplified by these four faculty members. Without such work, it is hard to see how any ongoing improvement is possible. *Critical Reading in Higher Education: Academic Goals and Social Engagement* is thus not only an eye-opening, in-depth study of an important theme in higher education. It is also an invitation to faculty from all fields to be part of a larger conversation and community of inquiry into one of the most important practices of academic and social life—one that is critical to the purpose of higher education in ways that Manarin, Carey, Rathburn, and Ryland explore with both candor and passion.

PAT HUTCHINGS

# Preface

THIS BOOK ADDRESSES a significant issue in higher education: how students read critically. Indeed, it is hard to think of an area of concern shared by more faculty across the disciplines. Faculty are concerned that students are unable to read and comprehend material, that students are unprepared to read for academic purposes, and that students do not seem to be engaging with what they are reading to the detriment of social or civic participation. We believe many faculty members want their students to read differently. They want them to read material for their courses more deeply and more critically. However, critical reading is important beyond the academic context; it is crucial for an engaged, thoughtful, and resilient society. Critical reading is about more than academic or economic success. Developing critical reading skills, we argue, is about developing capabilities for interacting with an increasing complex world. It is about influencing intellectual, emotional, and moral development—a huge responsibility that all faculty members share.

Yet most investigations into reading at the postsecondary level focus on (1) specific groups, such as developmental classes, English as a Foreign Language learners, or students with various disabilities; (2) specific types of reading, usually literary or online; or (3) specific moments in tightly controlled experiments, often from linguistic or cognitive psychology perspectives. The insights are sometimes hard to translate into actions that instructors from various disciplines can take to try to improve student reading.

This book on critical reading is intended for undergraduate instructors from various disciplines who are frustrated that their students don't read, or more accurately, don't read the way they are expected to in undergraduate courses. The chapters are accessible to faculty members without a specialized background in linguistics, psychology, or literature. Indeed, the focus in this text is not on the reading of literary texts done in an English class; neither is it on developmental reading done in an upgrading class. The focus is on the types of reading done in many different undergraduate classes across the curricula—nonfictional texts in a variety of genres, from scholarly articles, to textbook chapters, to personal essays and newspaper editorials. We believe that faculty from different disciplines and institutions may find our discussion of reading behaviors in different first-year classes illuminating.

Given this audience, we have five objectives: (1) We want to share information grounded in recent research about reading processes and intellectual development. This research comes from different disciplinary perspectives, from neuropsychology through composition studies, because reading is too important to focus on through one lens. (2) We want to describe how our students read, hoping that in these descriptions other instructors will find elements that they recognize. (3) We want to offer suggestions for how to improve reading in many classes, not just those devoted to skill improvement, because we believe that reading should, and can, be taught across the undergraduate curriculum. (4) We want to encourage instructors to grapple with the bigger questions about critical reading in higher education, questions that circle around the purpose of an undergraduate education. (5) We want to create a conversation about critical reading among instructors across the disciplines. Specifically, we want to move beyond complaints about what students can't do, to consider what might be possible, and to address what we would have to do collectively to make it happen. We situate this book in two theoretical strands: critical reading for academic purposes coming out of a liberal-humanist tradition and critical reading for social engagement with its connections to critical pedagogy and neo-Marxism. We make several claims about our students' ability to read critically and suggest these findings have larger implications across the undergraduate curriculum.

This book grew out of a scholarship of teaching and learning inquiry undertaken at Mount Royal University, a public undergraduate institution in Canada. American readers may wonder whether Canadian students are like American students in their reading behaviors or whether the national context is simply too different. We argue that there is such a diversity of institutions and students in the United States and in Canada that it is impossible to talk about the American student or the Canadian one. We describe our study in detail that is sufficiently rich so that individuals can judge whether our observations resonate with their own, but doing so assumes that individuals have read far enough in to recognize their students in our descriptions. We address broader issues of context in chapter 1, where we talk about some aspects of the Canadian and American systems, including Mount Royal's American-modeled general education requirement. In that chapter we also describe our decision to use the Association of American Colleges and Universities VALUE rubrics to place our observations in a larger framework that makes conversation possible. Although our inquiry is context rich and anchored in our classes, what we found is too important to leave there.

Our process began in 2010 with initial discussions about the power of collaborative inquiry. We decided to focus on critical reading because instructors across the disciplines see it as a foundational skill. As biology, history, political science, and English professors, we brought notably different assumptions about what reading is and how to foster it in the classroom. We chose to focus our inquiry on the first-year general education courses because students from across the institution take these courses. We wanted to see how students demonstrate critical reading, defined as "reading for academic purposes" and "reading for social engagement," in these first-year classes. We shared the same research question, protocol, data-gathering methods, and methodology. As such, this study also offers a model for interdisciplinary collaboration within a single institution. Despite the differences in our courses and our disciplinary backgrounds, we discovered more in common than we had expected. Like many faculty, we have long assumed that students know the basics of how to read and that if they do struggle with reading particular texts, they just need to be shown how to read more effectively. Then if they don't read the way we expect them to, it's because they haven't tried or didn't spend enough time on it. We have assumed that students share our understanding of what reading means and that they are affected by what they read, assumptions we have begun to question in this inquiry. The processes and outcomes of this project have been exciting, frightening, and productive.

As this is a scholarship of teaching and learning inquiry, we cannot separate our experience of the class from our findings; we reflect upon our own practices as teachers and describe how our practice has changed in addition to offering suggestions. Although our findings are anchored in our context, they have larger implications for critical reading in higher education. Faculty from different institutions, programs, and disciplines may find that our experiences resonate with theirs and will, we hope, find inspiration and provocation. We believe it is possible to create conditions where critical reading is more likely to occur; however, two serious obstacles are faculty assumptions about reading and faculty assessment practices. Critical reading is much too important to leave the higher education system as it is. This book concludes with a call to rethink the purpose of higher education to foreground the ethical and intellectual components of critical reading.

# Acknowledgments

WE WOULD LIKE to thank the following organizations and individuals. The Mount Royal Institute for Scholarship of Teaching and Learning served as a collaboration broker for this inquiry; in particular, we would like to thank then director Richard Gale, who started on this journey with us, and current director Janice Miller-Young. We would also like to thank all the facilitators of the Nexen Teaching and Learning Scholars program who introduced us to the scholarship of teaching and learning, which changed our scholarship and teaching practices immeasurably. We benefited from attending the Association of American Colleges and Universities Engaging Departments Institute and General Education and Assessment Conference, where we learned more about the VALUE rubrics and calibration processes.

We thank the Office of the Vice-President, Academic, and Provost at Mount Royal for the financial support that allowed us to attend these events. We thank the Office of Research Services and Faculty of Teaching and Learning for providing resources so that we could disseminate our findings to the Mount Royal community and beyond. Jim Zimmer provided encouragement throughout the process, especially when we really needed it. We thank the entire Department of General Education and especially its chair, Karim Dharamsi. Margy MacMillan read all of this book in manuscript form; we are grateful for her generosity and thoughtful and critical responses. Many colleagues at other institutions contributed to the final shape of this book through their feedback at various conferences, perhaps the most immediate form of peer review.

We thank the anonymous reviewers for their thoughtful comments on the manuscript, as well as the staff at Indiana University Press, including Rebecca Tolen, who brought this book into being. We are also very grateful for the support and guidance provided by the series editors: Jennifer Meta Robinson, Whitney M. Schlegel, Mary Taylor Huber, and, of course, Pat Hutchings. Finally, we would like to thank our friends and families, our colleagues, and, most importantly, our students who have so generously allowed us access into their academic world. We hope this study will ultimately benefit students and faculty who are interested in both academic success and social engagement.

# CRITICAL READING IN
# HIGHER EDUCATION

# Introduction

I𝐓 𝐈𝐒 𝐂𝐔𝐒𝐓𝐎𝐌𝐀𝐑𝐘 to begin a discussion about reading in higher education with lamentation—lamentation about declining skill levels, participation, and engagement. *To Read or Not to Read: A Question of National Consequence,* a 2007 report by the National Endowment for the Arts, makes three alarming, though not surprising, claims:

- Americans are spending less time reading.
- Reading comprehension skills are eroding.
- These declines have serious civic, social, cultural, and economic implications.[1]

Discussions about reading in higher education typically add academic implications to this list. Students cannot, we hear and sometimes say, read well enough to master disciplinary knowledge. Faculty members from different areas and institutions identify student difficulty with reading as a major barrier to learning. They talk about a necessary "transition" to college reading and college reading expectations, a transition with which many students struggle.[2] Forty-one percent of faculty members surveyed by the *Chronicle of Higher Education* felt that students were not well prepared to read and understand difficult material in college; an additional 48 percent felt students were "somewhat" prepared.[3] Once they are in postsecondary courses, students often can't, or won't, do the reading required. Richard Arum and Josipa Roksa note in *Academically Adrift: Limited Learning on College Campuses* that many students do not read very much and sometimes seek out courses with less rigorous reading and writing requirements, hardly news for those of us teaching in postsecondary institutions. Arum and Roksa identify a correlation between heavier reading requirements and improved performance on the Collegiate Learning Assessment,[4] but simply increasing the amount of reading is not enough to improve student learning, especially if we believe that students cannot comprehend what they do read. The National Endowment for the Arts reports that reading proficiency of college graduates has declined 20–23 percent between 1992 and 2003.[5] Yet most studies of reading at the postsecondary level can be divided into three categories: (1) those that focus on specific groups—developmental classes, English as a Foreign Language learners, or students with various disabilities; (2) those that focus on specific types of reading—most often online or literary; and (3) those that focus on specific moments in tightly controlled experiments—often from linguistic or cognitive psychology perspectives. These studies, though fascinating, are sometimes hard to translate into actions that instructors from various disciplines can try when faced with students who don't read or, more accurately, don't read in the ways we want them to read.

For this is the first crucial point about reading. There are many different ways to read—many ways appropriate for different purposes, all of them remarkable. As Stanislas Dehaene notes:

> At this very moment, your brain is accomplishing an amazing feat—reading. Your eyes scan the page in short spasmodic movements. Four or five times per second, your gaze stops just long enough to recognize one or two words. You are, of course, unaware of this jerky intake of information. Only the sounds and meanings of the words reach your conscious mind. But how can a few black marks on white paper projected onto your retina evoke an entire universe?[6]

Dehaene proposes a theory of neuronal recycling to suggest how, in the evolutionarily insignificant space of a few thousand years, the human brain developed the capacity to read. He argues that "learning to read induces massive cognitive gains" although probably at the price of other abilities now lost.[7] Maryanne Wolf explores this idea further: "The capacity of literacy for rapid-fire performance released the individual reader not only from the restrictions of memory but from those of time. By its ability to become virtually automatic, literacy allowed the individual reader to give less time to initial decoding processes and to allocate more cognitive time and ultimately more cortical space to the deeper analysis of recorded thought."[8] She worries that this "secret gift of time to think" will be lost to a generation expecting apparently instantaneous access to information on the Internet: "During the phase in their reading development when critical skills are guided, modeled, practiced and honed, they may have not been challenged to exploit the acme of the fully developed, reading brain: time to think for themselves."[9]

Much recent attention has been paid to how electronic interfaces affect reading behaviors and cognition. Popular books like *The Shallows: How the Internet Is Changing the Way We Think, Read, and Remember* and *iBrain: Surviving the Technological Alteration of the Modern Mind* tap into the fear that by losing the ability to focus attention for long periods of time on written text or to immerse ourselves in text, we are changing how we think and learn.[10] While researchers don't know whether reading online sources changes how people think, they do know that "the process of reading on screen tends to be cognitively different from the process of reading on paper, in terms of brain activation, the contextual environment, cognitive focus, comprehension, and reading speed."[11] Ziming Liu, for example, notes that people spend more time on scanning, less on deep reading.[12] But such variation in reading behavior isn't limited to the screen, as anyone who has flipped through a newspaper or turned to the index of a monograph can attest. Depending on the purpose of the reading, such behavior could be completely appropriate.

Many literary theorists have tried to describe reading, often, though not exclusively, in terms of literary texts. The literary text is frequently expected to produce an aesthetic response; it can be more difficult to read, thereby providing more scope for investigation; and it is the object of inquiry for a whole discipline. Wolfgang Iser, for example, begins *The Act of Reading: A Theory of Aesthetic Response* with the following observation: "As a literary text can only produce a response when it is read, it is virtually impossible to describe this response without also analyzing the reading process. Reading is therefore the focal point of this study, for it sets in motion a whole chain of activities that depend both on the text and on the exercise of certain basic human faculties. Effects and responses are properties neither of the text nor of the reader; the text represents a potential effect that is realized in the reading process."[13] Iser justifies the study of reading through the potential aesthetic response realized through the reading process. He goes on to posit "an implied reader" separate from any real reader: "No matter who or what he may be, the real reader is always offered a particular role to play, and it is this role that constitutes the concept of the implied reader."[14] The concept of the implied reader, "a network of response-inviting structures,"[15] involves a generalized, indeed a phenomenological, account of the reading process. Other reader-response theorists like David Bleich and Norman Holland try to address issues of multiple readings from multiple readers.[16] From the Russian formalists who argued about what makes a text literary, to the New Critics who proposed ways of teaching literature through "close reading," to various reader-response movements of the 1960s and 1970s, scholars of literature have struggled to make sense of the relationship between the literary text and reader.[17]

Patricia Harkin, tracing the history of reader-response theory in English studies, argues for the usefulness of that theory beyond the literature classroom. She argues for composition studies as a site for the teaching of reading but claims that "discussions of reading have been so thoroughly conflated with discussions of teaching literature, of the purpose of English studies, of the future of the humanities, of the politics of general education, of the definitions and uses of literacy, and so forth, that a pedagogical or curricular decision not to teach literary texts in writing courses became or entailed a decision not to teach reading."[18] Mariolina Rizzi Salvatori and Patricia Donahue also describe the competing disciplinary narratives between literary studies and composition studies but identify a renewed interest in reading in composition,[19] while scholars like Kathleen McCormick theorize reading with careful attention to the classroom, analyzing, for example, students' strategies and assumptions in a "Reading-to-Write" first-year writing course.[20] If, as Robert Scholes claims, "we have a reading problem of massive dimensions—a problem that goes well beyond any purely literary concerns,"[21] there is growing consensus that we have to teach reading somewhere—indeed, in this book we argue, everywhere.

Although readers, and sometimes theorists, associate different types of reading experiences with different types of texts (we "lose ourselves" in a novel but rarely in a menu), it is important to consider the purpose of reading—or rather the purposes, because there is rarely only one. Louise Rosenblatt, best known for her influential transactional model of reading, in which she argues that meaning is created through a transaction between text and reader, also describes reading on a spectrum from efferent (or informational) to aesthetic, claiming that a reader can move back and forth on this spectrum while reading a single text.[22] Rosenblatt draws attention to reading as "an event occurring at a particular time in a particular environment at a particular moment in the life history of the reader,"[23] and she calls for greater attention to what the reader does in "these different kinds of readings."[24] As we consider how students read and how we want them to read, it can be useful to consider how we read in different circumstances. John Guillory argues that scholars rely both on extensive and intensive reading; for scholars the crucial skill that cannot be replaced by a keyword search on a machine is learning "when and how to decelerate reading or to commence the slow labor of interpretation."[25] We do not, indeed we cannot, apply the same attention to everything we read, even when reading for a scholarly purpose; reading for pleasure involves different behaviors than reading for a test, and reading for a test varies based on the type of test. Does the test require pure recall of textual details, or is synthesis, application, evaluation, or analysis required? Most faculty, when pressed, would say they want students to read "critically," but what they mean by this term is often fraught with contradiction.

## What Is Critical Reading?

The term "critical reading" has two distinct traditions: reading for academic purposes and reading for social or civic engagement. Each definition comes from a philosophical tradition with incompatible assumptions about the nature of knowledge and the activity of reading. Critical reading is sometimes defined as reading for academic success. Reading critically in this sense involves the following:

- identifying patterns of textual elements
- distinguishing between main and subordinate ideas
- evaluating credibility
- making judgments about how a text is argued
- making relevant inferences about the text

The SAT exam, for example, uses the label "critical reading" for its sentence completion exercises (testing vocabulary) and for its reading comprehension section (recognizing tone, identifying organization, making inferences). Many textbooks on reading skills focus on this type of critical reading. Kathleen McWhorter, for example, has written a variety of reading texts aimed at slightly different levels: *Essential Reading Skills: Preparing for College Reading* with Brette M. Sember (4th ed.), a skills-based reading text, and *Guide to College Reading* (10th ed.), a whole-language reading text, are designed for a developmental college reading course and advertised as suitable for reading levels of students in grades 6–9; *Efficient and Flexible Reading* (10th ed.) is a text almost obsessively concerned with how quickly an individual can read texts at the level of grades 9–12; *Reading across the Disciplines* (6th ed.) includes a chapter from a psychology text so that students can practice reading something longer; and *Academic Reading: College Major and Career Applications* (8th ed.), tries to motivate students by connecting generic strategies to specific disciplines, grade levels 10–12+.[26] Consider the profitability of this critical reading marketplace if one author produces so many texts—and we haven't listed them all here—in so many editions. Some texts blend reading and study skills, emphasizing retention of information and offering test-taking tips. Students are trained to locate main ideas, distinguish between main and supporting ideas, recognize basic patterns of organization, and, at the higher levels, evaluate techniques and arguments. Often the focus in these texts is on the structure rather than content of what is read, but critical reading for academic purposes does not have to be a formal exercise divorced from content.

Texts like *Ways of Reading* by David Bartholomae and Anthony Petrosky, *Rewriting: How to Do Things with Texts* by Joseph Harris, and *The Elements (and Pleasures) of Difficulty* by Mariolina Rizzi Salvatori and Patricia Donahue provide students with strategies to engage with the content of academic reading, content that is often difficult not only in how it is presented but also in terms of the concepts.[27] These authors, coming out of an American composition studies tradition, acknowledge the constructivist nature of critical reading for academic purposes. Indeed, Bartholomae, in his influential essay "Inventing the University," argues that students construct the university each time they write for a class:

> The students have to appropriate (or be appropriated by) a specialized discourse, and they have to do this as though they were easily and comfortably one with their audience, as though they were members of the academy, or historians or anthropologists or economists; they have to invent the university by assembling and mimicking its language, finding some compromise between idiosyncracy [*sic*], a personal history and the requirements of convention, the history of a discipline. They must learn to speak our language. Or they must dare to speak it, or to carry off the bluff, since speaking and writing will most certainly be required long before the skill is "learned."[28]

Although Bartholomae is talking about students' academic writing, their academic reading is bound by the same imperatives. Bartholomae argues that successful writers must "imagine and write from a position of privilege. They must . . . see themselves within a privleged [*sic*] discourse, one that already includes and excludes groups of readers."[29] Critical reading for academic purposes involves students learning to see themselves as part of the included group of readers, an alien and potentially alienating experience. Joseph Harris argues that "one way to help such students imagine themselves as intellectuals, then, is to ask them to look closely at how they already go about reading the many various texts they meet from day to day—both in school and outside of it."[30] But Harris's focus here is acculturation into academic discourse through the familiar; he explicitly sets his work on demystifying critical reading and writing against what is sometimes called the "social turn" in composition studies, a commitment to developing critical consciousness in a Freirean sense.[31]

Our second definition of critical reading is associated with critical pedagogy and its commitment to democratic and socially relevant education, and, as Harris pointedly observes, this understanding of "critical" as "vaguely synonymous with *oppositional* or *progressive*" diverges from the first definition, "responds to and makes use of the work of others."[32] Cheryl Dozier, Peter Johnston, and Rebecca Rogers define critical literacy as "understanding the ways in which language and literacy are used to accomplish social ends. Becoming critically literate means developing a sense that literacy is for taking social action, an awareness of how people use literacy for their own ends, and a sense of agency with respect to one's own literacy."[33] In this tradition, critical reading involves the following:

- sifting through various forms of rhetoric
- recognizing power relations
- questioning assumptions
- engaging with the world
- constructing new possibilities

While most reading textbooks involve the first definition of critical reading, teacher education often focuses on the latter, using texts like Joe Kincheloe's *Critical Pedagogy Primer*.[34] Scholars like Patricia Bizzell and Ira Shor argue for a critical pedagogy that pays careful attention to the political potential of critical reading.[35]

Both definitions of critical reading address key features of the Association of American Colleges and Universities' (AAC&U) Essential Learning Outcomes and support the goals of liberal education.[36] Such goals include not only productivity but also resilience, creativity, and compassion. Both definitions require that the reader comprehend the text, what the AAC&U VALUE rubric for reading describes as "the extent to which the reader 'gets' the text, both literally and figuratively."[37] We argue that critical reading also includes the abilities to analyze and interpret the text, where analysis involves recognizing textual features and interpretation involves using those features and the context to make meaning. Successful critical reading requires the identification and evaluation of assumptions within the text and those of the reader. Both traditions of critical reading involve inference: the ability to connect material to other experiences and ideas, whether academic, social, or personal. The inference required in critical reading for academic purposes tends to focus on connections to disciplines or across disciplines. Some of these connections are made through recognition of genres. The inference required for critical reading for social engagement, on the other hand, tends to focus more on connections to experience outside the formal classroom. Critical reading for social engagement involves analysis of knowledge as a step toward participatory action. It involves a transformation; as Paulo Freire explains, "A critical reading of the texts and of the world has to do with the changes in progress within them."[38] Freire's words reveal a key distinction between the two versions of critical reading.

The two definitions come from different philosophical traditions with incompatible assumptions about the nature of reality and knowledge, a disjunction not often explicitly addressed in discussions of reading. Lisa Patel Stevens and Thomas W. Bean, in *Critical Literacy: Context Research and Practice in the K–12 Classroom,* are an exception. They identify the crucial distinction between critical reading, which "emphasizes such skill-based tasks as distinguishing fact from opinion and, at a more advanced level, recognizing propaganda in text," and critical literacy, which "forces us to explicitly discuss the ways in which text [and they emphasize all texts] is mediated as a tool of institutional shaping of discourses and social practices."[39] They identify, on one hand, a rationalist view of meaning in text and, on the other, a constructivist view of meaning created in the process of deconstruction and reconstruction. They note that "engaging in critical reading is a search for a verifiable reading, whereas critical literacy is the endeavour to work within multiple, plausible interpretations of a text."[40] The term "critical" is thus associated with both a means of resolving uncertainty to attain greater "institutional viability" and what Ira James Allen describes as "a mode of negotiating uncertainty."[41] Allen doesn't use the term "critical reading"—preferring "instrumental" and "real" reading—but his call for "true conversation," anchored in Hans-Georg Gadamer and hermeneutics, anticipates a renegotiation of privilege in terms of critical literacy: "Part of discerning privilege means, for me, making transparent reading habits translucent, turning them into visible sets of dispositions and practices to make difficult decisions about values. In particular the values to be negotiated are those that foster institutional viability within the specific context of the corporate university and the larger context of a capitalist world system."[42] Gina Cervetti, Michael J. Pardales, and James S. Damico argue that what we are calling "critical reading for academic purposes" is rooted in the liberal-humanist tradition of empiricism. Knowledge is gained through experience and reason; facts can be separated from inferences; reality is a referent for interpretation; meaning is created by an author. Reading involves uncovering what is in the text. In this positivist orientation the truth is out there; reading provides access to that truth through reason.[43] As Allan Luke notes, "There is a rationalist assumption at work [in this position]: that critique enables the identification of logical or factual error."[44] Reading for social engagement, as part of a tradition of critical pedagogy, is built upon foundations of neo-Marxist constructivism, where knowledge is always contested and ideological; reality is constructed through interpretation; meaning is continually created and recreated in the text and in the world.[45] Texts, including those authorized in the curriculum, "necessarily engage particular cultural and political standpoints" and "the shaping of what counts as reading can serve cultural and social class-based interests."[46] As Peter Roberts asserts, "Reading *texts* critically, from a Freirean point of view, necessitates, and is only possible through, a critical reading of a given *context*."[47] Reading involves interacting with word and world to transform both. These two approaches to critical reading may share a number of elements, but it is important to remember this philosophical contradiction about the nature of knowledge as it plays out around the goals of education.

What do faculty mean when we say we want students to read critically? What do we want them to do with the texts? Do we want them to read so that they can comprehend and retain information, or are we interested in what happens in their minds during the reading process? Do we hope that reading changes their interactions with the world? In Allen's terms, are we hoping to increase their institutional viability, or do we want them to "unlearn institutional viability as priority number one"?[48] Can we hope to do both? Does either really matter?

## Why Does Critical Reading Matter?

From a liberal-humanist perspective, critical reading is one of the tools necessary for the individual to succeed, sometimes against great odds, in society. It is a foundational skill for academic and economic success and a necessary condition for participation within a healthy democracy. Employers look for workers who can understand complex material: 89 percent of American employers surveyed in 2009 believed universities and colleges should place more emphasis on written and oral communication, 81 percent on critical thinking and analytic reasoning.[49] Both of these essential learning outcomes involve critical reading. The Conference Board of Canada begins its list of fundamental skills for employability with "Read and understand information presented in a variety of forms."[50] Students want financially and personally rewarding careers, careers often linked to degree completion,[51] and if students cannot read critically, they are more likely to struggle with program requirements. In the competitive environment of postsecondary education, institutions are both market and mission driven.[52] Faculty and administration want students to succeed within postsecondary education and beyond. Rhetoric about critical reading with this emphasis on success, however, oversimplifies both the reading process and its significance for the individual and society.

Critical reading has the potential to change who we are. Colin Harrison describes it this way: "Reading . . . is much more than gaining a skill: it is about learning to be. And it is precisely because this is such a difficult and sensitive subject to talk about that we avoid talking about it, and this leaves an enormous vacuum. Because reading is so important, that vacuum becomes filled by other discourses, and often these have an emphasis on skills, on employment, on the economy and on reading for practical purposes."[53] Harrison is not arguing against reading for practical purposes or gainful employment. He is arguing for recognition that reading cannot be reduced to a utilitarian skill. Reading influences "the kind of person we are capable of becoming."[54] Therein lies the radical possibility of critical reading for social engagement from a neo-Marxist perspective. Harrison explains:

> Critical literacy is different from literacy. Literacy, as most governments under-stand it, increases educational achievement levels, improves the job-market skills of the population and cuts down crime. Critical literacy does none of these things: critical literacy challenges what schooling is attempting to achieve; it makes people more likely to be confident and articulate workers, who are ready, when necessary, to challenge their bosses about working practices, about the ethics of production, about redundancies; and it makes those in prison able and more likely to complain about their conditions. . . . It is not difficult to detect the efficacy of a critical literacy programme: those in power become uncomfortable.[55]

Critical reading, from this perspective, shifts from being a tool to succeed within the system to a tool for challenging the system within a wider social or civic context. It becomes crucial in an era of increasing inequalities, disenfranchisement, and despair.

## So What Can Faculty Do?

Given the twin imperatives of critical reading, it is not surprising that many research-ers and teachers are interested in how students currently read and how to help them improve. Reading is a complex process of actions that are almost automatic for the proficient reader, yet college instructors often speak about how students read or don't read as if it were a single skill employed for a single purpose. Alice Horning notes:

> Many college teachers will say, if asked, that students are "illiterate." What they seem to mean by this claim is both that they can't read and that they don't read. That is, first, they lack the ability to read in the critically literate sense of being able to go beyond summary of main ideas to analysis, synthesis and evaluation. In addition, though, they are uneducated in reading, lacking experience working with extended texts and the world of ideas from which they arise. In this way, they mean that students are uneducated in ways that derive from reading a wide variety of materi-als and seeing varied points of view, research, and information relating to ideas or issues.[56]

Looking at the literacy research quickly reveals that reading is a bewildering combina-tion of perceptual, cognitive, and social factors. Schema theory, influenced by infor-mation processing theories, suggests that individual readers place new information within a scaffold of prior knowledge; however, prior knowledge by itself is not enough to account for differences between readers. Trying to explain these differences, many reading theorists have turned their attention to epistemic, social, and cultural factors involved in reading.[57] As different theories of how people learn are developed, literacy research and instruction emphasize different elements.[58]

However, it is also worthwhile remembering that the term "reading" covers a wide range of activities dependent upon purpose. By reading, do we mean simple comprehension of an isolated text, or are we looking for something more—placing text within a larger context, evaluating meaning, questioning assumptions, applying concepts, or engaging with the text? Even simple comprehension is not that simple. Elements like fluency, phonics, recognition of sight words, vocabulary, semantic context clues, identification of schema, motivation, persistence, comfort with ambiguity, self-regulated use of strategies, and metacognition influence students' comprehension of written text. It is only when readers struggle with texts that they are likely to become aware of different factors affecting comprehension.[59] Much research has been done in the K–12 setting on how to increase comprehension through a range of methodologies from identifying reading strategies and promoting metacognition to engaging students and encouraging integration.[60] As we will demonstrate in later chapters, postsecondary instructors can draw upon the insights that this work provides even as our contexts differ and our disciplines require different types of reading. Some postsecondary instructors may assume that students receive their critical reading instruction in a first-year composition class. And while such classes do provide close attention to texts, they cannot be expected to bear either burden alone. Disciplinary practices are too important and too varied even within the discipline of English;[61] however, scholars like Debrah Huffman, Arlene Wilner, Mariolina Rizzi Salvatori, and Patricia Donahue do offer insights that postsecondary instructors from many disciplines can draw upon.[62] Even on a general level, it is worthwhile considering what faculty members hope to achieve with the readings assigned. Do we assign readings because we want to transmit certain pieces of information to be remembered, or are we hoping that something will occur within the student's mind as a result of interaction with this text? And before saying "both," consider that research suggests integration comes at a cost to content memory.[63]

*Time to Act: An Agenda for Advancing Adolescent Literacy for College and Career Success,* the final report from the Carnegie Corporation of New York's Council on Advancing Adolescent Literacy, outlines not only the challenges but also strategies to improve literacy in secondary schools. It recognizes that professional development in literacy is important for all content-area teachers but that such development needs to "address the literacy demands inherently embedded within their respective disciplines and in the tasks they considered crucial for their students to accomplish."[64] However, postsecondary instructors across the disciplines, including those in English departments, hunger for help with students who struggle with reading. Most of us are not trained in literacy instruction; most of us don't remember how we learned to distinguish between main and subordinate ideas. Most of us are so close to our disciplines that we cannot easily articulate the ways we read in those disciplines. Some believe that specific courses focusing on reading skills are the answer, but reading skills taught in developmental English classrooms are usually isolated from disciplinary content. The idea, of course, is that students who learn these strategies will be able to transfer them to a new context, but the literature on transfer, let alone something as context-specific as transfer of reading skills, is not hopeful.[65] Such a view of reading relies on a transmission model of education, a model often found to be inadequate.[66] Greg Mannion, Kate Miller, Ian Gibb, and Ronnie Goodman argue that we need to move from thinking about literacy as transferable skills to literacies as emergent practices in social settings. They argue that skills don't transfer but, rather, resonate between contexts.[67] And the reality is that most students aren't in developmental reading programs. If faculty members across the disciplines want students to read critically, they need do something about it. A first step is to examine how students read. And so we did.

## Who Are We and What Did We Do?

We are four instructors from a variety of disciplines; we teach at Mount Royal University, a public undergraduate institution in Canada. As biology, history, political science, and English professors, we brought markedly different assumptions about what reading is and how to foster it in the classroom. Rather than explore critical reading in any particular discipline, we decided to examine how our students read in four different general education courses offered at the university: Controversies in Science; Texts and Ideas—Genocide; Communities and Societies; and Critical Writing and Reading. We chose to focus on these general education courses because they represent a cross-section of undergraduate students from across the institution. We hoped we would be able to see if there were any general patterns about how undergraduates read critically. Of course, the difficulty with examining critical reading is that, as Robert Scholes notes, "we do not see reading."[68] Whether in discussion or writing, all we have are oblique measures of how students read, but what these oblique measures indicate seems to challenge many of our assumptions about reading and education. Pat Hutchings identifies three common characteristics of the scholarship of teaching and learning: it is embedded in the discipline; faculty examine their own classes, practice as teachers, and context; and it has a transformational agenda. It is "scholarship undertaken in the name of change."[69] This scholarship of teaching and learning inquiry examines critical reading in the name of change.

Chapter 1 addresses the issue of generalizability. How can data from four Canadian classes say anything about critical reading more broadly? We believe our findings will resonate with many other instructors. This chapter provides the rich description necessary for others to judge whether aspects of our inquiry can influence their own practice. We sketch our national context in comparison with the American and British postsecondary systems. We briefly describe the courses we examined in this inquiry. These multidisciplinary courses fit within thematic clusters of Mount Royal's general education provision, but faculty elsewhere might find it useful to place them within a general framework of science, humanities, social sciences, and composition. In this chapter we also outline the parameters of our collaborative scholarship of teaching and learning inquiry. We collected more than seven hundred written artifacts, including all assignments leading to the research papers and reflective reading logs with the prompts "What?" "So What?" and "Now What?" We describe our methodology, including the development of hybridized rubrics based on the VALUE rubrics, inter-rater reliability exercises, and additional qualitative analysis of reading logs and research papers to provide a richer description of how our students read. Our collaboration revealed more similarities than we had expected given the differences in outcomes, readings, and assignments in the four courses.

The next three chapters explore elements of our rubrics, supplemented with other analysis. In each we place our findings in the context of the scholarly literature. We speculate on reasons for what we see. We offer some practical suggestions for moving students forward in particular cases; we suggest directions for future research into student learning. We do not lament.

In chapter 2 we address the question "Can Students Read?" by looking at indicators of comprehension, analysis, interpretation, and evaluation. Comprehension is suggested by the ability to summarize text; analysis, by the ability to use elements of a text; interpretation, by the ability to infer meaning; and evaluation, by the ability to identify assumptions. These elements, we believe, are necessary parts of both critical reading for academic purposes and reading for social engagement. We place our discussion within the context of schema theory and implicit models of reading. We divide our findings into good, not-so-good, and bad news. The good news is that most students were able to comprehend at a minimal benchmark level. We then examine why faculty often complain that students can't comprehend and suggest it has to do with elements such as evaluation of assumptions, a task that requires a transactional rather than transmission model of reading. Much work on evaluating assumptions has been done under the heading of critical thinking; we examine some of this work as it connects to working with written text. The chapter closes with a caveat: in all four courses we found no developmental pattern over the semester, despite our assumptions that we were helping students read critically. They could be coached to display particular traits in their writing about particular readings but did not demonstrate these traits when the explicit prompts were removed. We suggest that reading development requires epistemological shifts.

In chapter 3 we focus on reading for academic purposes by examining the roles that genre and integration of multiple texts play in critical reading. Teachers have long intuited the importance of genre recognition and integration for comprehension. We summarize some of the research on how these processes work before turning to our students' work. In this chapter we also take a closer look at the research paper as not only the genre through which students are most often expected to display their critical reading for academic purposes but also an opportunity for students to increase their reading skills, as research suggests that writing about texts improves reading. The longer essays, we thought, provided more scope for students to demonstrate critical reading and disciplinary differences. Student and instructor attitudes toward the research paper, however, can impede critical reading. After scoring the research papers according to the hybridized rubrics, we looked more carefully at the cited sources. We suggest that the traditional research paper assignment fosters a type of academic dishonesty, not in terms of plagiarism, but by parodying academic activity. The chapter concludes with some suggestions on how to improve critical reading for academic purposes, including a call to radically rethink the research paper.

In chapter 4 we examine the rubric elements for civic analysis of knowledge and connection to personal experience as necessary parts of critical reading for social engagement. We begin by reviewing our definition of critical reading and identifying recent calls for civic engagement and service-learning before turning to our data. Here we were confronted by an overwhelming absence of any indication of social engagement in the aggregate results. The specific manifestation varied by course area, but responses could be categorized based on actions students demonstrated. Indeed, we posit a taxonomy of absence: in order to engage socially with texts, students need to negotiate compliance, comprehension, identification, and generalization, but some students stop at different points during the process. We also examine what seemed to be happening when students were able to demonstrate indicators of social engagement in critical reading. We offer some specific strategies to help students negotiate the different levels of generalization required. We also suggest that teaching students to read for academic purposes may undermine our attempts to have them read for social engagement as disciplinary norms pacify students by redirecting attention away from content to form. We conclude the chapter with suggestions on how to improve critical reading for social engagement.

In chapter 5 we offer our own "What?" "So What?" and "Now What?" reflections on what we have learned. This inquiry has challenged many of our assumptions about how students read and what we are doing in the classroom. We describe the changes we have made, will make, or wish we could make to our courses. Change, however, cannot be limited to individual faculty practice if it is to be effective. We return to the idea of collaborative inquiry and scholarship of teaching and learning. The scholarship of teaching and learning must have as its ultimate goal changes in practice to improve student learning. Collaboration makes these changes more likely, especially when they challenge some of the assumptions of higher education. We need to become advocates for critical reading across our institution. But we also note the difficulty of integrating critical reading across the curriculum, of moving faculty from lamentation to action. We are particularly aware of the curricular space and time such fundamental skill development requires but argue that we cannot afford to continue the status quo. We argue for a radical rethinking of the purpose of undergraduate education to foreground the intellectual and ethical components of critical reading.

# 1  Different Courses,
## Common Concern

$A$NY SCHOLARSHIP OF teaching and learning (SOTL) project must grapple with the issue of generalizability. On the one hand, the scholarship of teaching and learning is strengthened by its grounding in real classrooms, with the messy, ill-structured, fascinating, and rich glimpses of student learning they provide. However, these class-rooms, situated in messy, ill-structured, fascinating, and unique institutions, cannot be easily compared within, let alone across, institutions. Practitioners of the scholar-ship of teaching and learning cannot assume findings are transferable across contexts. Liz Grauerholz and Eric Main, warning against the assumption that findings are gen-eralizable, describe teaching methods as "social acts informed by cultural traditions that become most meaningful when described in terms of specific histories and larger social contexts."[1] As Cheryl Albers notes, "It is sometimes difficult to reconcile this context-dependent characteristic of SOTL with the call to use SOTL to build an intel-lectual commons. . . . The quandary lies in how to use context-rich SOTL work to build a body of knowledge that influences practice."[2] Albers talks in terms of transfer, "not achieved through generalizing the results of context-bound investigations," but rather through collaboration and conversation.[3] In this book we describe our collaboration, hoping to extend the conversation and influence practice beyond our own classrooms. We do not claim our findings are generalizable beyond our institution or even beyond these specific class sections. We believe, however, that aspects of our findings will reso-nate with other instructors and may provide insights they can use in their own unique contexts. To facilitate this transfer, we must provide more details about our particu-lar context, the "'rich description,' which paints a detailed picture of the conditions of the study, allowing others to compare it to their own context."[4] This chapter pro-vides some of those details by outlining our general education provision, the reading requirements for each of these general education courses, and the parameters of our collaborative inquiry.

We teach at Mount Royal University, a public undergraduate institution in Canada. The Canadian postsecondary system has much in common with the American system, including a high degree of individual autonomy for faculty.[5] As in America, bachelor degrees are usually four-year full-time programs involving a major concentration of courses, some sort of breadth requirement, and a few electives. However, many students do not complete the program in four years. One trend over the last few decades has been more students working part-time to help pay for their studies. Although the Canadian government is a large funder of postsecondary education and increasingly wants a say in how its money is spent, Canadian students still pay a portion of the costs, so many of them have to work.[6] Unlike America, where students seeking to enter postsecondary study take the SAT or ACT, students entering the Canadian system do not take any sort of standardized national examinations, so there is no way to compare students across provinces. For better or for worse, students are admitted on the basis of their senior high school grades. In our province, Alberta, these grades are a combination of an individual teacher mark and a provincial examination mark.

Mount Royal is the smaller of two universities in Calgary, Alberta, with more than 13,500 students. Almost 80 percent of Mount Royal students come from the Calgary area; while there are some student residences, most students do not live on campus. They come, take their classes, and leave. The average age of full-time students is twenty-two, and more than 60 percent of students are women. Mount Royal prides itself on smaller classes, though "smaller" is, of course, a relative term. While 99 percent of classes have fifty or fewer students, the average class size is more than twenty-seven students.[7] The first-year general education courses we describe in this study are capped at thirty for Composition and thirty-five for the others; they are usually full.

In Canada universities tend to offer bachelor, and higher, degrees, while colleges tend to offer diplomas or transfer courses. Founded in 1910 as a college, Mount Royal is a relatively new university, as it has been offering four-year bachelor degrees since only 2008. As part of this transition Mount Royal adopted a new general education provision, moving from a purely distributive model of arts and science requirements to a hybrid model. Most universities in Canada have some sort of arts and science requirement; far fewer have a general education program, as general education has not received the same attention in Canada that it has in America. We do not have province-wide general education programs as happens in many states; we have not yet faced the same pressures for standardization, accreditation, and accountability. Many universities continue to rely on what Terrel L. Rhodes has called the "inoculation approach of the last century" with a collection of courses that is, in Ann S. Ferren's terms, "an amalgam created through accretion" rather than an intentional structure.[8] Mount Royal took advantage of its transition to a university to create a general education provision, examining and adapting different American models.

When this study occurred, Mount Royal's general education requirement was 30 percent of the bachelor degree, like many American models.[9] In *General Education Essentials: A Guide for College Faculty,* Paul Hanstedt discusses a vision of general education as foundational—the courses taken in the first year that develop basic skills to support the major in years two, three, and four—and contrasts that with a vision of general education occurring over the four years. He argues for the importance of an integrative model providing iterative opportunities for students to practice and extend skills.[10] Mount Royal implements what Hanstedt describes as a core-distributional model: foundational first-year courses followed by a number of distribution requirements; these distribution requirements are courses spread across the disciplines to provide the students with some educational breadth. However, while Hanstedt finishes off the model with a capstone course or courses, we don't. So if the core-distributional model can be described as "a good start and a strong finish but a 'muddle in the middle,'"[11] we are left in the muddle. Many, though not all, of our students take our foundation-level general education courses in their first year of study as we had hoped. Some wait until later in their degrees before taking these courses. Students may wait because they don't like general education or particular parts of it, or someone recommended waiting, or they want an "easy" course near the end of their program, or they take fewer than five courses a term but still want to move with their cohort through their major requirements. The university does not have the resources nor, to be honest, the political will to make all students take foundational courses at the beginning of their studies, even though these foundational courses are designed to develop key skills and introduce students to different ways of thinking about the world.

Our distribution requirements are quite similar to many American institutions. Robert Shoenberg, describing twenty-two statewide general education systems, notes that all of them require at least one writing course, a mathematics course, and some courses distributed across arts, humanities, sciences, and social sciences.[12] When our study was conducted, Mount Royal students had to take twelve courses divided across four thematic clusters: Numeracy and Scientific Literacy; Values, Beliefs, and Identities; Community and Society; and Communication.[13] These clusters are intended to be cross-disciplinary; however, faculty elsewhere may find it useful to think of them in terms of the STEM fields (science, technology, engineering, and mathematics); arts and humanities; social sciences; and writing, speech, media studies, and languages.

Each cluster of general education includes three levels of courses. Students needed to take one course from each thematic cluster for the first two levels; at the third level they needed to take four courses from at least two areas. Mount Royal hopes that this structure provides students with breadth as well as the opportunity to go deeper into areas of interest outside of their major concentration. At the foundation level students take specifically designed GNED-prefixed courses (GNED meaning General Education); at the second and third levels most courses that fulfill a general education requirement have a disciplinary prefix and are also intended to serve students majoring in that area, a situation that leads to some confusion about the identity of general education. Mount Royal created a Department of General Education to administer the foundation-level courses and oversee the entire general education provision; however, it is difficult to predict how students will move through the general education requirements beyond the foundation level, where they have limited choice.

The courses we examine in this inquiry are part of that foundation level. Because students from across the institution must take foundation-level general education courses, these courses offer a glimpse into student learning that goes beyond any specific discipline. In what follows in this chapter we briefly describe the learning outcomes, the types of readings, and the range of activities for each of these courses. We try to present this material in terms of what we thought we were doing to foster critical reading when we started this inquiry. Subsequent chapters provide more detail about what was really going on.

## Cluster 1: Numeracy and Scientific Literacy

> These courses aim to develop an understanding of the nature and methods of subjects in the health sciences, natural sciences, and mathematics, as well as assuring that students have the opportunity to acquire essential mathematical skills needed in postsecondary studies.[14]

At the foundation level students practice basic math skills, begin to use statistics, recognize mathematics and statistics as ways of reasoning, develop a "foundational understanding" of the nature of mathematical inquiry and the scientific method, examine both the development and limitations of technology, become aware of the scope of scientific disciplines, and develop skills needed to retrieve and evaluate scientific information. Not bad for a thirteen-week course when many students come with negative attitudes and high levels of anxiety about science and mathematics. And those students are in the same courses as science majors, who may resent having to take a foundational course in numeracy and scientific literacy. At the time we gathered data there were two choices for students at the foundation level in Numeracy and Scientific Literacy: they could take Scientific and Mathematical Literacy for the Modern World or Controversies in Science. The main difference between the two courses is that the second is organized around case studies.

Melanie Rathburn, a biologist, gathered data on students in her Controversies in Science course. After an introduction to numeracy and the scientific process, students investigated three topics: the efficacy of complementary and alternative medicines, the safety of nuclear energy, and the effects of oil sands development. Students completed readings from a variety of sources ranging from media articles, to popular science writing, to scholarly literature. The complexity and length of the readings determined the number of readings for each case, but each student was assigned at least two readings for each case, along with additional readings at the start and end of the course. To assist students with the scientific articles, Rathburn demonstrated how to read these articles during a class at the beginning of the semester. Students were instructed to read the same article, and then the entire class period was devoted to interrogating the reading and examining the different characteristics of scholarly articles. Rathburn discussed various approaches to reading these types of articles, how to interpret graphs and figures, how to read through the discipline-specific vocabulary, how to recognize and understand the main conclusions of the research, and how to evaluate the articles. She contrasted scholarly articles with other types of articles in an attempt to help students recognize different reading strategies they would need to use in the course.

The students' major research assignment involved three parts: an annotated bibliography of their two major sources, a series of questions that helped students to summarize and interrogate a particular experimental study, and a research paper that compared and contrasted how an experimental study was presented in the media. Having taught this course many times, Rathburn felt that students were usually quite competent in answering specific guiding questions about the readings. They could articulate sampling procedures, describe methodological biases, and understand the overall conclusions of their articles. She assumed that students could read when given some help in knowing what to look for through the guiding questions. This assignment was perceived to be so successful that all instructors teaching this multi-section course used the exact same assignment, with each student selecting his or her own topic of interest.

## Cluster 2: Values, Beliefs, and Identities

These courses provide students with the opportunity to critically explore the values, beliefs, and ideas that shape and are shaped by human experience. The understandings and sense of meaning expressed by individuals, communities, and societies through their art, music, literature, philosophy, and critical thought will be explored. Students will also have the opportunity to explore the various media through which cultural expression takes place. They will consider the impact of technology upon both the media and the content of cultural expression.

At the foundation level students explore cultural traditions, study texts of historical and contemporary significance in Western and non-Western cultures, appreciate different perspectives, examine issues related to personal identity and social interaction, and practice methods of study in the humanities and social sciences, including research skills. Perhaps because of the nature of the disciplines involved, there is much less standardization among the different foundation-level offerings in Values, Beliefs, and Identities than in the Numeracy and Scientific Literacy courses. At the time we gathered data there were nominally three choices for students at the foundation level in

Values, Beliefs, and Identity: Aesthetic Experience and Ideas, Texts and Ideas, and Cultural Perspectives on Science. However, the courses are shells; each instructor decides upon a particular theme and texts, which typically students do not know when they register for that particular section. Three characteristics are common to all versions: the course is text-based, texts are approached with an open mind, and there is a strong written component.

Glen Ryland, a historian, taught Texts and Ideas—Genocide. He selected this theme because of its ongoing importance in the world and the wealth of primary and secondary texts; he had taught iterations of this course before. The primary required texts were *Acts of Faith: The Story of an American Muslim, the Struggle for the Soul of a Generation* by Eboo Patel and *The Moral Imagination: The Art and Soul of Building Peace* by John Paul Lederach,[15] but students also read excerpts from Plato, Machiavelli, Martin Luther King Jr., Elie Wiesel, David Weiss Halivni, and others. Students read on average thirty-five pages of emotionally and cognitively difficult text a week. Usually there was not enough time to explore the intricacies of the text in class. Twice during the term, students were assigned different readings and took part in "expert corners." In this activity the class is divided into four groups of "experts," who carefully read one of four texts and discuss it as a group before teaching the content to a group of three other students, who have not read the text. Most times, however, students had read the texts prior to class and then discussed the texts together in class. Students also had to research a post-Holocaust genocide for a poster project and complete an analytical essay about a primary source for their research papers. Ryland provided extensive support about writing in this course, including workshops during class on the analytical essay. He assumed that students had difficulty seeing themselves as academic writers, and he did not pay as much attention to them as academic readers. Twice during the term, he spent about one-third of the class period discussing strategies for how to read texts, especially those that were challenging and scholarly.

## Cluster 3: Community and Society

> Through these courses students will explore the complex interlocking of interests and relations that constitute social life from the level of the local community through the globalized network of societies. Through the study of the interlocking of material, moral, and political factors informing society at all levels, students will have the opportunity to acquire skills enabling them to both understand and act in the world that they will be inhabiting as citizens.

At the foundation level students practice research methods; recognize factors that shape communities; place Canada within a global community; begin to learn about key political, social, and economic institutions and practices; consider moral obligations of individuals and societies; are introduced to historical, ideological, and theoretical perspectives on community and society; and debate issues about the quality of life in society. Of the four thematic clusters in our general education program, this cluster is most explicitly concerned with citizenship and social engagement, so if we are trying to foster "intellectual and civic capacities" in our students, as our official documents claim, this area bears a disproportionate burden for fostering civic capacity. At the time we gathered data, there were two foundation-level choices in Community and Society for students: one called Globalization and a second course called Communities and Societies. Communities and Societies was conceptualized as a series of expanding circles of social groupings from the personal, to local, to national, to global with all sections of the course following the same structure; since then it has been revised as a shell course focused on social problems to allow for more instructor autonomy.

Miriam Carey, who has a political science background, had taught Communities and Societies many times. She believed the course engaged students with significant issues by encouraging their sense of agency and responsibility. Carey organized students into small groups who worked together as study teams during the term. These groups developed their own identities; many even chose to give themselves particular group names. As different communities were examined, the class addressed themes of rules and responsibilities and considered problem resolution. Students read material from a course pack co-created by all instructors in the course. Readings included articles from the popular press, academic articles, and chapters from books. Students read between ten and thirty pages per week. During the class, students were encouraged to discuss class readings, first in their small groups and then in a more open class discussion. Indeed, students used class discussion to decide on a series of topics for the end-of-course research paper. These topics were sparked by class readings but required students to go into more depth than the class allowed. Given the engaged and engaging nature of the class discussions, Carey hoped students would actually begin to realize their social agency and power in the creation of small group, and whole class, communities; she was less focused on the academic purposes of critical reading. She did not draw attention to the different genres or provide specific instruction in how to read different texts. It was not, she said, an English course.

## Cluster 4: Communication

> These courses focus on the development of an undergraduate level of proficiency in written and oral communication across a range of media. They further facilitate the development of a capacity for critical reflection upon various communication media and their uses. This cluster of courses also provides the opportunity for study in languages other than English.

At the foundation level these courses focus on English composition. Unlike the other three areas of Mount Royal's general education provision, they do not need to have any interdisciplinary content but are charged with assuring undergraduate-level writing skills—something that is impossible in a thirteen-week unit. For many students the foundation-level general education course in communication will be their only writing instruction. At the time we gathered data there were three choices: Critical Writing and Reading, Writing for the Professions, and Writing in a Digital Context. By far the majority of students took the Critical Writing and Reading course because we offered so many more sections of it. That course, staffed by English instructors, used to be a composition course with readings. Although the Department of English added the idea of critical reading to the course's title for the general education provision, it remains a composition course with readings. Instructors select their own texts and approaches; however, all sections must include some sort of rhetorical analysis.

Karen Manarin, an English instructor, taught Critical Writing and Reading many times. She has been investigating different reading strategies for several years, and so explicitly included material about critical reading and metacognitive strategies in the syllabus and in the classroom. She provided students with the opportunity to practice and reflect upon different comprehension strategies; she also guided students through rhetorical analysis of different texts, because it is, after all, an English course. Students read a variety of nonfictional essays taken from an anthology, *Landmarks,* the sort of reader commonly used in first-year writing classes; they also used *They Say/I Say: The Moves That Matter in Academic Writing* by Gerald Graff and Cathy Birkenstein, which provided them with practice for putting their ideas in conversation with texts.[16] Most essays read were short, the longest only fifteen pages. Students would typically read two or three essays a week and then would do some type of activity with those readings in each class. For example, students would outline the essay's structure, identify topic sentences, discuss rhetorical strategies, look for logical fallacies, and consider stylistic choices. Grammar and documentation instruction were also provided. In this section of the course, students worked on the same topic for three different assignments during the term. They were asked to create a position paper, an annotated bibliography, and a research paper on a topic they felt passionate about. Manarin hoped the sequence would help students with their reading and writing skills.

Our approaches and these four courses are not unique in our institution, nor, we suspect, elsewhere. Many places have some sort of scientific literacy component in their general education program. University is a time for struggling with big ideas and difficult texts, as is the case in our humanities-type cluster. Civic engagement has received more attention in general education and higher education overall in the last decade. A writing requirement has been a constant in most general education programs over the past century. Indeed, it is precisely because these approaches and courses are not unique that what we discovered about student learning in these particular classes is important. We initiated this project because we were frustrated by some students' reading behaviors; we assumed they all could read, or if they couldn't, it was someone else's problem, not ours; sometimes we thought students just weren't trying; we didn't understand why some students didn't seem to "get it"; we thought we were fostering critical reading in our classrooms; we were somewhat complacent.

## A Collaborative SoTL Project

Even though we thought we were doing a fine job, we were curious about how our students read. So we designed a collaborative SOTL inquiry across the four courses.[17] We shared the same research question, gathered comparable assignments, and conducted the analysis using the same protocols. We wanted to see how our students demonstrated critical reading for academic goals and social engagement.

We gathered students' written course work in the January to April 2011 term; as part of the institutional review board's conditions for approval, we did not know until after the courses were finished which students had agreed to participate. Participation rates for three of the four courses were similar: Controversies in Science, 76 percent; Community and Society, 79 percent; and Critical Writing and Reading, 77 percent. Participation among students in the Texts and Ideas course was much lower, at 31 percent, perhaps because of the emotionally charged nature of many of the readings. Overall, 72 students participated in our study by allowing their course work to be examined for indicators of critical reading. Although at first glance the sample seems small, we examined more than 700 written artifacts in various genres. In each course, students wrote on average 10 reading logs, of at least 250 words each, using the prompts: "What (is the reading about)?" "So What (does it mean)?" and "Now What (are you going to do with this information)?" The reading logs received comments but no grades beyond participation. We also collected all assignments leading up to the research papers and the research papers themselves.

The scholarship of teaching and learning always involves ethical issues because of the dual (at least) role of teacher and scholar. Indeed, institutional review boards' policies on research involving human participants can help us think through some of the issues that must first be addressed, including gaining free informed consent, minimizing the possibility of coercion, citing student work, and protecting confidentiality.[18] But ethical issues don't end with the official approval. The scholarship of teaching and learning contains what Pat Hutchings calls "dilemmas of fidelity, attempts to balance competing goods—and to do so in a context without clear norms or rules."[19] Is the primary concern in the classroom setting following the research protocol, or is it providing whatever the students seem to need most at that particular moment? Collaborative scholarship of teaching and learning magnifies those issues, because choices made by the individual instructor affect more than the individual class. In terms of the collaborative inquiry, what do you do if one team member has time to assign only nine rather than ten reading logs? What do you do if one team member has students respond to a foreign film with subtitles for one of the reading logs rather than a written text? Reading a film critically requires many of the same elements as reading a text critically, especially evaluation of assumptions and creation of inferences; however, there are many different processes at work as well. Although the reading logs about the film were longer and particularly rich, perhaps because of the medium, we chose to exclude that data from this study.[20] We also decided, after the fact, that because we were looking for larger patterns of engagement in critical reading, the variation of nine or ten reading logs was unlikely to make a substantive difference in our analysis.

We analyzed the written work in several stages, using as a starting point the Valid Assessment of Learning in Undergraduate Education (VALUE) rubrics for reading, integrative learning, information literacy, and civic engagement created by the Association for American Colleges and Universities (AAC&U). We did not use the VALUE reading rubric exclusively, because we wanted evaluating assumptions and making inferences to be addressed explicitly in our rubrics as they are two crucial elements for critical reading. We deliberately did not share the AAC&U rubrics with the students. They were never intended to grade student work within an individual course; rather they were intended to be used as an institutional tool to assess student learning across the undergraduate experience. For this inquiry we wanted to capture a snapshot of what was happening in these classes with our regular readings, activities, and rubrics; this was not an exercise in course redesign. We did not know if students would demonstrate improvement according to the rubrics over a thirteen-week semester and didn't want to discourage them if there was no improvement. And as we graded assignments for the course, we assessed more than just reading. Examining the assignments for this collaborative inquiry was a different experience from marking those same assignments earlier when our focus was to provide students with formative feedback for future assignments. In the analysis of data for the inquiry, however, the AAC&U rubrics offered a way to assess critical reading across the disparate disciplines, and they provided a common framework when we were examining indicators of critical reading in markedly different content areas. They also helped us place information about our students' reading abilities within a national—indeed, for us, international—set of expectations. They gave us a vocabulary with which to describe what we were seeing, and they also helped us identify elements that were not captured by the rubrics.

After the courses were over, we examined all the VALUE rubrics, discussing the language of the different descriptors and eventually coming up with our own hybrid models, selecting those elements that seemed central to critical reading for academic purposes and for social engagement.[21] Critical reading is more than the decoding of literal meaning embedded within a text. We met, discussed, defined, and clarified terms to construct our categories. We decided upon four categories that are consistent across the two definitions of reading:

- Comprehension (from the VALUE reading rubric)—the ability to summarize text and recognize its implications
- Analysis (from the VALUE reading rubric)—the ability to recognize and use features of a text to support understanding
- Interpretation (from the VALUE reading rubric)—the ability to construe meaning from a text and recognize different ways of reading

- Evaluation (from the VALUE information literacy rubric)—the ability to identify and analyze one's own and others' assumptions

We believed that evaluation would be particularly important in critical reading. We also felt that successful critical reading would require high levels of inference, although the type of inference would vary depending on the purpose of reading. Critical reading for academic purposes would likely require students to be able to make connections between different texts and types of knowledge. Therefore, our Critical Reading for Academic Purposes rubric also included the following:

- Recognition of Genres (from the VALUE reading rubric)—the ability to recognize different types of texts and how to use them;
- Connections to Discipline (from the VALUE integrative learning rubric)— the ability to draw connections across disciplinary conventions.

These categories provide glimpses into the processes readers use to construct meaning beyond basic comprehension by using inference, but the type of inference we were looking for here was primarily academic. Critical reading for social engagement, on the other hand, involved issues of agency. Here the inferences were more likely to connect to the community and personal experience. So our Critical Reading for Social Engagement rubric included the following:

- Analysis of Knowledge (from the VALUE civic engagement rubric)—the ability to integrate academic work and community or civic engagement;
- Connections to Experience (from the VALUE integrative learning rubric)—the ability to connect academic knowledge and relevant life experiences.

Thus, our rubrics, Critical Reading for Academic Purposes and Critical Reading for Social Engagement, each contained six indicators of critical reading.

We did not change the language of the rubrics, because we wanted to participate in the "common dialogue and understanding of student success" that the AAC&U framework offers. However, we did combine the two "milestone" categories in the middle, as it was often difficult to distinguish between the two when examining student work. So the hybrid rubrics have "capstone," "milestone," and "benchmark" categories. Using the rubrics, we began at the highest, or capstone, level and assessed student work against each subsequent descriptor. We assigned a zero (0) if the written piece contained evidence that the introductory or benchmark level of performance was not achieved: a student spoke to a particular category but failed in his or her attempt. We also created a category called "absence" if there was no evidence that a particular category was attempted. We assigned a score for each indicator holistically but then went back to identify particular pieces of evidence to support that score. We also decided to record our judgements using worksheets, which allowed for easier comparison later. This formal protocol helped us understand one another's qualitative judgments.

Once the rubrics were created and the protocol designed, we met to assess inter-rater reliability on our use of the rubrics. We assessed pieces of anonymous student work individually with the rubrics and then compared our findings. Our ratings during these trials were remarkably similar. Differences were discussed, and decisions were clarified. The biggest discrepancies were in our interpretations of what we thought the students meant to say rather than focusing on what the students had actually written. By checking our ratings with one another, we felt more confident that the rubric scores were more than idiosyncratic judgments. We read and coded the data from our classes independently and then met periodically to discuss our analysis. Working with the rubrics allowed us to see patterns that otherwise might have been lost in the richness of the data, but it also became clear that the rubrics were not sufficient in themselves. Here we could see the difference between "planned working" and "emergent working," in Lorraine Walsh and Peter Kahn's terms.[22] We needed to become aware of what the rubrics couldn't show; in other words, we needed to read critically.

In the midst of data analysis we realized that the rubrics were not capturing everything. We chose to use supplemental analysis of the research papers and reading logs to provide a richer description of how our students read, recognizing that all we had were oblique measures and that we did not always agree about what those oblique measures suggested. We were deep in what Judith Davidson Wasser and Liora Bresler call "the interpretive zone": "a place where multiple viewpoints are held in dynamic tension as a group seeks to make sense of fieldwork issues and meanings."[23] As we examined the research papers, we knew that we needed to check as many of the students' sources as we could, not for plagiarism, but for glimpses into how those sources were read. We could not apply rubrics about reading if we had not read the original documents, a realization that undermines our usual grading practices. We recognized that we habitually had been making assumptions about how students read sources that we were unfamiliar with based on how they integrated them into their writing. As we examined the reading logs, what wasn't evident was sometimes as interesting as what could be measured by a rubric. Only by returning to the data—developing lists of significant statements, grouping them into themes, writing textural and structural descriptions, and trying to capture different aspects of reading through writing—could we begin to make sense of what was happening in our classrooms.

Before we turn to our discussion of findings in the context of research about reading, we want to unpack some of our assumptions, including compliance. Before attempting to answer "Can students read?" in the next chapter, we briefly look here at a different question: "Do students read?" Like many faculty members, we believe that keeping up with assigned reading is important for student success in many disciplines. Celia Popovic and David A. Green report that this assumption is supported by data from American and British institutions.[24] However, faculty members also don't think their students are keeping up with the reading, as witnessed by the extensive advice to faculty on how to increase reading compliance, from quizzes, to reading groups, to modeling reading or note-taking strategies.[25] As Bryan D. Brost and Karen A. Bradley observe, explanations for noncompliance often focus on student ability; they assert that instructors often perpetuate noncompliance by not using the reading effectively to support learning and by repeating the material in lecture.[26] In Brost and Bradley's case study, as in our inquiry, response papers were written after the material had been discussed in class, so students could avoid reading by relying on class discussion.[27]

Keenly aware of this possibility, we tried to pay attention to details in the reading logs that signaled to us that students had engaged with the text itself. Students were also encouraged to take their responses beyond what was discussed together. Sometimes students juxtaposed their understanding of the reading before and after discussion, sometimes they offered interpretations that were at odds with what had been discussed in class, sometimes they confessed not reading, and honestly sometimes they bluffed. We also note that research suggests that journals in which students write responses to readings increase compliance, even if the journals do not necessarily increase compre-hension.[28] So we assume that students who were able to refer to specific details from the readings in the reading logs had read the assigned readings, although they may not have comprehended them in any depth and may not have been able to remember details later, a type of reading required when studying texts for examinations.

Another assumption we held until well into the data analysis was that students in different courses would display much different reading behaviors appropriate to the variety of texts and assignments. Indeed we first imagined this project as a compari-son of reading behaviors across the general education program depending on course content. After all, literacy instruction has been shifting from more generic approaches to disciplinary literacy. A similar emphasis on disciplinary understanding can be seen within the scholarship of teaching and learning, particularly in the "Decoding the Disciplines" movement.[29] Surely students would read scientific articles, eyewitness accounts of genocide, newspaper articles, and personal essays quite differently, espe-cially given the outcomes and activities of the four courses. Our first reaction was surprise at how similar responses seemed to be across the four courses.

To check whether our gut reactions matched the data, we took a closer look at the distribution of rubric scores for the reading logs in the four courses. We analyzed the data using Pearson's chi-squared tests of association. We constructed a contingency table for each variable of interest, those that characterize reading for both academic purposes and social engagement, and evaluated the levels of student performance (capstone, milestone, benchmark, failure, and absence) for each of our courses. For each variable we found significant differences (all $P - 0.001$) among our courses, but a statistically significant difference is not necessarily a meaningful one. Although we had a large sample size ($n = 587$), these statistics should be interpreted with caution, as there were some instances where only a few students were ranked within a particular category, or all students were ranked in the same category. For example, in our analy-sis of reading for social engagement, most students (85 percent) in the Controversies in Science course didn't even attempt to connect their readings with aspects of civic engagement. Thus, most reading logs were ranked as demonstrating an absence of this aspect of social engagement, with the remaining students distributed across the remaining categories of proficiency. To ensure that failures and absence rankings were not driving these significant findings, we also analyzed our data using only capstone, milestone, and benchmark levels of student performance. A similar pattern emerged; there were still significant differences among our courses with respect to student performance for all variables of interest. It is not surprising that there were differences: the courses have different foci, texts, and instructors. It is also important to remember that despite our attempts to be consistent in how we read the student work, we were still four people making complex qualitative judgments on oblique measures of reading. Yet the reading responses across the four courses seemed so similar to us when we talked together. Despite statistically significant differences among courses, we still saw general patterns.

In the chapters describing our findings, we present rubric scores in bar graphs broken down by course for each element of critical reading identified in the hybridized rubrics. These charts make visible some of the key similarities and differences in student reading performance among the courses. In each chapter we discuss similarities, point out areas of prominent differences, and suggest explanations for these observed patterns. Our collaboration revealed more similarities than we had initially expected given the different outcomes, readings, assignments, and instructor styles in the four courses. Of course, we were dealing with first-year general education courses, and although many of the students had already entered programs or declared majors, they were probably not deeply enculturated in these disciplines at that point. As individual researchers, we could never have seen these similarities, nor could we have seen the differences among courses. Noting the time commitments, effort required, and emotional investment in collaboration, Wasser and Bresler take an instrumental position in terms of the cost: Is the collaboration worth it? "Does it serve to deepen and enrich the interpretation? What evidence do we have that it does so?"[30] In this inquiry, collaboration was well worth the cost, as the following chapters will demonstrate.

# 2   Can Students Read?

CAN STUDENTS READ? On one level the answer must be, Of course, they wouldn't be in university if they couldn't. Usually we think of reading instruction as something that happens when children are young. Emergent literacy, the process by which toddlers make crucial connections between world, sounds, and print, sets the stage for the decoding processes of early literacy with specific attention to areas like phonics, spelling, fluency, and vocabulary.[1] When employers, governments, and faculty complain that postsecondary students today just can't read, for the most part they are not talking about decoding skills (although decoding remains a serious challenge for many students with a print-related disability); they are talking about the ability to make meaning out of complicated texts and to apply that knowledge in different contexts. These concerns have intensified over the past decade perhaps because of anxiety over how pervasive electronic interfaces seem to be. Popular books like Maryanne Wolf's *Proust and the Squid: The Story and the Science of the Reading Brain* (2007), Nicholas Carr's *The Shallows: How the Internet Is Changing the Way We Think, Read, and Remember* (2010), and Mark Bauerlein's *The Dumbest Generation: How the Digital Age Stupefies Young Americans and Jeopardizes Our Future; or, Don't Trust Anyone under 30* (2009) suggest that behaviors like texting and Internet surfing may change how we read and think.[2] Certainly our students recognize both positive and negative impacts of technology on their understanding: "I know that technology has affected the way that I read and process information. In ways it has brought me down because it is easier to google a question rather than get information from a textbook. At the same time, it can help me because I really like visuals and often I can find YouTube or other visuals on the internet to provide support to a topic I may not understand." Electronic interfaces have the potential to limit and to enhance understanding, but we don't really know how electronic interfaces affect cognition. Nor do we know whether these students, en masse, demonstrate a lesser, or even a different, capacity for reading than generations that have gone before.[3] We are only starting to know more about cognitive processes involved in different types of reading and the activities that seem to trigger these processes.

This chapter explores the four categories that are consistent across our two definitions of critical reading. We believe that regardless of whether individuals are reading critically for academic purposes or for social engagement, they will demonstrate the following abilities:

- Comprehension—the ability to summarize text and recognize its implications
- Analysis—the ability to recognize and use features of a text to support understanding
- Interpretation—the ability to construe meaning from a text and recognize different ways of reading
- Evaluation—the ability to identify and analyze one's own and others' assumptions

We took descriptors for the first three categories from the VALUE reading rubric and the fourth from the VALUE information literacy rubric, because critical reading, like critical thinking, has at its heart the careful examination of assumptions in preparation for informed action, to paraphrase Stephen Brookfield.[4] In what follows, we briefly situate these four elements, all of them essential for critical reading, within theoretical models of reading before attempting to answer our chapter's title: "Can Students Read?"

Reading involves many cognitive and, increasingly recognized as crucial, noncognitive elements. As James Paul Gee notes, reading research in the 1980s and 1990s began to shift from a relatively abstract focus on the individual's mind to situated cognition; he argues that "literacy needed to be viewed as embedded in multiple socially and culturally constructed practices, not seen as a uniform set of mental abilities or processes."[5] While information-processing models of reading led to the development of schema theories, built on the idea that the reader places new information within an abstract structure composed of prior knowledge, such theories do not adequately account for readers reading in a naturalistic environment. Indeed, as Mark Sadoski, Allan Paivio, and Ernest T. Goetz observe, proponents of schema theories tend to rely on isolated experiments involving sentence integration, bizarre or ambiguous texts, and perspective studies; however, prior knowledge, by itself, is not enough to explain differences among readers.[6] The three researchers argue for a process of cognition involving both linguistic and nonlinguistic elements, including imagery and affect. Schema theory can be a powerful heuristic for instructors seeking to understand how their students read; it is a way to think about how individuals construct meaning.[7] This construction cannot be purely cognitive nor value-neutral, because, as Mary B. McVee, Kailonnie Dunsmore, and James R. Gavelek write, "language is a way of doing things in the world."[8] They argue that "all cultural activity is imbued with and linked to power; therefore, schemas can assist a learner in accessing relevant knowledge, or culturally situated schemas may cause confusion or even precipitate resistance. Such is the political nature of schemas."[9]

♆ One relevant construct with the potential to increase or impede critical reading is the reader's implicit model of reading. Gregory Schraw and Roger Bruning, examining motivation to read, define implicit models of reading as "tacit, yet systematic beliefs about the reader's perceived role as a reader."[10] They identify two models: transmission, characterized by the belief that the text contains the meaning, and transaction, characterized by the belief that meaning is constructed from the text by the reader, but they also argue that all adult readers hold both beliefs to differing extents. Their research suggests that transmission beliefs have little effect on reading ability, while transaction beliefs seem to increase engagement and reading success, leading them to advocate for explicit modeling of transaction beliefs. David Yun Dai and Xiaolei Wang examine the connections between readers' implicit models and their need for cognition, which "in the context of reading is expressed as a reader's tendency to engage in deep understanding of the text, build a well-integrated situation model, and enjoy the processes and outcomes of the cognitively demanding comprehension activity."[11] This suggests that a transactional model of reading is important for critical reading, whether for academic purposes or social engagement. However, Dai and Wang argue, "Transactional and transmission beliefs may reflect different levels of cognitive sophistication that is more domain general rather than domain specific, that is having less to do with specific types or genres of reading and more to do with cognitive complexity implied in transaction versus transmission models."[12] If so, an individual's ability to engage deeply in a text may be less a matter of linguistic competence than of intellectual development. By "intellectual development" we do not mean intelligence; rather, we are referring to the work of William G. Perry, Marcia B. Baxter Magolda, and others who suggest that individuals go through a series of attitudes about knowledge, from dualist to committed, or absolute to contextual.[13] These epistemological stages play a role in implicit models of reading. An individual who believes that knowledge is the collection of information is unlikely to have a strong transactional model of reading but may be able to extract information from a text using both memory-based and constructionist processes,[14] although perhaps with greater effort. Tracy Linderholm notes that readers who are less skilled "do more re-reading and read much more slowly, and thus put in more effort, when reading for study purposes" compared to skilled readers who de-emphasize rereading in favor of comprehension-monitoring strategies.[15] It  can be a vicious circle where less skilled readers employing a transmission model of reading may try harder, achieve less success, and become less likely to trust their own understanding of content, reinforcing transmission model beliefs at the expense of transactional ones.

As we looked at the VALUE reading rubric,[16] we noticed this distinction between transmission and transactional models in the descriptors for the Comprehension, Analysis, and Interpretation categories. The benchmark level of student performance for Comprehension is "Apprehends vocabulary appropriately to paraphrase or summarize the information the text communicates"; for Analysis the benchmark is "Identifies aspects of a text (e.g., content, structure, or relations among ideas) as needed to respond to questions posed in assigned tasks"; and for Interpretation it is "Can identify purpose(s) for reading, relying on an external authority such as an instructor for clarification of the task." Each of these descriptors involves activities that someone holding a strong transmission model of reading should be able to complete. Milestone and capstone levels require the student to demonstrate increasingly more transactional activities, requiring different cognitive processes. Thus, Comprehension, Analysis, and Interpretation categories reflect different implicit models of reading across the levels. This is not the case with the Evaluation category, from the VALUE information literacy rubric.[17] There the expectations described at the benchmark level imply a transaction model: "Shows an emerging awareness of present assumptions (sometimes labels assertions as assumptions). Begins to identify some contexts when presenting a position." Right from this benchmark level, the student is expected to do more than mine the text for information. Someone with a strong transmission model of reading may struggle with the reflection required in this task. And, honestly, we don't teach transactional reading in any systematic way; we just assume students can do it when asked.

Armed with our hybridized rubrics, we began to reread all the reading logs created for the courses, trying to determine through these oblique measures whether our students were able to read course material critically and where they seemed to succeed or struggle. Remember, the reading logs were designed so that students would describe what they read, what it meant, and what they were going to do with that information (the "What?" "So What?" and "Now What?" prompts). We divide our findings into good, not-so-good, and bad news.

## The Good News: Comprehension, Analysis, and Interpretation

The good news, the really great news, is that the majority of students in all four courses were able to comprehend course readings at a minimal benchmark level; a significant number comprehended at higher levels according to the VALUE rubrics (see fig. 2.1). There are some differences among the rubric scores for the four courses; most noticeably in this case, the number of responses that were judged to be at the benchmark rather than milestone level for the Critical Writing and Reading course can be explained by the different disciplinary expectations on the part of the English instructor of the group. However, a general pattern emerges. By far the majority of students in these first-year courses demonstrate benchmark or milestone performance in Comprehension.

In response to the "What?" prompt, students were usually able to identify topics and main claims, even in texts that were difficult—for example, a scientific article from a scholarly journal. It is important to note, however, that the reading logs were

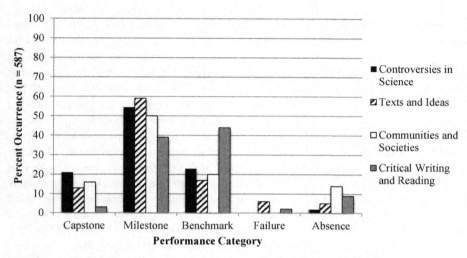

FIGURE 2.1. **Comprehension:** Most students were able to understand the text well enough to identify important information and to make at least some inferences about context.

completed after class discussion of the particular reading, so those students who may have been unsure of the content or who hadn't read the reading were able to confirm or revise their understanding of the article based on that discussion. Indeed, many students referenced the role of class discussion in their reading logs. They said things like "I was a little confused after reading the article, but coming to class and discussing it with my group and the class kind of helped me (a lot). I feel that I have a decent understanding now, whereas before I didn't." Class discussion was not a free-for-all. We tried to reinforce particular behaviors we thought were important through targeted questions and activities. Discussion seemed particularly important when the reading was saying something that the students didn't expect, perhaps a symptom of the dangers of schemas as aids to understanding. For example, poetic language or rich description often caused difficulties, a finding that won't be surprising for instructors of English. However, as David Bartholomae and Anthony Petrosky contend, "In an academic setting, difficulty is not necessarily a problem. . . . The work can be hard to read because the writer is thinking beyond the usual ways of thinking."[18] Difficulty is too often presented as a problem caused by a deficit, in the writer or in the reader, but it can be reframed as "a point of departure for a long and satisfying journey of the mind," to quote Mariolina Rizzi Salvatori and Patricia Donahue.[19]

Salvatori and Donahue identify many types of difficulty the students shared, including "difficulties posed by readers confusing a text's surface with its depth," "difficulties posed by a strangeness of content or formal arrangement," and "difficulties posed by ambiguity."[20] One student, reflecting on his reading processes, talked about the "limbo of thought" that a certain essay provoked until class discussion and further reflection: "It was not until our class discussion that I truly understood what Menzies [the essay's author] was trying to portray. I became slightly trapped by her descriptions and symbolism and the whole point of the essay was almost completely lost on me. But by living in the moment and trying to imagine her story, I was in a way doing exactly what her essay was trying to push, being without doing." Here the class discussion allowed this student to recognize his initial confusion as an important part of the reading experience; by reflecting upon his struggle to find meaning, he came to a deeper understanding of the author's purpose in writing an essay that resists closure and a tidy moral. The first reading, bewildering and imaginative, took on new significance through conversation and rereading. Class discussion provided an opportunity for students to think about a text retrospectively rather than in the moment of first reading. It forced students to slow down, to read "intensively" in John Guillory's terms.[21] And if, as Bartholomae and Petrosky argue, rereading is "the best way to work on a difficult text,"[22] discussion allowed students to take a closer and more critical look at targeted passages of a text with scaffolding that promoted transactional activities. This scaffolding could include activities such as annotating a text, writing about reactions to specific passages, and reading passages out loud to experiment with tone.

Given this level of reading support, we're not sure why almost 10 percent of reading logs showed significant misunderstandings of the text even when students were present for discussions that identified the thesis or main claim of the text. Perhaps part of the issue is the transmission model of reading, where miscues found in the text are still more authoritative than the discussion. Discussion clarifies meaning, but individuals must be willing to recognize and revise their initial impressions, something that is more difficult for those with strong transmission models of reading. After all, if the meaning is hidden there in the text waiting to be pulled out, how can a person know when he or she has found it? Or perhaps some students saw the reading log as an opportunity for commentary rather than comprehension. For example, in a reading log for a chapter from a sociology text about changes in the Canadian family, one student said nothing about the chapter or the changing characteristics of families, instead launching into a discussion of her own family. In this case, personal resonance displaced textual content, even when the student was directly asked to describe "What?" she had read. This student chose not to comply with that first question. Is this demonstrating a lack of comprehension or something else? Possibly the student hadn't completed the reading and so didn't have enough content knowledge to answer; talking about her own family, then, could be a compensatory move. However, the disconnect between answer and question might also be the result of the reader's goals, which are not necessarily the same as the instructor's.

Paul van den Broek and others have developed the idea of standard of coherence to explain how readers' goals affect reading processes and levels of comprehension. Predictably, readers who have a study goal are much more concerned about coherence in text and comprehension than readers who have an entertainment goal, who seem to focus more on making associations to personal experiences.[23] How did our students view the course texts? In all four courses, they were not explicitly tested on the content of the readings, and we know, as instructors and as former students, that students are more likely to skim readings for class than for an exam.[24]

At the same time, however, students knew they had to write about the course readings, and research shows that writing about a text helps increase reading comprehension, something composition theorists have argued for a long time. For example, Salvatori and Donahue promote "writing to read pathways," where students "trace their reading paths, to reconstruct the various reversals, re-tracings, and difficult negotiations that they inevitably experience as they attempt to think the thoughts of another, learn from those thoughts, resist or reject them, dialogue with them—and much more."[25] Writing can improve reading. Steve Graham and Michael Hebert's meta-analysis of empirical reading research suggests that "writing about a text proved to be better than just reading it, reading and rereading it, reading and studying it, reading and discussing it, and receiving reading instruction."[26] The form of writing matters. In order of increasing effect, Graham and Hebert advocate having students answer or ask questions about the reading in writing, take notes about the reading, summarize the reading, and write extended responses, both personal and analytical. While some students seemed to view the reading log prompts as simple questions to be answered as efficiently as possible, most used them—especially the questions "So What?" and "Now What?"—as an opportunity to write extended responses to the readings.

These responses demonstrated that many students were not only able to comprehend the reading well enough to summarize the text, but they were also able to manipulate the ideas of the readings in terms of analysis and interpretation. If Analysis is seen as taking a text apart or "recognizing and using features of a text to build a more advanced understanding of the text's meaning," Interpretation involves "determining or construing the meaning of a text or part of a text in a particular way based on textual and contextual information."[27] For example, students in Critical Writing and Reading found an essay about language in biology textbooks difficult to get through, but they could still comprehend it.[28] This essay by anthropologist Emily Martin was originally published in a feminist academic journal, so it had an ideological dimension that made many students uncomfortable; it was longer and more dense than many of the other readings in the course; it also had a lot of references and endnotes. Although many students did not enjoy the reading, most of them were able to identify relationships between textual features as the author built her argument (Analysis). In addition, many students were able to identify interpretive strategies, or ways of reading, depending on purpose (Interpretation).

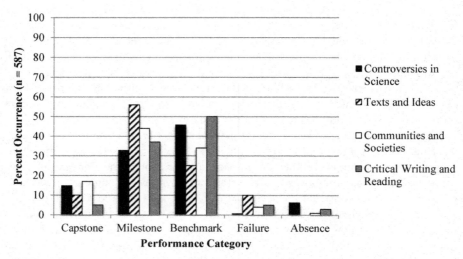

FIGURE 2.2. **Interpretation:** At the benchmark level, students were able to demonstrate reading for purpose by answering the specific prompts; sometimes they described deliberately choosing interpretive strategies to meet their purpose.

At a benchmark level a student would say something like the following: "My favorite strategy for reading and understanding a story, article, or essay is using imagery. To be honest I had a lot of trouble imagining this because of the depth Martin went into. So I turned to questioning. The more I questioned what Martin was saying, the more I started understanding." This student goes on to link the language of sperm and eggs to a larger, and mostly implicit, argument about men and women, successfully identifying the argument as relying upon metaphor. The student self-consciously adjusts reading strategies to increase comprehension but also can identify aspects of the text. He hasn't moved yet to evaluating how these aspects support the argument, nor has he demonstrated awareness of a range of interpretive strategies based upon particular communities of readers. His response fits the benchmark descriptors for Analysis and Interpretation.

Contrast this response with another student's: "I read this essay with some scrutiny. Being that I am interested in the field of science, I found Martin's take on society's accepted version of the egg and sperm system to be different and new. I had always just adopted the perspective that was reflected in my textbooks. Martin's essay really expressed the necessity for skepticism in science. We cannot just accept everything we're told." This student has an advantage; she has taken biology courses and places Martin's essay in a disciplinary context. She situates herself in a particular community

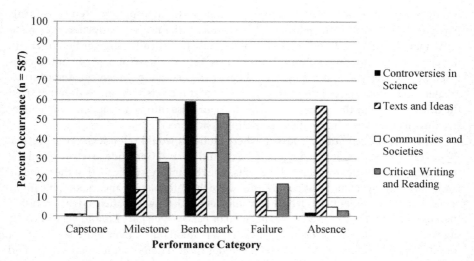

FIGURE 2.3. **Analysis:** Students in three of these first-year courses demonstrated the ability to interact with different aspects of the text, often recognizing relationships among these parts or aspects. Students in Texts and Ideas—Genocide did not attempt to analyze what they read.

of readers and recognizes different ways of reading the same texts (Interpretation). She also evaluates specific textual features in the argument. For example, she talks about how the factual evidence appeals to the reader's sense of logos and provides a more nuanced explanation of the text, linking the metaphor not only to men and women's roles in society but also to gender discrimination in science (Analysis).

A few students were even able to find the humor in Martin's presentation of a serious topic. This doesn't mean the students necessarily agreed with her argument. Some students offered rationales for their disagreement—for example, "There are much more blatant and serious incidences of gender bias in our lives." Others understood but then chose to dismiss the essay with misrepresentation: "It has made me think about gender stereotypes and the ways in which we have been taught about sexual education, although the majority of the information presented in this essay I do not agree with and I feel is relatively generalized." The essay may be many things, but it is not generalized, as it focuses on the specific language of fertilization in biology textbooks, carefully listed in seventy-one endnotes. But this student's response still demonstrates that he read and understood the essay.

Even though the reading logs for all four courses demonstrated at least benchmark levels of Interpretation (see fig. 2.2), the results for Analysis were very different in one of the four courses (see fig. 2.3). Students in Texts and Ideas—Genocide did not demonstrate an attempt to analyze in many of their responses. Remember, this particular course had a much lower response rate, with only nine students agreeing to participate in this study, and these students were scholastically stronger than many in the class, as measured by not only their grades but their level of engagement in class discussion as well. If anything, we would have expected these students to demonstrate greater levels of Analysis. However, the content of this course was much different from the other three, and thus the course provides a glimpse into what happens when affective dimensions of reading influence reading behaviors.

In contrast to the other courses, where students would often identify aspects of the text in the reading logs, students in Texts and Ideas—Genocide rarely divided the texts into parts, let alone evaluated the texts. The reading logs indicate that the students comprehended the texts; most could summarize the information and make some inferences. However, students tended to describe details that caught their attention rather than examining the text as a whole made up of parts: "One part I found very interesting was . . . ," or "As far as content goes, what has stood out to me would be . . . ," or "I found it interesting how. . . ." They talked about these details as information they had not known before, explicitly positioning themselves as lacking knowledge or expertise. They repeatedly said, "I did not realize." Some of the details they identified were emotionally charged: "I am also concerned with the children who were killed innocently. They were not given the choice to even enjoy life and liberty [sad face emoticon]." The emoticon is jarring when we read the response, probably because of its association with text messaging. Emoticons are sometimes dismissed as decorative and trivial,[29] but the sentiment expressed here is not trivial. This student is trying to describe deep concern for a vulnerable population; her words do not seem to be enough, so she adds a conventional symbol. Another student described weeping as she read. Again and again, they said, "I don't understand how this could happen," as they grappled with the concept of genocide. Struggling with emotional content and ethical dilemmas, the students did not have the necessary distance or authority to analyze the text. They could not break it into its component parts, because they were transfixed by individual elements.

Ryland has since become more intentional when introducing students to the process of analyzing texts with uncomfortable or unfamiliar themes, in part by using classroom discussion. After his students identify and summarize key parts of the text ("What?"), Ryland probes for contextual and linguistic knowledge to help analyze and interpret details. With additional information, the students seem more comfortable handling the texts. Ryland has discovered, however, that students need repeated prompting and modeling of textual analysis before they become comfortable when analyzing challenging texts on their own. Naming the discomfort may also help students recognize that, far from being a sign of disrespect toward a text or author, analysis is a way to more fully engage with what the author wants to say and ultimately, perhaps, to change behavior. As one student said, "Had we read and paid attention to Lemkin, would things (genocidal outcomes) [have] been the same . . . [?] Had I analyzed what got me into certain predicaments maybe I'd learn. Or maybe not. Who knows!" We do not know how to read the student's tone. Grammatically, the comment "Who knows" should end with a question mark; if it ended with a period, we might read resignation into it, the equivalent of "Whatever." But what does an exclamation point, only the second one in this student's reading logs, suggest?[30] We choose to believe that he not only identifies but also emphasizes the potential power of analysis, of critical reading, to change our world.

Across the four courses, students did not always demonstrate equivalent levels of Comprehension, Analysis, and Interpretation in a particular reading log. Sometimes a student who did not summarize text was still able to demonstrate features of Analysis and Interpretation; sometimes a student was able to summarize details but was unable to place those details into a larger context for meaning. For example, one student in response to an article about bitumen extraction from *National Geographic* was able to report on details presented: "The article that I read involved a native man who lived near Fort McKay. His people didn't have telephones, electricity, etc. so they were living a very traditional lifestyle. These people (including the man's grandpa) gathered cranberries and hunted bison and moose for food. His grandpa had a wood cabin and used a trail for trapping. One day when the man came to the cabin and trails, he found they have been demolished by oil companies. These areas would be used as oil mines (I think) and for other oil company interests." From the description, it is obvious that the student had read the article and was able to comprehend the basic vocabulary, but he was unable, or unwilling, to discuss why these details were presented or what the article meant. Other students were able to recognize the technique of using a character to create a personal connection with the reader: "[The author] wrote in a way that used the story of a particular man who grew up to see the oil sands develop. This added emotion into the oil sands in a way that I have never seen before—they used this man as a relatable point of interest rather than a guilt trip from environmentalists or business people (although the article did touch on these aspects)." Consider these two responses—one student identifies information found in the reading but seems hesitant, given the parenthetical "I think," to make any inference about content, let alone risk analysis or interpretation; the other identifies a particular technique, judges its rhetorical efficacy, and explicitly compares this text with other discourses about the oil sands. The second student seems willing to risk a commitment in commenting on the author's choices. Perhaps willingness to risk is a key element of critical reading. Certainly some risk is required for a transactional model of reading: the individual must risk constructing meaning. However, in most university assessment, instructors do not reward, and sometimes penalize, the student who risks but fails; the less skilled reader may decide it is safer to stay at the literal level rather than risk something more.

Thus far, with the exception of analysis for those in the Texts and Ideas—Genocide course, we were pleasantly surprised by our students' performance according to the VALUE rubrics. Students were consistently demonstrating benchmark or above performance in these first-year classes. Sometimes they would score dramatically lower on a particular reading response as different readings caught or failed to catch their interest, or they failed to read at all, but overall, students were comprehending, analyzing, and interpreting. Why, then, were we left with the feeling that something was missing? That students were not reading critically?

## The Not-So-Good News: Evaluation

While our students could, for the most part, comprehend, interpret, and analyze required texts, we were startled by the rubric results for the Evaluation category. This category involves awareness of assumptions and contexts (see fig. 2.4). Again many reading logs scored at or above the benchmark level, as students demonstrated at least emerging awareness of assumptions and contexts. We also note that many students demonstrated lower levels of Evaluation than of Comprehension, Analysis, and Interpretation. Remember, however, that the VALUE descriptors for Evaluation involve a transactional model of reading at the benchmark level. Although disappointing, it's not surprising that students who were at benchmark level for Comprehension, Analysis, and Interpretation may have slipped below that level for Evaluation, because the activities described suggest different models of reading. More surprising were those reading logs that showed no evidence of students considering assumptions or contexts despite class discussions that focused on these elements in all four courses. We do not know why there were more "failure" scores in two of the courses and more "absence" scores in the other two. It may be simply a matter of instructor interpretation or course focus; for example, the Controversies in Science course emphasized looking for bias in different sources of information, and students tried, often unsuccessfully, to identify assumptions, explaining the higher rate of failure there. However, taken together, the failure and absence categories for Evaluation are alarming. Without even an emerging awareness of assumptions, there can be no critical reading.

At first we thought that perhaps students had difficulty with assumptions when they agreed with the authors, because often it is easier to see an assumption you don't share. However, many students had difficulty with assumptions whether or not they agreed with the author. For example, in response to Nicholas Carr's "Is Google Making Us Stupid?" one student wrote: "The internet is [a] wonderful source of information for research. It opens up a world of information as the author mentions. Google's mission is to organize the world's information and make it universally accessible and useful."[31] This statement is a misrepresented quotation from the article. Carr quotes Google's website; the student quotes Carr's quotation without realizing or, if that is too strong, acknowledging that Carr doesn't agree with Google's vision of itself. After all, those words exist in his article. The student does not respond to the challenge put forth by Carr in all those other words in the article; she does not even seem aware that they disagree.

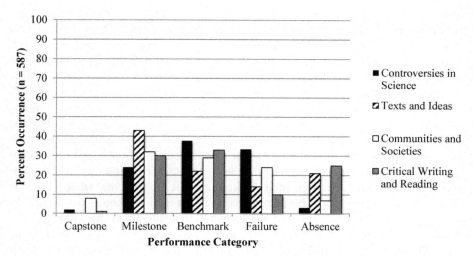

FIGURE 2.4. **Evaluation:** While many reading logs provided evidence that students were showing awareness of or questioning assumptions, a disturbing number of reading logs showed no evidence that students considered assumptions or context while reading.

Agreement with the author leads to its own issues in terms of evaluating assumptions, as many students accept the claims at face value. For example, students reading a sermon by Martin Luther King Jr. restate King's main idea and its implications for the audience as well as personally for the student, but they do not evaluate the claims beyond saying they are "significant," "important," and "very powerful." Students find it difficult to be critical of King and his ideas, perhaps because of his posthumous reputation. Involving students in a class discussion that compared the ideas expressed in King's essay with Malcolm X's ideas allowed some students to begin to read more critically:[32] "Ultimately, I think that 'hate' and feelings of animosity are best conquered with 'love,' but violence is necessary to defend yourself when it is staring you in the eyes. ~~Both wanted equality.~~" Here the student is struggling to reconcile two irreconcilable attitudes about violence, both of which he agrees with; he recognizes that both men wanted racial equality, but that similarity is (literally) crossed out by their differences. Unfortunately, the response ends there; we do not know if this student was able to identify the contradictions within his response.

In Controversies in Science one of the assigned readings was especially useful in highlighting students' reluctance to evaluate information critically. In fact this reading, "Cigarette Smoking: An Underused Tool in High-Performance Endurance Training," also generated many emotional responses.[33] Students have been told for years about the negative consequences of smoking, and although this article had "Satire" written across the top (it was published in the holiday issue of the *Canadian Medical Association Journal*) and the abstract pointed out how information can be misused, many students read the article without challenging its conclusion: that smoking can be beneficial for endurance athletes. After all, the article came from a respected scientific journal and contained research from other respected scientific journals. Even though many students knew the conclusion didn't make logical sense, they never drew inferences about the message. They said things like "I do not believe one thing that this article states. I am shocked that this article is promoting smoking. There is so much evidence for negative repercussions of smoking especially in sports. I don't understand how something so ridiculous can be published in the science community." The student recognizes dissonance between what she knows about the topic and what the article is claiming but does not use this dissonance to reflect upon the context of the article. Other responses were even more disappointing in that students seemed to accept the conclusion: "I believe that these scientists need to conduct further experiments on the use of cigarettes in athletes. I believe that legal medicines should be used or some sort of natural product to get the same results as cigarette smoking. Polls should be conducted in order to see if this would be publicly accepted." Instead of evaluating the claim, this student uses three strategies of deflection from the uncomfortable conclusion in quick succession: get more evidence; find another, less objectionable product; and go with popular opinion. Notice also the repetition of "I believe" as the student hedges what might be interpreted as criticism of the published piece. Critical reading requires identification of contexts as part of evaluation of information, and, thankfully, many students were able to recognize the ridiculous conclusion and specifically reflected on the need to read critically: "This article claims that cigarettes offer the same benefits that athletes seek from other illegal and dangerous methods. These benefits are: an increase in serum hemoglobin, increased lung volume (by COPD [chronic obstructive pulmonary disease]) and weight loss. Given the context of the paper, its intent is to demonstrate how selectively chosen and properly worded scientific research and facts can become misleading and even lead to incorrect conclusions." Here the student is able to construct meaning by paying attention to what the article says and doesn't say, and why, in order to move beyond a literal reading to a critical one. How, then, can we get more students to this place?

Earlier we suggested that critical reading, whether for academic purposes or social engagement, has at its heart the evaluation of assumptions. Much work on evaluating assumptions has been done under the heading of "critical thinking," although what people mean by that term varies across the disciplines. Stephen Brookfield provides a helpful summary of the emphases of five traditions of critical thinking: logic and language tricks examined in analytic philosophy; the deductive method of the sciences; the pragmatism of examining student experience; the psychoanalytic belief in a core or authentic self; and the political imperative of critical theory.[34] Our two definitions of critical reading, one coming from a liberal-humanist tradition of empiricism and one coming from a neo-Marxist tradition of ideologies structuring knowledge, draw on different aspects of these five traditions of critical thinking. Sometimes aspects are shared by both definitions; for example, it is hard to imagine critical reading for academic purposes or social engagement that did not pay careful attention to logical fallacies in an argument. Brookfield argues, "Whatever discipline one teaches in—from statistics to theology, physics to romance languages—the point of getting students to think critically is to get them to recognize, and question, the assumptions that determine how knowledge in that discipline is recognized as legitimate."[35] With that aim we have moved away from a transmission model of reading, whether we are teaching critical reading for academic purposes or for social engagement.

Brookfield suggests that critical reading requires "understanding the text in terms the author sets"; "conducting a critical analysis of the text," including identifying and evaluating assumptions; and "taking a position."[36] Too many of our students did not address the middle step, perhaps because we did not explicitly ask them to do so in the reading log prompts. Our students jumped from understanding the text to taking a position. Those students who did identify assumptions tended to do so when they felt discomfort with what the text claimed. For example, in response to an essay by Gary Genosko criticizing hockey,[37] one student began to identify relevant contexts for his reactions: "I realize the author is trying to make points about some of the things he finds negative about the NHL [National Hockey League], and I think maybe I just don't really care about what he's saying. Or maybe it's that I'm taking offense to what he's saying as he makes comments about a sport I've loved my whole life that I don't care to hear. Most of what he was saying left me feeling a bit angry and defensive, and as far as essays go, I don't particularly like reading them when they bring up these feelings!" Notice how the student starts with a simple rejection but circles back to consider his assumptions and his preferences. He prefers not to feel uncomfortable. Contrast this with another angry reader of the same essay: "Another complaint Genosko made in his essay was the fact that there are no homosexuals or women in the National Hockey League or that they don't have a competitive league they can play in. The National Hockey League is a league for the best hockey players in the world to play. If there was a woman that was good enough to play, she would be allowed to play." He conflates two very different arguments from the text, one about the homophobic environment of professional hockey and one about sexism, before making unexamined claims about meritocracy. Instead of evaluating information critically or reflecting on his own reactions, he lashes out.

Brookfield argues that critical reading must include awareness of emotional response, because "as we read work that challenges some of our most deeply held assumptions, we are likely to experience strong feelings of anger and resentment against the writer or her ideas, feelings that are grounded in the sense of threat that this work holds for us." Explicitly identifying such feelings as "the inevitable accompaniment of undertaking any kind of intellectual inquiry that is really challenging" may help provide students with not only reassurance but also a tool to help them find assumptions, within the text and within themselves.[38] However, students also have to know that we want them to do so. In her Critical Writing and Reading course, Manarin was struck by the difference between two reading logs based on scholarly articles students had selected for their research papers. In one of the logs there was very little connection to other material read or to life experiences; there was also little evidence of evaluation of assumptions, with roughly a third of the responses scoring at the benchmark level or higher (5 out of 17 at benchmark, 1 out of 17 at milestone). In the second, written two weeks later, two-thirds of the responses reached the benchmark level or higher, with many more at the milestone level (3 out of 15 scored at benchmark, 7 out of 15 at milestones). At the time, Manarin interpreted the change as the result of students becoming more engaged in the research topics, an interpretation she no longer believes (for reasons that will become evident in the next chapter). Looking back, she speculates that the difference might stem from a small exercise completed immediately before that second reading log was written. Students were asked to practice integrating quotations in a paragraph, so they were instructed to select specific statements from their sources that they agreed or disagreed with and explain why. The reading log prompts were the same, but their level of engagement in evaluating assumptions in this particular case was not. When explicitly given permission to evaluate and interact with the ideas, most students could. If only it were all so easy.

## The Bad News: No Developmental Pattern

We must confess that in all four courses we found no developmental pattern in reading over the semester despite our assumptions that we were helping students read critically. We discussed readings, explained information, modeled strategies, commented on their readings, and encouraged their writing about their readings. Individual reading logs showed increasing or decreasing levels of comprehension, analysis, interpretation, and evaluation, depending on whether a particular reading was more difficult, or perceived as more interesting, or whether something else was happening at the same time. But when we looked at the data across the four courses over the term, we saw no evidence that students had improved in any category. Neither did we see evidence that they had declined—a horrifying, though not often considered, possibility. Manarin, with her disciplinary background of English, took the news the hardest; after all, most justifications of English as an academic subject of study include its supposed ability to improve reading skills. Carey, by contrast, never expected that students' reading skills would improve dramatically over the course of a thirteen-week period, with many other learning outcomes expected simultaneously. Perhaps if reading development requires an epistemological shift, it is too much to expect significant reading improvement over the course of a term. Perhaps incremental progress is unobservable and large leaps become evident from time to time. We have all had the experience of seeing students in later terms who seem to read and understand differently. Perhaps individual elements of critical reading must be practiced until what literacy experts call "automaticity" occurs: cognitive and metacognitive processes are coordinated with little conscious effort.[39]

## Can Students Read Critically?

We can create conditions where critical reading is more likely to occur by providing opportunities for guided practice. If critical reading implies more of a transactional model of reading, we can make this explicit and practice features of this model through class activities and assignments. Some composition texts, such as *Ways of Reading: An Anthology for Writers; Rewriting: How to Do Things with Texts;* and *The Elements (and Pleasures) of Difficulty,* offer scaffolds to promote transactional reading.[40] However, it is also important to recognize that, by themselves, these texts and these activities may not produce decontextualized skills that are productively transferred.[41] Rather than see transfer as replication or application of knowledge (knowledge transfers out to a new problem), researchers like Daniel M. Belenky and Timothy J. Nokes-Malach suggest that transfer is interpretive knowledge (knowledge transfers into a new situation and prepares students to learn).[42] The two researchers demonstrate that student motivation and achievement goals play a significant role in transfer. Transfer as preparation for learning is more likely to occur if individuals attribute value to what is learned, regardless of the type of learning activity. Individuals with lower achievement orientation can improve transfer with targeted learning activities, although the effect may not last. Belenky and Nokes-Malach question what would be required to turn "such adopted goals into more stable orientations."[43]

Unlike some, we believe that most students see value in reading even if they do not read very much or very well.[44] In a survey of 120 general education students at our institution, 85 percent claimed reading was relevant to their lives, and a stunning 80 percent agreed or strongly agreed with the statement: "In the area of reading, my confidence level is very high."[45] Perhaps students are recognizing that they can understand text on a surface level of comprehension while we are hoping for something more, but perception is also a tricky measure, something to bear in mind when judging the efficacy of interventions. For example, based on anecdotal comments in these four classes, some students believed that their reading had improved even though the evidence suggested it hadn't. Perhaps they were saying what they thought we wanted to hear; perhaps they actually felt more confident, and, after all, confidence can lead to greater persistence and self-efficacy, which can lead to increased performance;[46] or perhaps there is a disconnect between perception and performance. Tracy Linderholm and Adam Wilde note that although college students try to match reading strategies to reading purpose, their choices "are not always effective in altering actual comprehension performance."[47] We also recognize that students could be coached to display particular traits in their writing about particular readings but did not demonstrate these traits when the explicit prompts were removed. For example, students can identify a faulty premise in a text and argue against it when explicitly directed to do so, but won't demonstrate that behavior with subsequent readings if the prompt is not there. These findings have significant implications for curricular design and research protocols. We cannot rely on student or instructor testimony about what works nor assume that just because students can do something, they will. Students need to see value in the activity consistently across many classes, and for many students the accepted currency is grades. Students may value reading, but the question becomes, How do we encourage them to value critical reading, a more difficult activity, and help them make effective choices about how and why they read?

## Lessons Learned

- Students can comprehend nonfictional text with at least benchmark proficiency; what many faculty call a lack of comprehension may be students struggling with evaluation of assumptions.
- Evaluation of assumptions requires the individual to interact with the text in a way that may be difficult for those with strong transmission models of reading.
- Students can be coached to display particular traits in writing about their reading. They can be prompted to demonstrate higher levels of evaluation based on assignment requirements.
- Prompted levels of engagement did not remain when the prompts were removed.
- Students' reading skills did not improve over the course of a term. If reading development requires epistemological shifts, we need to take a longer and more coordinated approach to critical reading.
- Activities to promote a transactional model of reading can be implemented but must be valued across the curriculum to encourage productive transfer.

# 3 Critical Reading for Academic Purposes

W<small>HILE THE MAJORITY</small> of our students displayed comprehension of required texts with at least the benchmark level of proficiency—and remember these are first-year courses, after all—we have all worked with students across the levels of an undergraduate degree who just don't seem to "get" the required readings despite being able to comprehend all the words in order. The reader's implicit model of reading, whether they see reading as transmission or reading as transaction, plays a role in critical reading. Certainly one issue is the evaluation of assumptions. Another is the creation of relevant inferences, to both academic and personal experience. We want our students to make connections and to go "deeper." In foundational work on deep and surface levels of learning, Ference Marton and Roger Säljö distinguish between those students who, when reading, focus on the text itself versus those who focus on what the text was about.[1] Although some scholars like Tamsin Haggis have critiqued assumptions within the deep/surface paradigm, it has been a very powerful metaphor, because, as Graham Webb says, "Everyone could agree that a deep approach to learning was desirable and good."[2] However, beyond describing levels of engagement with text as deep or surface, how can we describe the type of reading we hope students do in our classes? We identify the following characteristics of critical reading for academic purposes:

- identifying patterns of textual elements
- distinguishing between main and subordinate ideas
- evaluating credibility
- making judgments about how a text is argued
- making relevant inferences about the text

Some of these characteristics are captured by the measures of Comprehension, Analysis, Interpretation, and Evaluation discussed in the last chapter; however, critical reading for academic purposes also requires high levels of inference, where "inference" is the ability to make connections between different texts and types of knowledge. When looking at critical reading for academic purposes, we pay particular attention to Recognition of Genre (from the VALUE rubric for reading) and Connections to Discipline (from the VALUE rubric for integrative learning).

Teachers have long intuited the importance of genre recognition for comprehension of academic texts. By "genre" we do not mean merely the basic distinctions between fiction and poetry that students were exposed to in their high school English classes; nonfictional prose, the type of reading students do in most postsecondary courses, can also be divided into genres. Understanding what something is—whether a newspaper editorial, scholarly article, textbook chapter, web blog, or encyclopedia entry—is often the first step in understanding what it says. Yet, as John Bean notes, "Students do not understand that prose styles, discourse structures, and argumentative strategies differ from discipline to discipline or from historical period to historical period. Just as they do not adjust their reading speed to differences in purpose, they do not adjustment [*sic*] their reading strategies to differences in genre."[3] Bean goes on to provide a series of suggestions to help teachers create an environment where students can become better readers for academic purposes, most of which involve trying to get the student to become more aware of the reading process and interact with the text, thus supporting a transactional model of reading. Composition scholar Debrah Huffman also calls for attention to how students read nonfiction text, including text other than essays. She claims that there are multiple kinds of reading: attentive, expressive, interpretive, evaluative, comparative, and projective.[4] However, when she examines textbook reading instruction, interpretive reading instruction dominates across her sample, perhaps because of historical links to literary interpretation.[5] Some textbooks, like Eric Henderson's *The Active Reader: Strategies for Academic Reading and Writing,* are built around explicit instruction of the conventions of academic prose with the hope that these conventions can be translated into students' academic writing. Henderson even divides academic prose into three main categories: A for Arts, essays concerned with the interpretation of ideas perhaps applied to a primary source; B for Biology, to represent scientific research; and C for Critical Evaluation, to represent synthesis research. He suggests that the typical student research paper, with its emphasis on synthesis, summary, and evaluation, is like a Type C essay, a claim we will challenge later in this chapter.[6]

Recognition of genre conventions by itself is not enough to demonstrate critical reading for academic purposes. The student who knows where to find information within an article may still not understand that information because of the rhetorical context and what Bean calls the cultural codes of the text: "background information, allusions, common knowledge that the author assumed that the reading audience would know."[7] But simply advising students to look up what they don't know doesn't work if too many terms and references are unknown or if the reader doesn't have a firm *to many interruptions*

grasp of the conventions.[8] If there are too many interruptions to the reading process, as the individual looks up yet another name or term the reading itself can grind to a halt, a problem that may have less to do with persistence and more to do with epistemology and identity. After all, if academics, with years of experience reading for academic purposes, feel discomfort when reading outside of their disciplines because they do not see themselves as legitimately part of that conversation, how much stronger must the discomfort be for students who do not even recognize knowledge creation as a conversation occurring within a particular framework of concepts?[9]

The processes by which readers synthesize texts to create knowledge have been widely studied. Latricia Trites and Mary McGroarty, for example, suggest there is a distinction between basic comprehension, as measured on traditional reading tests, and what they call "reading to learn" and "reading to integrate."[10] Reading to learn, they explain, requires readers to "integrate and connect information presented by the author with what they already know."[11] To do so, students must form both a situation model, which can be described as a mental representation of information that doesn't depend on the specific words and sentences, and a text model of rhetorical features.[12] Students must be able to place information from a text within a schematic framework involving these two models; however, much of the reading students do in our classes requires that they also make connections among texts. Charles A. Perfetti, building on research about how students interpret multiple historical documents, posits a documents model that includes a situation model as well as an intertext model that marks relationships among texts.[13] Trites and McGroarty suggest that reading to integrate is a more difficult task than reading to learn because of the multiple models involved.[14] The two types of reading, both included under our Reading for Academic Purposes category, might even compete for the same limited cognitive resources; M. Anne Britt and Jodie Sommer, for example, suggest that integration comes with a cost to content memory.[15] But the issues involved with reading to learn and reading to integrate are not only cognitive.

Ivar Bråten and Helge I. Strømsø examine the role of personal epistemology—beliefs about what knowledge consists of and what the individual's role is—in reading to integrate.[16] While much research has been done on the role that prior knowledge plays in an individual's ability to integrate multiple texts,[17] Bråten and Strømsø suggest that epistemological belief may be more important than prior knowledge: "Not only knowledge itself, but also personal beliefs about knowledge and knowing, may enhance or constrain the understanding of multiple texts." They go on to claim that "an important aspect of constructing meaning across texts seems to be that people believe that their role as readers and learners authorize [*sic*] them to build new complex knowledge through their own effort to integrate information."[18] They are describing a transactional model of reading, although they don't define it as such. Bråten and Strømsø recommend that students' beliefs about knowledge be explicitly targeted in reading instruction.[19] Many disciplines value the ability to construct knowledge from

*beliefs about knowledge*

sometimes contradictory or ambiguous sources. Indeed William Perry and others have placed epistemological development on a continuum from naïve certainty through relativism to evolving commitment, but shifting individuals along the continuum is easier said than done.[20] Research suggests that simply asking students to build an argument based on multiple documents does not improve comprehension. Laura Gil, Ivar Bråten, Eduardo Vida-Abarca, and Helge I. Strømsø report that undergraduate students who were asked to summarize documents performed better on comprehension questions than those who were asked to write argument essays with those same documents. Those students with high prior knowledge were able to integrate sources in an essay, while those with lower prior knowledge were not.[21] If prior knowledge and personal epistemology are key factors in reading for academic purposes, a research paper assignment intended to help students build a knowledge base will not help those students who are struggling.

In each of our four courses, students completed two main reading tasks: the class readings we read and discussed together and the material read for individual research papers. Class readings were reported in the reading logs, with the common prompts of "What?" "So What?" and "Now What?" The research papers, however, took different forms as is common across disciplines. Indeed, Betty Samraj notes that the research paper genre is "a heterogeneous genre with a number of sub-genres."[22] This variety itself can cause confusion among students.[23] The research paper tasks across our courses ranged from nine hundred to two thousand words with different levels of scaffolding and autonomy. Students in Controversies in Science built upon an earlier assignment in which they had compared a pair of articles on a controversy; for the research paper, they used their initial articles and added more research. Students in Texts and Ideas—Genocide were required to do a textual analysis of a primary source informed by scholarly secondary sources. Students in Communities and Societies created researched arguments, choosing one question from a series of five possibilities generated by the class. Students in Critical Writing and Reading selected individual topics to work on through the whole term; the research paper was an extension of an earlier opinion piece on the same topic. Each of us felt that the readings assigned for and discussed in class would develop students' knowledge base, reading to learn, while the longer essays would provide more scope for students to demonstrate reading to integrate.

To examine reading to learn and reading to integrate in our students' work, we turned to the AAC&U VALUE rubrics.[24] We paid particular attention to the Genre category from the reading rubric and Connections to Discipline from the integrative learning rubric. Reading to learn requires interplay between the situation model and the text model. It is difficult to measure an individual's situation model, the mental representation of content, but a reading's genre provided a proxy for a textual model. The Genre category describes behavior that ranges from "Uses ability to identify texts within and across genres, monitoring and adjusting reading strategies and expectations based on generic nuances of particular texts" at the capstone level to "Applies tacit genre knowledge to a variety of classroom reading assignments in productive, if unreflective, ways" at the benchmark level.[25] For us, the difference between the categories was in the level of awareness the student demonstrated about rhetorical features that would affect how the material was read and evaluated—for example, recognizing that a newspaper editorial involved a different standard of detail and different purpose than a scholarly article. The Connections to Discipline category from the integrative learning rubric describes behavior that ranges from "Independently creates wholes out of multiple parts (synthesizes) or draws conclusions by combining examples, facts, or theories from more than one field of study or perspective" at the capstone level to "When prompted, presents examples, facts or theories from more than one field of study or perspective" at the benchmark level.[26] In some ways the Connections to Discipline category could be named "Connections *among* Disciplines." Because our students were, at least nominally, at the beginning of their postsecondary studies and might not have yet selected a discipline, we read this category as connections among any courses or even disparate readings. With that framing we then saw the main difference among categories as the level of initiative the student took in making connections as well as the ability, at the capstone level, to synthesize information. We did not assume students would be able to synthesize information read in these courses, but we hoped for connections, especially since our general education program is supposed to develop a multidisciplinary base for the development of disciplinary knowledge.

## Reading Logs

We described earlier our surprise that we saw so many common patterns in the reading logs given the differences in course foci, readings, and assignments. Levels of genre recognition, however, were noticeably different among the courses (see fig. 3.1). All four courses used a variety of nonfictional texts, including autobiographical essays, textbooks, newspapers, and scholarly articles. These different genres involve different reading experiences and require different reading strategies. However, students in two courses, Communities and Societies and Texts and Ideas—Genocide, rarely mentioned genre at all. Students in the other two courses, Controversies in Science and Critical Writing and Reading, often recognized genre if only to label the type of text they were reading—for example, "I read the scholarly journal" or "This speech is lengthy." This type of labeling was, unsurprisingly, most common in the Critical Writing and Reading course, where different rhetorical strategies and patterns are part of the course content.

Some students were able to move beyond simple labeling to articulate how the generic conventions affected their reading experiences: "Knowing that this reading was a speech instead of an essay, I read it a little differently. As the author would be

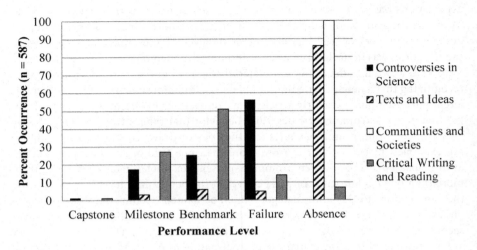

FIGURE 3.1. **Genre:** Students demonstrated very different levels of genre recognition among the four courses.

telling his speech to an audience, I tried to imagine his tone, his mannerisms and the emotions he would have been feeling while delivering it." Here the student recognizes that genre affects how something is read, identifies distinctive features of the specific genre, and makes a strategic decision to focus on particular elements when reading. Most students in Critical Writing and Reading did not seem to have such an awareness of the impact of the text situation on the reading experience, but it is a first-year course, after all. In Controversies in Science much attention was given to evaluating different types of scientific representation, and although students were armed with criteria to differentiate among genres, many students incorrectly labeled articles as "scholarly" or "scientific" when, in fact, they were from magazines or other popular press formats. The high number of failures in the Genre category according to the hybridized rubric for students in Controversies in Science can be explained by this mislabeling of the genre. In their course work, students examined popular and scholarly articles, paying particular attention to misrepresentations from either misunderstandings or attempts to mislead the reader. For example, one student wrote: "The pro nuclear article is written by a person who is biased toward nuclear power and may be leaving negative facts out of the article. Even though that is true, his points are still valid in my opinion." By understanding the genre of the reading, this student felt confident to question the author's motivation and biases, even though the student supported the overall conclusions of the article. Thus, genre was part of the conversation about the controversies and played an important role in helping students to assess and evaluate the facts and opinions in the readings. It is not surprising, then, that many students in these two courses recognized genre as a factor in their reading logs.

Much more surprising is the lack of reference to genre in Texts and Ideas—Genocide and Communities and Societies, even though both courses required a wide variety of readings. In Texts and Ideas—Genocide, for example, students had to read everything from eyewitness accounts to Plato, but they did not mention genre in their reading logs. In Communities and Societies students did not pay attention to genre as having any impact on the content presented. They rarely labeled the text, but when they did, everything was referred to as "an article" regardless of the genre. The instructors of these two courses, Ryland and Carey, did not spend much time in class talking about genre expectations and rhetorical conventions. These students were unaware of the rhetorical features that shape their reading experiences or, perhaps more accurately, were unaware that rhetorical features are worth commenting on or paying attention to except in specific contexts like an English class. We can trace the differences across the four courses to the emphasis the instructor placed on genre in class and to the students' desire to provide what they thought the instructors were looking for, an important academic skill. The variation among courses also demonstrates that students can learn to recognize genre if explicit attention is given to it in class. If, as theorists of reading suggest, reading to learn involves an interplay between situation models and text models, we should pay some attention to rhetorical features in all classes.

Reading for academic purposes involves not only reading to learn but also reading to integrate. When we looked at the reading logs using the Connections to Discipline category, we expected that students would refer to examples, facts, or theories from other readings, courses, or fields of study, especially given the multidisciplinary nature of these general education courses. Many reading logs did not contain connections between readings in the course and material learned in other courses although students were prompted to make connections in class discussions (see fig. 3.2).

In the reading logs, students often did not even make connections between readings in the same class, a particularly troubling pattern for the instructors of three of the four courses: Controversies in Science, Texts and Ideas—Genocide, and Communities and Societies. These multidisciplinary courses are designed to expose students to multiple perspectives on significant issues, and yet the reading logs showed very few connections. For example, one of the reading logs in Controversies in Science was based on students' readings of two articles that took opposing views on the use of genetically modified foods. Many students resisted the idea of making connections and discussed the articles as if they were completely unrelated: "The first article by Chaudry seems to show much more scientific evidence and procedures that take place during a DNA mutation. However, the second article does give a first hand [sic] look at those taking part in the agricultural industry (farmers)." This student felt it was necessary to say something positive about each article rather than using the content of each article

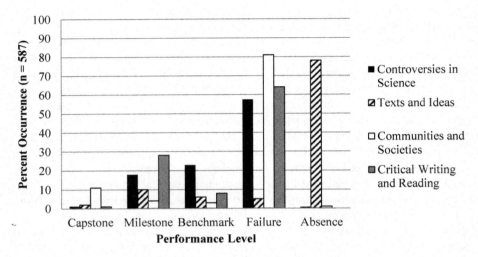

FIGURE 3.2. **Connections to Disciplines:** Many students did not make connections between the specific readings and other academic material.

to inform his reading of the other. The multidisciplinary courses showed remarkably little interdisciplinarity in how students read. Critical Writing and Reading, on the other hand, does not take a multidisciplinary approach; although the specific readings come from different disciplines, it is primarily a composition class. The readings for Critical Writing and Reading were not organized in thematic units, unlike those in the other three courses, so we expected significantly fewer connections because there were fewer opportunities for students to make connections between readings about a particular subject. Yet we did not see this pattern in the data. In all four courses, the majority of reading logs did not contain evidence of any attempt to make connections among perspectives, disciplines, or even readings.

Faced with these puzzling results, we believe the issue was the reading log itself. After all, the reading log prompts—"What?" "So What?" and "Now What?"—did not explicitly authorize students to make connections. Perhaps we would have observed more integration if we had specifically asked for it; after all, the benchmark level description is "When prompted, presents examples, facts and theories from more than one field of study or perspective." We realized that students did not extrapolate connections made in class discussion into their writing, itself a useful finding. They saw the reading logs as stand-alone assignments, asking them about each reading in isolation even when the readings addressed different aspects of the same issue. So at least part of their failure to read to integrate was our fault, our unspoken expectations of what we would have done if we were them.

## Research Papers

Given the embarrassingly non-integrative nature of our reading log prompts, we then turned to an assignment we felt would lead to both reading to learn and reading to integrate: the research paper. We believed that the longer essays provided more scope for students to demonstrate critical reading and connections to disciplines. The research paper is not only the genre where students are most often expected to display their critical reading for academic purposes but also an opportunity for students to increase their reading skills, as research suggests that writing about texts improves reading.[27] The research paper itself, however, is a strange, amorphous genre that can cover everything from a literature review to argument essay.

This is not a new insight; indeed, composition specialists have fretted about the nature of the research paper for decades, in part because they are often charged with teaching it in so-called service courses. Too often the research paper is an exercise in form, specified differently, and apparently arbitrarily, from class to class, instructor to instructor. In 1982 Richard Larson famously called the research paper a "non-form of writing."[28] He argues that the generic research paper has no substantive or procedural identity; teaching as if it does misrepresents both research and writing activities, implying that research is something required only on occasion and that research looks the same in different disciplines. Betty Samraj, among others, has sought to outline the conceptual and discursive patterns of research papers in various disciplines.[29] Still, at the first-year level, most instruction into research papers occurs in composition classes. Carra Leah Hood, surveying 166 postsecondary institutions in America, suggests that more schools are offering alternative research assignments, such as the researched argument or an annotated bibliography, in an attempt to combat the "genrelessness" of the traditional research paper.[30] However, the emphasis in many cases remains on mastering a form or set of skills rather than exploring concepts. This emphasis can be seen assignments like the mock research paper, where students make up their sources,[31] or in the amount of space in the research assignment handouts devoted to requirements of manuscript submission rather than the intellectual work of doing research. Alison J. Head and Michael B. Eisenberg conclude their analysis of 191 research handouts from different disciplines collected on twenty-eight campuses with the claim that "most students lack a seminal understanding about what conducting research means as a form of intellectual inquiry and discovery."[32] They suggest that adding situational and information-gathering contexts may help and assert that "many of the handouts . . . had evolved into their own genre—a step-by-step process with standards and conventions that ended up defining research as more of a linear checklist than an iterative process that requires critical thought, curiously ongoing discovery, and tenacity."[33] Robert A. Schwegler and Linda K. Shamoon note, "Students view the research paper as a close-ended, informative, skills-oriented exercise written for an expert audience by novices pretending to be experts. No wonder then that students' papers often roam freely over the subject area, are devoid of focus, and loaded down with quotes."[34] Sherry Lee Linkon, referring specifically to literature professors, makes a claim that can resonate with many faculty: "For us, research is a process of exploration and discovery, not merely a matter of collecting supportive quotes."[35]

As experienced instructors, we were aware of these issues. We knew that the intellectual engagement we experience when doing our own research is unlikely to occur within the artificial confines of the classroom. We knew that students focus more on how to get a good grade than on the ideas explored. We were aware that sometimes our emphasis on the finished product obscures the processes of research and that students were likely to read their sources with a particular argument in mind. We knew they were likely to collect supportive quotations, or when given explicit directions to do so, quotations they could argue against. Yet we still believed that the research paper assignments, in their various forms, would require students to read more broadly and more deeply. Even pulling together supportive quotations, we thought, would require reading to learn and reading to integrate for an academic purpose.

So we turned to scoring the research papers according to the Critical Reading for Academic Purposes rubric. The research papers themselves were not unusual; all of us had assigned these types of papers before and had been pleased with the results. Indeed, we were pleased this time too, because many papers were interesting and had received good grades. But, of course, we were judging them primarily on how they were written and how the arguments were organized. As we worked with the rubric, it quickly became apparent that we really couldn't tell how or what students were reading without reading those sources ourselves. So we began the labor-intensive process of reading each source cited, or at least all of those we could find. We were looking not for plagiarism, but for how each source was used. Was there evidence of critical reading?

As we read through the sources, we kept track of the type of source, how often it appeared in the research paper, how it was used, what part of it was used, and whether there was evidence of the student's comprehension. We also wrote summary statements for the research papers before returning to our initial score on the rubric to see if our opinion had changed. Our methodology here was influenced by the Citation Project, a multi-institutional investigation of how students in first-year composition classes use their sources.[36] Leading a team of twenty-one instructor-researchers from across America, Sandra Jamieson and Rebecca Moore Howard focus on how students integrate their sources into papers rather than how they read those sources; however, as all we have are the oblique measures of reading, we use some of their distinctions as proxies. We can see only how the student chose to use a source in an essay, which may or may not correspond to how the student read that source; however, we believe that general patterns of comprehension emerged. One of the key concerns in the Citation Project is whether a student chooses to quote, "patchwrite," paraphrase, or summarize material used. Howard defines patchwriting as "copying from a source text and then deleting some words, altering grammatical structures, or plugging in one-for-one synonyms." Although it is often seen as a type of plagiarism, Howard argues that patch-writing is a learning strategy used by nonexperts.[37] Miguel Roig has demonstrated that even professors are more likely to patchwrite when paraphrasing difficult-to-read paragraphs.[38] As Howard, Tricia Serviss, and Tanya K. Rodrigue note, if patchwriting "is a sign of uncertain comprehension . . . [and] summary is a sign of source compre-hension . . . copying and paraphrasing are not necessarily a sign of either. Copying does not require comprehension of what one copies, regardless of whether the copying is marked as quotation and cited. Paraphrase does require comprehension, but usually only of a sentence or two."[39] Bearing these distinctions in mind, we set about recording how our students referred to sources within their research papers as a first step toward understanding how they read those sources.

The percentage of sources that were summarized by students varied widely among the four courses, from an astonishing zero in Communities and Societies to an equally astonishing 43 percent in Texts and Ideas—Genocide.[40] The other two courses were in between, with 16 percent of sources summarized in the Critical Writing and Read-ing research papers and 30 percent in Controversies in Science. The zero, however, is consistent with Howard, Serviss, and Rodrigue's analysis of eighteen papers written by sophomore students in a research writing class at a large, private, comprehensive university. Here at Mount Royal, in first-year general education classes at a public undergraduate institution, students did not regularly summarize, except in the case of Texts and Ideas—Genocide. In that course students were given strict parameters to follow in the research task: they had to do a textual analysis of a primary source sup-ported by two scholarly secondary sources. Those research assignments that allowed more latitude in number and type of sources used and that focused more on arguing a position rather than explicitly anchoring the assignment in a source required less sum-mary, so students summarized less often. If summary requires deeper comprehension of sources, we may be able to manipulate comprehension by creating research assign-ments that require summary, but there are also different types of summaries.

A closer look at the summaries created for Text and Ideas—Genocide reveals that in many cases students were summarizing historical or biographical details, mate-rial that was easier to comprehend, rather than concepts. Indeed, students some-times slipped into descriptive summary rather than critical analysis. For example, one student, writing about Bishop Clemens van Galen's 1941 sermon against the Nazi euthanasia program, summarizes the historical facts provided in secondary sources about the sermon but doesn't move beyond those facts. It remains an essay about the secondary sources rather than an analysis of a primary text supported by secondary sources. He grasps the main ideas of the sermon but doesn't consider in much detail how those ideas were presented. Indeed, he doesn't quote from the primary text at all. He uses sources about the text, including reference books and *Encyclopedia Britan-nica*. Another essay examining the role of the Christian Church during the Rwan-dan genocide relies upon summarizing what happened to a thirteen-year-old girl who sought sanctuary in a church. The language is clear, the details compelling, but there is little analysis of the ideas. At times the student seems to mine secondary sources for quotations about the Rwandan genocide. Again, the quotations are presented without analysis. Describing the essays written for Texts and Ideas—Genocide, Ryland observes that few score well on the rubric criteria. He found basic comprehension, analysis, and interpretation in most of the essays, with a few students reaching into the milestones, but the essays show little evidence of critical reading of the sources, which were accepted at face value. There was virtually no recognition of genre, a noteworthy omission given the distinct types of sources that were the focus of most of the essays (a poem, a documentary film, a bishop's sermon, eyewitness accounts, a war report, and memoirs). Although the essays imply that the students were not critical or reflective in their reading of sources, they demonstrate that the students had read the sources cited, which is not clear in the essays written for the other three courses.

In Controversies in Science, again a course with strict parameters for the research assignment, we saw a related pattern. Students in that course were building on pairs of articles, one popular and one scholarly, that they had already read and answered questions about. Rathburn's assignment prompt explicitly reminded students of this earlier assignment, with its goal of increasing comprehension of the articles. For the research paper they were asked to do additional research, but they were also told that they needed to summarize the two articles "by clearly explaining the science and the evidence for their conclusions." The idea underlying this assignment was to get students to recognize that miscommunications and misunderstandings of scientific information can contribute to incorrect perceptions and facts among the general population. To accomplish this goal, students compared the original scientific information with how that information is presented in the media to assess the accuracy and errors that might be contributing to misinformation of the public.

Although most students picked scientific studies that were on topics relevant to their everyday lives, such as the amount of sleep required, benefits of energy drinks, role of exercise, and consumption of alcohol, some students chose more complex topics and sometimes studies that presented controversial information. For example, one student examined the new treatment for multiple sclerosis (MS) called Chronic Cerebrospinal Venous Insufficiency (CCSVI), which is based on deficiencies of blood flow within the brain. This student summarized a recent scientific study that examined differences in intracranial blood flow among participants with and without MS in order to determine whether blood flow differs among the groups. The student clearly comprehended the article and the statistics and was able to clearly articulate the main conclusions of the scientific study: "They found no significant differences regarding internal jugular venous outflow, aqueductal cerebrospinal fluid flow, or the presence of internal jugular blood reflux (Sundstrom et al., 2010). Using specific statistical analysis . . . none of the measurements indicated a p-value less than 0.05. In conclusion, they found no evidence confirming the suggested vascular MS hypothesis."

As the instructor reading this paper, Rathburn was excited that a student, a non–science major, obviously comprehended a complex medical article and had a fundamental understanding of statistics. The student then compared these scientific findings with media articles that correctly discussed lack of scientific support for this treatment, but she also included articles that discussed the implications of these findings: a lack of government funding for the treatment. She concluded her paper with contradictory statements. Her final paragraph began with: "There are countless media-based presentations of this subject and the majority are not presented accurately," and her final sentence stated: "However, the Canadian Institute of Health Research says there is still lack of evidence of the safety and efficiency of the procedure. The public is being misled as it would appear this is a cure for MS, when in fact it is a treatment, which may benefit some patients." From the start of the research process, the student was clearly approaching the paper with a preconception that this was an effective treatment, and even in light of the overwhelming evidence that the student clearly presents to show this is not a treatment for MS, she sticks with her initial views and rejects the evidence. She has read and understood the main articles; she has read and understood additional material; she may even have read to integrate. However, she has not read to learn, because she is not willing to shift preconceived beliefs, even in the face of evidence she accurately presents. What do you do with that? Where does this resistance to critical reading come from? Would explicitly tracing out assumptions, perhaps writing down a hypothesis and then listing evidence that supports or disproves it, help the individual recognize the contradiction?

Most students in Controversies in Science (16 out of 22, or 73 percent) were able to read and summarize their main sources, although they often relied on data-mining statistics and isolated quotations for the additional research they were asked to do. For example, one student examined two articles on trustworthiness between genders, but the student's additional research consisted of one isolated statement from a media report: "According to The Telegraph, the London Science Museum says the average male tells 1092 lies in a year and will likely not suffer from a guilty conscience in comparison to a typical woman." Although this claim is related to the topic that the student was investigating, it contributes nothing to the student's discussion of the two articles. Another student wrote his paper on the nature-nurture debate—specifically, the role of genetics in shaping social relationships. This student was examining the idea that friends are determined through genetics and used an isolated quotation to support his description of how genes work: "A gene tells your body how to make a protein, then that protein interacts with other proteins to make the parts of your body work. More specifically, genes tell your brain how to function." Although what the student wrote is correct, albeit a simplification, the student obtained this information from a study examining diversity among dog DNA, not a source that relates to this topic other than the mention of genes. It is likely that the student found this article using a very limited keyword search but still decided to cite information from this source, even after realizing the article focused on canine DNA. Students tended to rely on strategies like keyword searches for their additional research, perhaps because it was more efficient in terms of time spent. These findings are consistent with Mark Emmons, Wanda Martin, Carroll Botts, and Cassandra Amundson's in-depth analysis of six freshman research papers. They describe papers that have surface plausibility and rely on easily accessible information that have been selected to prove a predetermined thesis.[41] Such data mining and Google trawling can lead to misunderstanding or at least misrepresentation of the text cited.

Howard, Serviss, and Rodrigue observe, "*Students are not writing from sources; they are writing from sentences selected from sources.*"[42] They wonder "not only whether the writers understood the source itself but also whether they even read it."[43] Our study suggests many of them haven't, at least not beyond the abstract and opening paragraphs. Many students limited their engagement with the source to the first paragraph or two. Quotations and paraphrases often came from the abstract, the first sentence, or the literature review. There was little evidence that students had read the entire text, particularly in the two courses where students had greater flexibility in the research paper assignment. In Communities and Societies students were asked to create a researched argument selected from a list of topics generated by the class; topics ranged from the role of students' associations, to immigration in Canada, to global gender equality. In Critical Writing and Reading each student had selected a topic to work on during the entire term, presumably something he or she was interested in and already knew something about. Students were then asked to build on an earlier paper, either going deeper into one aspect or exploring the context surrounding that topic; they were instructed to use at least three scholarly sources, and examples were provided. Despite, or perhaps because of, our attempts to engage student interest by allowing them more flexibility, many students did not demonstrate evidence of comprehension. Honestly, they didn't have to in order to complete the assignment successfully. Instead of summarizing, many of them relied upon isolated statistics or sound-bite quotations, which were often taken out of context in a way that misrepresented the original source. So while students in Texts and Ideas—Genocide and Controversies in Science misrepresented 15 percent and 16 percent of texts cited respectively, students in Communities and Societies misrepresented 37 percent of sources and those in Critical Writing and Reading, 29 percent. These students did not necessarily misunderstand the original text; indeed, we have no evidence that they even read it. In many essays a consistent pattern can be seen: sources used just once—often from the first paragraph or abstract, many times the first sentence or even the title, or an isolated statistic without information about what the statistic means. No wonder student essays sometimes are strangely general; after all, first sentences are often generalizations.

Once we looked more carefully at the sources selected, we noticed that some students demonstrated considerable resistance to the idea of research. For example, in

Communities and Societies one student tackled the topic of changing family values in Canadian society as exemplified through the growth in multicultural marriages. Although she cited six sources in her four-page paper, three of them were websites: one was an online dictionary; one was from a blog, "Hubbynet, Marriage Help for Husbands: Helping husbands cope since 2000!"; and the third was a web page about interracial marriages on Angelfire, a website that offers people "free space" on the web. There is no indication on the site of who wrote this page or why; the address is a puzzling www.angelfire.com/space/cropcircles. Of the other three texts she used, two were from the 1990s, and one was clearly a text she had as a result of being a student in a course offered at Mount Royal, as it was written by two of our colleagues in an identifiable program. In her research paper, she quoted from her sources eight times; only one of the quotations exceeded one complete sentence. Nor did her quotations explain or add anything to the argument she was trying to craft. The majority of them were phrases or partial sentences plugged into her own text, often framing the cited authors as authorities in the subject area, and nothing more. This student clearly understood the tasks associated with drafting a research paper, and on the surface she appears to have mastered the skills of finding vaguely relevant, if unreliable or easily accessible, sources. Her paper read as many others do: as a string of quotations that she hoped would look and sound good enough to pass muster.

Sometimes, and this is perhaps more frightening, these essays are very good. Consider, for example, an essay on whether there is a global understanding of gender equality. It is beautifully structured with clear definitions of gender equality and global understanding; the student makes an interesting argument with specific examples and apparently reliable statistics. She used literacy rates, average salaries, and seats in legislatures as indicators of gender (in)equality, suggesting a strategic and evidence-based approach to her question. Carey's despair, and embarrassment, over the grade assigned surfaced only in the post-evaluation examination of sources. This essay cites eleven sources, but only one of them is used more than once. Five of the sources are websites from which the student has pulled statistics. She quotes the first sentence of three of the sources and claims to paraphrase an idea from another source, but the source doesn't include that idea. A quotation from another source is wrongly attributed but again comes from the first page of the source. And an online dictionary is used. How much reading was done for the paper? Carey notes that when she started to track down student sources, she began with Mount Royal's library databases to little avail; then she started googling keywords and found virtually everything her students had used. For example, the second quotation in the gender equality paper was cited as coming from a source not found in the student's reference list; when Carey googled the phrase to find out where it did come from, 236 sites popped up with exactly that phrase. To see if the source the student cited showed up at all in that list, the instructor then added a name associated with it to refine the Google search—the source the student cited was found on Facebook.

But, you might say, I can tell when students haven't done a lot of reading, when the essay is superficial. With more than fifteen years of teaching essay writing, Manarin thought she could tell, until she took a closer look at the sources. Manarin's assignment sequence had students working on the same topic all term. Students had to propose a topic that interested them; then they wrote to convince her that they had the passion and expertise to develop that topic; they wrote position papers to outline their opinions before researching the topic; they wrote annotated bibliographies to summarize their research and help them identify patterns in the research; and they wrote their research papers. Add to the sequence a set of exercises, both individual and peer, designed to help them view research as a conversation or argument. Some students used sources to build an argument, but most of the pieces used come from the first sentence, first paragraph, a bulleted list, or even the title.

One paper listing thirteen sources, including five scholarly articles, seemed to demonstrate the student was interacting with her sources and developing an argument, until Manarin realized that seven of the sources, including all five articles, were misrepresented. In some cases the articles were selected for their titles. The web sources, relevant and far less difficult to read, were used only for generalizations. Far from reading sources, learning from sources, and integrating them, this student apparently created a paper and then added the sources in, quite well actually. The saddest part of this example is that this particular student is a good reader; at least she consistently scored at the benchmark level or higher on comprehension, analysis, and interpretation for the reading logs.[44] She didn't have to comprehend texts to get a good mark on the research paper assignment, so she didn't. Rebecca Moore Howard describes how her pedagogies have changed over the past twenty years as she came to realize that the primary issue with how students use sources isn't comprehension; it's that students "are engaging shallowly with their sources, usually working only with sentences gleaned from the first pages of the source."[45] These papers can look good on the surface and may even look better than a paper in which the student struggled to comprehend sources because he or she actually read them.

Manarin compared the paper that cited thirteen sources, carefully integrated but apparently unread, with a relatively clunky paper that demonstrated little integration of four sources. Each of the four was addressed in a separate paragraph, but the student had clearly read beyond the abstract in each case and had attempted to place information in a new context, sometimes failing. Although there were some errors in the in-text citations, it was possible to trace what she cited to where she found it. She used each source more than once. She quoted more often than she summarized, perhaps because she didn't feel confident in her ability to represent the content. Sometimes the summary was rather general, and sometimes the details she selected didn't help her argument along, but she didn't misrepresent her sources. She had used only four sources, but she read and apparently understood them.

Which paper deserved a higher grade? How often do we grade a research paper based on what it looks like? Having traced through the sources, Manarin found herself reevaluating the rubric scores for five of eighteen papers, mostly from the milestone range. She worried about whether these papers deserved a different, whether higher or lower, grade than they received. In some cases they did; in others they didn't, because we do not mark only reading when we are marking a research paper. However, we should not fool ourselves into thinking we can mark reading by marking format. If the research paper assignment is intended to promote critical reading for academic purposes, whether we define that as reading to learn or reading to integrate, it is failing. Worse, it promotes a false idea of what research involves.

Eric Henderson claims that most student research papers involve synthesis, summary, and evaluation;[46] perhaps this is the faculty member's intention, but the reality, we argue, is very different. The traditional research paper assignment seems to be teaching a type of academic dishonesty, a parody of academic activity. These faux research papers often looked fine on the surface and had been rewarded with higher grades because we assessed for technical proficiency rather than intellectual depth. Faculty members do not have time to comb through all of the sources cited for all of the papers to be marked. Having students hand in copies of the sources used, perhaps with quotations or paraphrased material highlighted, might help us identify what they are using from where, but it probably won't help students read critically for academic purposes. Students are creating these faux research papers because that is what we have told them to do, explicitly in our handouts—"find and use at least three sources"—or implicitly in our assessment practices.

## Critical Reading for Academic Purposes

If critical reading for academic purposes involves reading to learn and reading to integrate, faculty need to spend much more time on making explicit the intellectual work involved in these two activities. They also need to emphasize that it *is* work, that reading complex material, learning from it, and placing it in context with other work is difficult. What would reading to learn look like in a particular context? How can students create the situation models and text models that will help them integrate and evaluate new information with what they already know? Explicitly modeling in class how we read unfamiliar texts may help; students may need to see us struggle on occasion. However, since much reading for academic purposes is driven by the grade, at least at the undergraduate level, we must also reconsider our assignments and our assessment practices. Perhaps a place to begin is with the academic purpose, recognizing that there are different purposes for reading in an academic context.[47] Students are asked to read to synthesize existing knowledge, to evaluate information, to develop capacity, perhaps even to create new knowledge, but our assessment processes often lump all of these purposes together, with the hope that students will also demonstrate that they can find relevant sources, integrate those sources within their written work, and build a coherent and appropriately cited argument. Perhaps with all of these tasks, faculty and students lose the focus on reading. Faculty need to make some difficult choices about what they want their students to do and how they plan to assess it.

Much of the discussion in this chapter has focused on our attempts to help the individual read critically in his or her academic studies. Our assumptions include individual agency within a competitive environment. Students are often motivated by grades, and we can use this motivation to reward or discourage certain behaviors, which may or may not become habitual. The next chapter has a broader, and some would argue more important, focus: how to foster critical reading for social engagement. There our assumptions include the importance of a literate citizenry, the need for collective action, and the recognition that many aspects of education and schooling, including postsecondary experiences, maintain a status quo that privileges some at the expense of many. We explore what critical reading for social engagement looks like in this environment.

## Lessons Learned

- Just because students can read doesn't mean they will; it may be more efficient not to.
- Faculty need to identify and communicate which academic purposes the readings and assignments are intended to serve. Is the goal to build new knowledge, synthesize existing knowledge, or develop particular capacities?
- Critical reading for academic purposes can be impeded by students' assumptions about assignments and our assessment practices.
- If summary requires deeper comprehension of sources, we may be able to manipulate comprehension by creating research assignments that require summary.
- Traditional research paper assignments emphasize how to find and use information rather than how to read text and understand ideas.
- Emphasizing the intellectual processes of reading, including the role genre plays in understanding, rather than the technical details of the final product can facilitate critical reading for academic purposes.

# 4 Critical Reading for Social Engagement

Wᴇ ʜᴀᴠᴇ ᴛᴀʟᴋᴇᴅ about the difficult choices that are necessary when we promote critical reading for academic purposes given the variability of those purposes. The situation becomes even more complicated when we consider critical reading for social engagement within the context of the postsecondary institution. After all, critical reading for academic purposes can be seen as an act of domestication, where students are trained to become institutionally viable in order to reproduce academic disciplines, often at the expense of their own sense of agency. In *A Pedagogy for Liberation* Ira Shor and Paulo Freire identify a dichotomy between reading for academic purposes, what they call "reading the words," and reading for liberation, or "reading the world," in North American education: "Students withdraw into passive noncompliance or offensive sabotage in response to a disempowering education, this dichotomy of reading from living, of intellectualizing from experiencing."[1] Without minimizing the need for rigor, critical reading for social engagement necessarily involves interaction with, rather than reproduction of, patterns of knowledge in the service of something more— more than the individual, more than the discipline, and more than the institution.

The call for liberal education that reaches beyond the institution to the community or communities has taken on more urgency in the last decade because of economic and political pressures. In America this call often involves the terminology of civic engagement and "service-learning."[2] Reports like *A Crucible Moment: College Learning and Democracy's Future,* from the National Task Force on Civic Learning and Democratic Engagement, insist that all sectors of education should "reclaim and reinvest in the fundamental civic and democratic mission."[3] The Bringing Theory to Practice project, with its recent monograph, *Civic Provocations,* and the Campus Compact coalition of almost twelve hundred institutions committed to civic engagement and service-learning are only two of many such initiatives. However, David Scobey notes:

The civic turn has tended to take as normative, or at least as unexamined, the assumptions of the traditional paradigm of undergraduate education: that our students are fulltime and full of time, committed for a compact number of years to an educational experience in which they traverse the general education to major journey as a unified trajectory; that they have the time, space, and money for intensive, unpaid community-based learning; that they are taught largely by regular, fulltime faculty who can undertake the hard work of community-based teaching, sometimes with the aid of paid civic-engagement staff; that the melding of public work and academic work is anchored in an "in-here" campus world that reaches out to partner with a locally bounded "out-there" community world.[4]

These assumptions don't fit most undergraduate students in North America. We know that community-based learning is one of several high-impact educational practices that can increase not only student engagement but also academic achievement; we also know that the majority of students do not participate in such a practice, especially if they are from historically underserved groups.[5] Data from both the National Survey of Student Engagement and the Cooperative Institute Research Project suggest senior students are more likely to participate in community-based learning than first-year students, but even then engagement is sporadic at best.[6] Students struggle with course work and part-time jobs in which they work full-time hours as they juggle family and personal commitments. In a specifically Canadian context, there are few civics courses, little co-curricular focus, and limited opportunities for learning through some type of community service, although there is interest. For example, the Canadian Alliance for Community Service-Learning has been expanding, but it still involves around fifty programs nationwide as opposed to Campus Compact's twelve hundred institutions. Demands on resources, including both student and faculty time, have been a barrier. And, unlike the American postsecondary system, there is not a widespread perception of crisis in higher education among the public, governments, or institutions in Canada.[7] Few external pressures exist to increase student learning and engagement, and there are powerful disincentives: inertia, nostalgia, self-interest. High-impact practices that might lead to social engagement take time and resources from everyone involved. For the most part institutions lack a coordinated approach to social engagement, instead relying on "inoculation," whereby faculty hope exposure to issues through readings and discussion will lead to systemic changes. However, while social engagement is difficult to achieve within the confines of an academic institution, critical reading for social engagement is just as difficult, if not more so. This chapter exposes our efforts and our failures to have students read critically for social engagement.

Reading for social engagement includes many of the same elements as reading for academic purposes: it requires comprehension, analysis, interpretation, and evaluation. In addition, however, it requires connections between knowledge and civic engagement and participation or, on an even more basic level, knowledge and personal experience. Critical reading for social engagement requires the integration of both word and world, in Freire's terms.[8] To try to capture these elements, we added two categories to our base rubric: Analysis of Knowledge from the VALUE civic engagement rubric and Connections to Experience from the VALUE integrative learning rubric. We discussed whether or not to include more items from the civic engagement rubric but decided not to for several reasons. Part of our decision was based on our context: as Canadians we do not share the American vocabulary relating to civics and rhetoric about democracy even though we share many of the same goals. Our general education program is supposed to develop "civic capacities" in our students, but institutionally we have never defined what that means. "Social engagement" is not usually part of our vocabulary of instruction. The VALUE civic engagement rubric is also heavily weighted toward action, as indeed one would expect. We were just looking at oblique measures of reading; some students might indeed demonstrate commitment to public action, but we were unlikely to see it based on the information we had. So we selected "Analysis of Knowledge," where the capstone level is described as "Connects and extends knowledge (facts, theories, etc.) from one's own academic study/field/discipline to civic engagement and to one's own participation in civic life, politics, and government," and the benchmark level is described as "Begins to identify knowledge (facts, theories, etc.) from one's own academic study/field/discipline that is relevant to civic engagement and to one's own participation in civic life, politics, and government."[9] Because at least nominally these were first-year courses, we took "one's own academic study/field/discipline" to mean any reference to material from other courses or any academic field. Again, we collapsed the two milestone categories together in our initial analysis of written artifacts.

We wondered whether this category would capture all the connections that could lead to social engagement. We wondered if the "world" we hope students will connect to texts is more about personal engagement and less about social engagement at this point in their studies. An earlier study by Carey demonstrated that students can integrate scholastic and personal material when prompted to do so.[10] So we added the category "Connections to Experience" from the VALUE integrative learning rubric. The descriptor for the capstone is "Meaningfully synthesizes connections among experiences outside of the formal classroom (including life experiences and academic experiences such as internships and travel abroad) to deepen understanding of fields of study and to broaden own points of view," while the descriptor for the benchmark is "Identifies connections between life experiences and those academic texts and ideas perceived as similar and related to own interests."[11] Again we collapsed the two milestone categories. We felt that the prompts for the reflective writing—"What (is the reading about)?" "So What (does it mean)?" and "Now What (are you going to do with this information)?"—would encourage students to make the connections that are so necessary for social engagement, but we were wrong.

As we began to score student reflective pieces according to the Critical Reading for Social Engagement rubric, we quickly noticed what would become an overwhelming

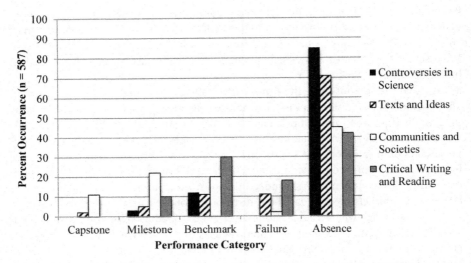

FIGURE 4.1. **Analysis of Knowledge:** Few students related the readings to civic/social engagement as reflected in the Analysis of Knowledge category. The majority of students did not even attempt to discuss social engagement.

trend: students were not demonstrating benchmark levels of Analysis of Knowledge; they were not even failing to achieve that level. Rather, there was little evidence of any attempt to identify knowledge relevant to civic engagement in response to readings that we believed demanded a social response. In the Controversies in Science course, readings included those that centered on the efficacy of complementary and alternative medicines, the exploitation of the oil sands, the safety of nuclear power, and the implications of genetically modified foods. In Texts and Ideas—Genocide students were asked to read excerpts from classic texts on power, policy statements, eyewitness accounts, memoirs, and books on religion, violence, and peace building. In Communities and Societies students were led through widening levels of their own communities and societies, with readings selected to help them find their places, power, and responsibilities within those contexts. In Critical Writing and Reading students read and wrote about discrimination, the gendered language of textbooks, and AIDS in Africa among other things.

Asked to identify the "What?" "So What?" and "Now What?" of readings about gender politics, technological advancements, and civic responsibilities, many students who had read and understood the text did not even acknowledge the possibility of social engagement. Based on 587 reading logs, 58 percent of the students showed no recognition of social context; with an additional 7 percent the social context was acknowledged but refused. For example, in response to an essay about sexist language

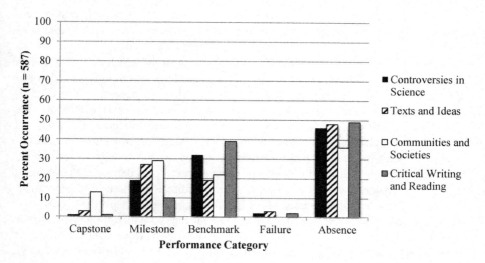

FIGURE 4.2. **Connections to Experience:** Results from the textual analysis examining students' connections to experience. In their reading logs, many students did not attempt to make connections or draw any parallels with their personal experiences.

in textbooks, one student said, "I found it an odd topic to discuss because honestly, I've never thought about it before. It's not overly important to me because I don't particularly care what kind of language biologists use and how it is a reflection of male/female roles." This woman understood the main claim about sexism in textbooks, recognized that the author was also making a larger social claim, and discounted it as unimportant to her personally. Another student writing about the same essay said, "I am going to tuck this down in the corner of my brain reserved for interesting but irrelevant information to my life. Not saying it's not a relevant issue in our culture, I just don't plan on losing sleep over it." Sixty-five percent of readings logs written by the students did not make the benchmark level for Analysis of Knowledge from civic engagement (see fig. 4.1). We turned to the category of Connections to Experience, expecting that here at least students would make connections between texts and their personal contexts when explicitly asked to do so—"Now What (are you going to do with this information)?" Here the responses were significantly better, with 28 percent of the students performing at the benchmark level, 26 percent above, and only 2 percent who in their reading logs attempted but failed to connect their knowledge. However, in a stunning 44 percent of responses, students demonstrated no attempt to make connections between the readings and life experiences in reflective writing (see fig. 4.2). The rubrics could not show us what students were doing, only what they were not doing. We were confronted by an absence in the aggregate results.

We then set about trying to make sense of this absence by returning to the reflective logs, reading and rereading them. Moving away from the particular content of the logs related to the subject matter of the readings, we began noticing variations on actions. We started to map what we saw happening in the logs for which students had demonstrated "failure" or "absence" in the categories Analysis of Knowledge and Connections to Experience, eventually coming up with a taxonomy of absence.[12] Students demonstrated variations across the four courses, but the overall pattern was the same. Based on what students were doing in their responses, it seemed like they could get stuck at compliance, comprehension, identification, or generalization. Of course, compliance with the reading task and comprehension are not specific to reading for social engagement, and we continue to work on increasing students' participation in and comprehension of reading. Problems with identification of issue and generalization were more specific to the issue of reading for social engagement. In what follows, we explain each of the categories in relation to social engagement, noting symptomatic variation in the four courses. We also examine what happens when critical reading for social engagement appears to be successful, hoping to find some elements that can be reproduced in other contexts.

## Compliance

It seems counterintuitive to talk about compliance as being necessary when discussing a definition of critical reading linked to critical pedagogy, but there can be no critical reading if there is no reading. As far as we could tell from the details reported in the reading logs, most, though not all, of our students read the texts we discussed in class. When students hadn't read, they would often admit it in the entries. For example, one student opened a reading log with "I feel that I should be honest and tell you that I did not read the article. I feel this is better than me making up aspects about the reading." This student went on to reflect how not reading the article affected how she was able to participate in class and promised to read the article later so that she could "gain understanding of what was discussed in class." We don't know if she did. The amount of reading completed for the research papers was less than it was for texts discussed in class, as we discussed in the previous chapter. Shor and Freire describe a culture of silence and a culture of sabotage in which students resist reading in response to the domination of a disempowering education.[13] Ira Shor claims, "Domination is more than being ordered around impersonally in school, and more than the social relations of discourse in a transfer-of-knowledge pedagogy. Domination is also the very structure of knowing; concepts are presented irrelevant to reality; descriptions of reality achieve no critical integration; critical thought is separated from living. This dichotomy is the interior dynamic of a pedagogy that disempowers students politically and psychologically." According to Shor, "This dichotomy destroys student enthusiasm for knowledge."[14] We suggest something a lot more pragmatic and less interesting.

Students often do not read because they don't have to, and it's difficult, and they're busy. When Brian D. Brost and Karen A. Bradley examined the reading habits of students in senior-level elective courses, they discovered that the main reason students don't read is because of how instructors use, or don't use, the readings.[15] Consider the student in Communities and Societies who commented: "My prof. in my Monday class even posts audio recordings of most longer texts he requires us to read. It's nice but it doesn't improve my learning . . . only my laziness." There are, of course, many different reasons to assign readings, including transfer of information, and if we assume students can't or won't read, we may choose to resort to alternate means. However, such solutions do not help students' ability to read critically or foster the types of self-reflection theorists believe reading makes possible: "The dynamic interaction between text and life experiences is bidirectional: We bring our life experiences to the text, and the text changes our experience of life. . . . Sometimes we emerge after this immersion into other worlds of thought . . . with an expansion of our capacity to think, feel, and act in new and courageous ways; but wherever we are led, we are not the same."[16] Listening does not provide the same possibility for immersion, because the pace is already set; there is no time to hesitate, think, or reflect. Nor do such alternatives to reading provide students with the opportunity to remake knowledge and power: "Reading is rewriting what we are reading."[17] Critical reading for social engagement calls for much more than passive reception or consumption of texts, but it does start with reading.

## Comprehension

Having read, students needed to be able to comprehend the text in order to engage with it in a meaningful way. Most students' reading logs demonstrated comprehension with at least benchmark proficiency, although that level may have been influenced by class discussion. Occasionally students had read and not understood the main claims of a piece as evident in their reading logs. More often they would report on strategies they relied upon to increase their comprehension, particularly rereading or class discussion. From the perspective of social engagement, however, we would like to draw attention to the difficulty students may face in comprehending material that contradicts the master narratives of their lives. While much research has been performed on applying schema theory to comprehension, examining how new information is placed within an existing framework, researchers have increasingly called for theories that allow for more nuanced understanding of affect and personal epistemology.[18] Expectations can impede understanding. Students in Critical Writing and Reading, for example, had significant difficulty understanding an autobiographical essay by Heather Menzies; seven of fourteen reading logs did not indicate student comprehension after guided class discussion about the essay had occurred. In the essay, Menzies uses childhood memories of planting trees to reflect on the importance of taking time to be present in the moment rather than always striving for something else. However, several students read her essay as promoting the value of hard work, even after the thesis was identified and key passages and techniques were discussed in class. For example, one student proclaimed: "From this essay, I have learned that there are some things in life that need to be done, but in order to achieve, you have to work hard. Not everything comes easy. I will take this message and incorporate it in my daily routines and start to work harder and more efficiently in everything that I do," precisely the opposite of what Menzies advocates. The possibility that Menzies is criticizing a work ethic that leaves "No time for rest and contemplation. No time for rooting and taking root. No time for remembrance and reciprocity" is not even considered.[19]

In this context it is worthwhile considering research on the intellectual development of college students. If students move through a series of developmental stages from dualism through relativism and into the evolution of commitments, as William G. Perry suggests, their inability to comprehend an unexpected thesis may spring not from misreading the words of the text, but from student attitudes about knowledge, authority, and identity. But if students aren't yet able to recognize and accommodate contradictions, it is surely higher education's role to nudge them along within a supportive framework, elements of which have been described by Lee Knefelkamp and Patricia M. King and Karen Strohn Kitchener.[20] King and Kitchener distinguish between critical thinking and reflective thinking, arguing that reflective thinking includes consideration of epistemic assumptions; they also argue that "the development of reflective judgment is the outcome of an interaction between the individual's conceptual skills and environments that promote or inhibit the acquisition of these skills."[21] King and Kitchener identify key elements of these environments appropriate for different stages of development: assumptions, goals, difficult tasks, developmental assignments, and support.[22] Perhaps taking the time to explore the contradictions between students' assumptions and Menzies's actual meaning would have helped more students comprehend the essay. Without the ability to accept the thesis, even as something to argue against, there was little chance of critical reading for social engagement.

## Identification

For most students, however, difficulty in critical reading for social engagement came not in compliance or comprehension, but in identification or generalization. By "identification" we mean simply the ability or willingness to identify the issue in the assigned reading. There are three common reasons for this failure to identify an issue based on the patterns we observed in the reading logs. First, the prompts—"What?" "So What?" and "Now What?"—may have simply failed. Perhaps in our desire to allow for different responses without undue influence, we did not signal acceptable models, so even those who saw an issue did not identify it as such. If we had asked "What is the issue in the reading?" rather than "What is the reading about?" we probably would have received more responses signaling elements of reading for social engagement. However, there are two other factors worth considering. The first, connected with the issue of the prompts, is student expectations in terms of epistemology and genre; the second is students doing something else, whether writing about other aspects of the reading or reading for other purposes.

In terms of student expectations, we saw a number of responses that suggested that students did not hold constructivist epistemologies, which makes reading for social engagement, with its assumptions that language is not transparent and that reality is shaped by language, more unlikely. A constructivist epistemology is not synonymous with a transactional model of reading, but a transactional model does require some elements of constructivism. As we described earlier, some students seemed to be demonstrating a strong transmission model of reading rather than a transactional one. Instead of believing that "their role as readers and learners [authorizes] them to build new complex knowledge through their own effort to integrate information,"[23] many students saw the text as the repository of knowledge, a characteristic of early stages in the Perry scheme. This pattern occurred across the courses. In Texts and Ideas—Genocide students sometimes accused a text of complexity rather than trying to engage with morally ambiguous material: "It's too hard to understand." The text contains the information and therefore the problem. When the content is complex, ambiguous, or contradictory, students see this as a failure of the text to deliver information. There may also be issues of affective resistance if students feel stupid when confronted by something they do not understand. In Communities and Societies students could comfortably identify contestable terms and understand that the definition of terms is highly influential in shaping an argument, but a larger conception of reality as constructed in the readings eluded them, and, to be fair, Carey did not present a constructivist position. In Critical Writing and Reading some students rejected the idea that language, whether related to gender bias in a biology textbook or nicknames of professional hockey players, might make a difference to reality. This belief that the texts hold the knowledge seemed strongest in Controversies in Science.

Despite the course title, the students generally believed that scientific information is objective, and they didn't internalize the readings in the way that constructive epistemology suggests. They didn't view science as unbiased, because recognition of author bias was a major focus of the course. Even with the recognition of bias, students didn't interpret the readings in a personal way; they just rejected the readings outright, pointed out flaws or problems with the author's methodology, or called for more information. Very few students challenged interpretations or conclusions of the author. For example, after a reading promoting the benefits of genetically modified foods, one student responded to the reading with the following: "Obviously, there are potential economic benefits and even nutritional benefits but there is no really scientific evidence that shows the exact negative side effects. And with the academic work that was or has been done was seemingly done improperly. We need more research on GM foods." Although the reading advocated a particular viewpoint and the student was able to acknowledge there was another side to the issue, she interpreted the absence of supporting information for that opposing argument as a lack of scientific evidence. The student continued to make claims that more research is needed but did not understand what evidence even exists. This was a common occurrence in Controversies in Science: when students were confronted with a one-sided argument, they defaulted to the claim that more research needed to be completed and didn't try to consider the current state of science. Students' assumptions about the objective nature of the readings may also have been perpetuated by the introduction of new terminology that they had to struggle with. Although most students didn't directly comment on terminology in their reflection papers, classroom discussion often began with questions that centered on clarification and explanation of terms. Cognitive load theory explains how our working memory has a limited capacity to process new information.[24] Perhaps the lack of social engagement that we observed can be partly explained by these limitations; students were focused on a basic understanding of the text rather than a higher-order analysis of the content. Or it may have been influenced by their preconceptions about science as neutral truth, those same preconceptions the course itself was designed to complicate. Students would often side with articles that "had references" or "contained detailed diagrams" or articles that were "very neutral with his writing." We cannot assume that a score below the benchmark level indicates a lack of ability; it may indicate that student assumptions about knowledge and particular courses clash with our own, especially when we are not explicit about our assumptions and expectations.

In some cases the rubric score below benchmark simply indicated that the student was doing something else during that particular reading log, an important caveat when using the VALUE, or any, rubrics. Sometimes we saw students who clearly had read and understood and who, based on other responses, were capable of making the civic and personal connections necessary for social engagement but who chose to write about other aspects of their reading process or to read for other purposes. For example, in Communities and Societies, in response to an essay about global problems and opportunities by Jeffrey D. Sachs,[25] a student responded, "The only problem I had with the article was the part about Kennedy. Wasn't he President when the Vietnam War started and during the invasion of Cuba by the CIA?" The reading mentioned Kennedy briefly under the topic of "learning from the past," principally to note his "Strategy of Peace" address at the American University in 1963, in which he urged global solutions to global problems. The student seemed caught up in the confusion he felt over Kennedy's roles, with the former president presented in the reading as a forward-thinking global leader in direct contrast to the student's own understanding of Kennedy's more apparently aggressive military stances. What seems at first like a tangent to the content of the reading might be the student trying to make sense of that content.

Responses that indicated the student was focused on elements other than social engagement were most prevalent in the Critical Writing and Reading course. Students often read for style, probably because the course content focused on how assigned texts were written. For example, an English major in Critical Writing and Reading was able to make connections between knowledge and civic engagement with at least bench-mark-level proficiency in seven of her ten reading logs; in two instances this engage-ment inspired her to write poems outside of class on social issues. However, writing about Stephen Lewis's keynote address "AIDS in Africa,"[26] she analyzes his diction and rhetorical strategies rather than his ideas, saying, "I am totally in love with his diction."

Another student, one of only a few demonstrating critical reading for social engagement in the research paper, commented in response to the same essay: "Now what am I going to do with it? One part of the essay surfaces more than any other to me. It's the part when Lewis describes the 'pipedream' (p. 305). I know what the word means, and found it humorous that Lewis would use such street level slang to describe the bottom line of an issue to an academic and international audience. His use of the slang makes me more comfortable to use the same types of words in writing of my own." This particular student, a sociology major, was especially interested in AIDS. She had lived in a neighborhood that was infamous for high drug use; she knew some-one who was HIV-positive and taking antiviral drugs; and her research paper was on safe injection sites; however, you would not know anything about these connections from her response. Instead, she chose to focus on the rhetorical strategies and style of the piece, perhaps because of the context in which she read it: a class on Critical Writ-ing and Reading taught by an English professor. She chose to read in a more academic way, even on an issue that usually engages her personally and socially. When asked in a follow-up interview whether the readings encouraged any changes in thinking or behavior outside the course, she answered again in terms of style:

> It's just, in a sense, it freed me. . . . So the way that influences me is that I feel like I have the confidence to be able [to] write things like Atwood wrote and still hand them in to a professor or be almost a little bit more casual or more bold in my state-ments to a professor in my writing. For example, in a sociology paper I wrote what I really felt. I wrote about how girls wear short skirts and they're showing more mid-riff and teen girls look more sexual, and I was really bold and borderline crass in the way I said that to him because I wanted to get the point across. And reading a piece like Atwood's gave me the confidence to be able to do that in my writing instead of just pussy-footing around and trying to sound just common in what I was saying. So that's what I picked up from exposure to the pieces.

Reading, even reading for style in this case, provided this student with the confidence to be able to "get the point across" in an argument about a social issue by providing the permission to write in a less academic way. However, her argument is still limited to the academic task and rewarded with the academic currency of grades: "I thought he would just slam me on the paper, but I must have done better than I thought because I walked away with an A. So he liked it." Notice that she doesn't end with a statement about the essay's effectiveness, but with her instructor's opinion, as if the grade has less to do with her performance than his preference. Does this response demonstrate reading for social engagement within an academic context or co-opted by an academic context? We hope it demonstrates capacity for future engagement outside of the academic context. And as Shor and Freire note, education within the academy cannot be the lever for transforming society. That doesn't mean it cannot develop "critical curiosity, some political awareness, democratic participation, habits of intellectual scrutiny, and interest in social change,"[27] what we will talk about in the next chapter as "combined capabilities," to use Martha Nussbaum's term.[28] If we want social engagement within this academic context, we need to unpack the assumptions about knowledge and expectations students carry into particular courses.

## Generalization

Most troubling for us were those students who, having identified an issue in their reading logs, went on to generalize too little or too much for even the possibility of social engagement. Here we saw many examples of what Perry describes as "Positions of deflection," especially "Escape," where the student "exploits the opportunity for detachment and retreat offered by [late multiplicity and relativism] to deny responsibility through passive or opportunistic alienation," and "Retreat," where the student "entrenches in dualistic and absolutistic structures."[29] Perry associates these positions with the early stages of college student development, but they can be seen in many other contexts when individuals are confronted with material that makes them uncomfortable. When we first started looking at the many students whose reading logs scored failure or absence on our measures of social engagement, we were overwhelmed by the variety of responses among those who had identified an issue but refused to go any further. After reading an article about the impacts of oil sands, one student discussed the importance of understanding the issue and its implications but when asked to respond to "Now What?" replied: "Nothing. The oil companies show no signs of slowing." This was the student's entire entry for this question; he clearly understood the article, but his response indicates that he is overwhelmed and sees no way to effect change. Many students expressed distress, resignation, apathy, resentment, self-righteousness, and boredom. Beyond the emotional state and specific content, responses could be divided into those that demonstrated insufficient or excessive generalization. Among students who generalized too little were those who over-personalized their responses to the readings or sank into their own immediate experience. Among students who generalized too much were those resigned to the current state and those who displaced responsibility for the current state onto others. Neither pattern of generalization allowed for critical reading for social engagement.

On the one hand, sometimes students claimed to be too personally invested to move into questions of social engagement. After all, many of our students are from the so-called Millennial generation, sometimes talked about in terms of entitlement, consumerism, or even narcissism. Reading about the disadvantages of an elite education in Communities and Societies, one student proclaimed: "Well, I still want to go to an Ivy League school for my PhD. Why? 1 word: money, and my love of all things it buys. I would love to better mankind but let's be real. Money buys everything today. I'm not saying money is everything in life, but without it you go nowhere. . . . What can I do but conform and do what the system demands and make money. At least until I turn 50, I will work for money." This student clearly identifies a series of issues: inequitable education, humanitarian impulses, capitalist drive, and peer pressures. The student also claims to want to put off social engagement until the unimaginably old age of fifty. It is difficult to tell how much of this response is a pose. This student was older than many first-year students and noted various positions on social engagement throughout the term. For instance, he was a strong advocate of political participation and voting in particular, and he chastised the "younger generation" for apathetic disregard of its political power. Later in the term he queried his own ecological irresponsibility, confessing how frequently he drives to the mountains to enjoy his favorite sports while simultaneously suggesting we all need to be more environmentally conscious. His ambivalence addressed both his own successes and failures in terms of social engagement, and he was highly critical of the failures of those around him. Aware of the issues, critical of self and others, he explicitly refuses engagement.

We also saw responses in which students explained how the readings had nothing to do with them because they just weren't interested in the topic, whether child care, politics, education, or gender roles. They didn't see the relevance to their lives, even when it seemed clear to us. And merely telling them it was important was not a successful strategy, because a number of students indicated in no uncertain terms that they have heard it all before: "Thinking about how decisions are made by those set in power, I feel that my apathy, perhaps, could be related to desensitization. I care less about who runs my country and more about why it doesn't matter. Perhaps I should invest more interest into political stances and become involved in who really reflects my beliefs." This student, responding in Communities and Societies to a reading on political culture and socialization, realizes that he should care, should invest interest, should become involved, but probably won't. Community activists like Dave Meslin argue that the issue is not apathy, but rather systematic attempts to discourage engagement.[30] Perhaps this student's self-identified apathy, or reluctance to get involved, does not indicate lack of generalization, but instead is a symptom of excessive generalization, in which case the solution might be to push toward specific actions and issues rather than a political stance more generally.

Certainly the most common pattern we saw in responses that scored below the benchmark was excessive generalization, often in the form of resignation or displacement, or both. Across the four courses, students did not think they could make a difference, although what this looked like varied by course. In Controversies in Science some students expressed being overwhelmed by environmental challenges; many of the responses talk about how powerless they felt: "It's really starting to hit me, the impact of oil in our world. I can't help but wonder what we are going to do. It's like being stuck between a rock and a hard place, we need it but it's hurting us, we can't think of anything better or anything more convenient or efficient. I feel as though for society to really step back and make a change something more drastic than dying ducks is going to have to happen." But notice how the change is society's, not the student's, and the change has to be dramatic in response to crisis rather than incremental. They do not see their world as malleable—to use the student's words, they are "between a rock and a hard place."

Other students expected that someone else, or technology itself, would save them. This was especially true for students who were discussing whether nuclear power was safe, at a time that coincided with the Fukushima nuclear disaster of 2011. After reading a text that argued against the use of nuclear power, one student commented: "The arguments against seem unfounded and largely unsubstantiated except for evidence given by large scale disasters such as Chernobyl and Three Mile Island. Because of the huge technological advances made in the last two decades, there is no reason to fear nuclear power, as it should be noted that any form of power generation can be dangerous under the right circumstances." Despite news coverage and class discussions of the disaster at Fukushima, this student defaults to technological optimism and a universal claim—"any form of power generation can be dangerous." Another student responded to this same reading by deflecting responsibility onto government: "If nuclear power is as terrible as they say, why would a government allow it since without the public, the government doesn't exist so doing things that destroy the public is highly illogical." Here the necessity of social engagement is discounted because someone else, the government, will take care of us. Although the student acknowledges that the government exists because of the public, there is no recognition that the government is constituted by us. Nuclear disaster is such a catastrophic event it is difficult for anyone to find individual agency; however, the possibility of agency must begin with the willingness to consider information rather than reject it out of hand.

We also saw a number of responses indicating a type of social Darwinism, sometimes regretted, but seen as inevitable. For example, in Texts and Ideas—Genocide, one student reflects on Thucydides and Machiavelli with the following:

> As long as people are willing to embrace violence, they will always be in a position of power over those who won't or who are weaker than them. . . . The strong will take advantage of the weak, and it is viewed to be natural or as something that will always happen. I wonder, will this always be the scenario with humans? As long as there are inequities in the world, I fear this may be the case. It always lightens my heart to see people break this mould though and gives me hope for the future of man and our society.

Note the repetition of the word "always" throughout the entry. There is a glimmer of hope at the end: some people can break this mold, although the student does not include himself in that company. The student is able to acknowledge personal affect—"lightens my heart"—but not action. Instead, he demonstrates a sort of resignation.

In Communities and Societies this resignation came up again and again in the responses: "Personally I feel powerless and confused as to a solution or action to take"; "There is nothing we can do"; "Honestly, I figure not much will really change"; "I believe this is a huge problem with this and future generations"; "I wish the world would come together and make a positive change through cooperation, but I just don't think it is going to." Instead of agency the students expressed helplessness. Sometimes this helplessness is redirected into fatalism; something is inevitable and therefore not to be regretted: "We aren't sad that we don't live in caves anymore so why dread leaving small towns?" What might be seen as a social problem is redefined as necessity or inevitability in a teleological sense, where human progress is always good.

The movement to redefine something as unpleasant but necessary can be particularly dangerous, as an exploration of genocide demonstrates. Genocide seems beyond the scope of individual agency, although it reveals the moral necessity of social engagement. The course Texts and Ideas—Genocide had the lowest student participation rate in this study, at 31 percent, or nine students. We suggest the lower participation rate has to do with the emotionally charged readings of the course; many students, we believe, did not feel comfortable enough to share their struggles with painful and ethically challenging material with us. The nine students who did agree to participate tended to be academically strong students who performed well in the course. But even here students tended to shy away from personal engagement into generalization.

The following three reflections are by the same student and show thoughtful engagement with the material being read; however, the student does not wish to consider personal social engagement with the implied issues that come to mind as she reads. Reading John Docker's assessment of Raphael Lemkin's work to define "cultural genocide,"[31] this student reflects on the history of US slavery and the Canadian treatment of its First Nations people, not the main topic of the article, but a connection that the student makes in reading: "I never really thought about what happened in the US with slavery or what happened with the Indians as genocide until now. Docker pulled out this interesting piece of Lemkin's work and maybe he has an opinion on it too. I think that if more time and energy got focused on proving this [slavery and efforts to change the culture of a people] as genocide, the politics of Canada and the world would [be] entirely different." Having considered the larger issues, the student then deflects these issues by stating, "I don't really have a stand on this yet, but perhaps after next class I will." In the next class, when the issue of the Canadian treatment of the First Nations was debated, this student reflected on the question of protecting the "freedoms" of both First Nations and "Whites" but again deflected any possible personal social engagement onto nonhuman agencies: "My response to this is that something needs to be done proactively to prevent our world from slipping back into our old, seemingly less accepting ways and keep moving forward. I think this can be done with resources we already have, media, conventions, speeches, and education programs, but the focus needs to be on opening eyes to the issue." Notice the evasive language in the response: something needs to be done by someone; the world is progressing; we already have resources; awareness, a passive "opening eyes," is enough. The student is not willing to move beyond generalization toward agency in this case; however, she is capable of reading for social engagement on other topics. When reading a sermon by Martin Luther King Jr. on "loving your enemy," this student reflected on King's statement that "Hate destroys the very structure of the personality of the hater."[32] This student thought about the implications for bullying in schools and then concluded that this reading may have relevance to her training as a nurse: "Using this simple sentence and building a campaign around that to end bullying would be helpful. Instead of using the typical 'bullying hurts others' campaign, this might hit home for bullies. By using an idea that if you're a bully YOU will be changed might have more of an impact on the bullies. In our community nursing course we're discussing community development and I think that if I ever chose a community nursing setting this would be an interesting project." The student relates the material to her own discipline of study and possible personal action. Reflecting on a single sentence from the reading, this student is able to integrate academic knowledge across courses and to the community in terms of personal agency. In the terms of the VALUE rubric for civic engagement, she "connects and extends knowledge (facts, theories, etc.) from [her] own academic study/field/discipline to civic engagement and to [her] own participation in civic life, politics, and government."[33] She has not moved to action yet, and may never do so, but the capacity and the plan are there.

Why is such critical reading for social engagement possible in one case and not the other? Students were more likely to make personal connections to Martin Luther King's sermon, perhaps because it had a practical theme students could relate to even when they disagreed with him, perhaps because it seemed less overwhelming than the horrors of genocide, or perhaps the rhetoric of a popular sermon by a celebrated figure has greater appeal than an academic text. This particular student was also able to draw upon a disciplinary identity and framework to find a place for social engagement, and this student, probably in her late twenties, had a greater degree of confidence than what we might expect in first-year students. The greater the personal distance from the issues at stake, the less likely students are to think about social engagement. All of these factors may tell us something about how students become more socially engaged.

## Critical Reading for Social Engagement

Freire talks about the importance of generalization in critical reading as part of an oscillation between reading the world and reading the word: "One critical exercise always required in reading, and necessarily also in writing, is that of easily moving from sensory experience, which characterizes the day-to-day, to generalization, which operates through school language, and then on to the tangible and concrete."[34] We witnessed this oscillation in responses that demonstrated critical reading for social engagement. In such responses students were able to make personal connections with some detail from the reading, make a generalization to a different context, and then pull back to specific action—as is the case of the nursing student who applied Martin Luther King's words to the problem of bullying to imagine an intervention. Also note the connection to identity, whether personal or disciplinary, involved. However, if that identity is threatened by the reading—for instance, by being accused of complicity in racism or sexism—the reader is more likely to back away from social engagement into defensive posturing. Students weigh the risk of taking the discussion deeper and then make choices. We also need to recognize the issue of the timing of knowledge,[35] and the possibility for future capacity even if it is not demonstrated when we expect it. And we need to consider the issue of academic context. We offer suggestions below for intervention in two main areas: issues of scope and issues of academic expectations.

Students seemed to struggle with the large problems they were faced with; they didn't understand how they personally could make a difference with climate change, genocide, poverty, or global aid. One approach to developing such understanding in students is to embed the big issues within a local context, perhaps by having students investigate college campus conflicts.[36] We are not suggesting that general education courses cover only local issues; after all, college is a place for exploring big ideas and big problems, and depending on the student's discipline, these foundational courses may be one of the few places where these ideas can be explored from interdisciplinary perspectives. We are suggesting that the big ideas be explicitly presented in a way to help students oscillate between generalization and specific experience. For example, students across the four courses explicitly noted the importance of class or small group discussions in terms of facilitating their understanding of the readings. Scaffolding a greater sense of empowerment and agency within those discussions might help students generalize in appropriate ways about their own power to change even small things, like their own behavior. Instructors could easily become more intentional about facilitating that kind of connection, which might then facilitate social engagement in a variety of ways. We might simply spend more time assisting students to understand that they have choice when it comes to taking action, or not, in their own lives. One student in Communities and Societies reminds us of this: "I guess it is important to critically read material so that we can take the concepts and apply them to real life. . . . We can learn a lot from doing research but only if we truly understand it and then apply these concepts to our everyday life. It is one thing to read something and understand it but a total different thing to take this knowledge and change your actions and behaviour because of it. Makes me question if I should change my actions and behaviour after I read something." By being more intentional and explicit about facilitating our students' power and agency, we may facilitate their social engagement.

Part of this facilitation, we suggest, is modeling our own struggles to read critically in terms of social engagement, which involves a certain amount of risk both for us and for them. Freire warns, "If you appeal to the students to assume a critical posture as readers, as ones who re-write the text being read, you risk the students not accepting your invitation, and their intellectual production declines."[37] But without this invitation, intellectual production may stagnate. Ryland tries to model the process of moving from generalizations based on personal knowledge to interpretation based on research, which then impacts a reflection on meaning. For example, when reading David Weiss Halivni's allegory, students usually struggle with the author's metaphors.[38] After letting the students work on providing their own interpretations, Ryland stops the class to recount his first reading of the allegory. Students usually participate by identifying key metaphors they think should be addressed. Usually he sees a few nods from students as he applies his initial reading of the story. Next, he provides contextual information from his own research of the metaphors, and students begin to see that his initial reading appears inadequate and possibly even misguided by assumptions he had made. The class then discusses alternative interpretations. Ryland ends the discussion on Halivni's text by turning to his complex questions about failed redemption in the face of the Holocaust, how Halivni appears to be arguing that the Holocaust undermines religious faith. As a result of our research on student reading, Ryland has added one final step: without providing his own conclusions to Halivni's text, he ends the class by asking the students to rewrite their reflections on the subject. Students now take this text much deeper than they have in the past and often discuss implications beyond those necessarily intended by the author.

Sometimes students who are pushed to consider implications may slip into anger and defensiveness. Moments of difficulty may contain the seeds of understanding, as Mariolina Rizzi Salvatori argues,[39] but how do we nurture those seeds? Does it mean allowing students to retreat from difficulty on occasion, or is that just an easy way out for all of us? In Critical Writing and Reading both male and female students tend to react negatively toward anything they label as feminist, because they believe sexism is a thing of the past, or inevitable, or irrelevant to how they live their lives. While discussing "The Female Body" by Margaret Atwood with her class,[40] Manarin described her own reading processes, confusion about particular references, images and examples that came to mind, irritation with the author, and amusement at particular jokes. Student responses, usually very resistant to this essay, were surprisingly positive as they witnessed her struggles to understand the text. Yes, there were still the few who rejected Atwood's argument about the objectification of the female body by attacking the author—"If I wanted to hear someone bitch and complain, I would hang out with my mother more"—but there were fewer outright rejections than usual. There weren't many direct connections to action either, but perhaps the seeds were there. That possibility could be nurtured with activities that asked students to engage with the essay in a less academic way.

Indeed, the issue of academic expectations is a stumbling block when it comes to reading for social engagement; assumptions about the neutrality of knowledge are heightened by the academic genres of the institution. We have already discussed some of the issues involved with expectations for the research paper; here we would like to take a few moments to describe a reflective paper in the Communities and Societies course based on the following prompt: "What do the concepts of community and society mean to you, and how do they apply to your life?" The objective of this assignment was to get students to consider their own place and power. Several students referred to concepts from the readings, but students were discouraged from using academic research. Instead they were encouraged to use their own voice to articulate their understanding and experiences. For example, many could relate to the concept of social capital and discussed it in terms of their own communities:

> The concept of community is one that I find more appealing; the community in which I live is [a] great example of social capital at work. The sidewalks are shoveled daily and not necessarily by the homeowners in each house. . . . The entire attitude of the community is one of help your neighbor, not of a competition (well Christmas lights and Halloween decorations don't count). . . . The concept of social capital is fantastic, and one that I believe makes being part of a community infinitely more valuable and desirable. . . . The more formal nature of a society which at times feels forced makes my membership in it less appealing.

Not surprisingly, the student feels closer to a specific community rather than the more abstract society, but the student is also applying the more academic concept of social capital to help explain her experience in that community.

Another student uses the reflection paper to describe his growing awareness of his place in society:

> Before entering the classroom of my Communities and Societies course I had never really thought about the concepts of what a community or a society is. . . . I think that being a contributing member of a community is what really makes you a part of it. Without participating in it how can you feel a sense of belonging to a community? . . . Although it's apparently a controversial subject I do believe that Canada is a society that I belong to. I am governed and abide by the countries [sic] laws and rules; I contribute to society by furthering my education, working and paying taxes. I consider this contributing to society because I'm engaged in the resources my society has to offer. I'm privileged enough to live in a society where I have the opportunities to seek higher education, can get a job and have a say in societal affairs. I can vote for who I want to make decisions, and if that person doesn't win an election I have the right of free speech to express my thoughts, values and beliefs in a respectful way and be heard.

In this passage the student argues that belonging to a community depends on engagement with that community before claiming that he belongs to Canadian society. By extension, then, his membership in society depends on engagement. He participates in a social contract, bound by rules and responsibilities, but he is also granted certain opportunities. He can learn, work, vote, and "have a say in societal affairs" even when he disagrees with authorities. He connects knowledge and experience to make claims about social identity as a citizen. He does not interrogate this social contract more deeply, by considering, for example, whether "the resources society has to offer" are available to all, but he connects academic knowledge to social engagement. Not all of the essays were as optimistic as this. Some students expressed concern about declining community engagement; some worried about the influence of technology on community. Informed, but not constrained, by their readings, students began to place themselves within communities and consider strategies for social engagement.

The social engagement scores on the reflective papers were significantly higher than those for the research paper. Many students spoke passionately about what they had learned from sports teams, clubs, or extracurricular groups when they were younger. Many noted their ongoing volunteer activity within these communities of belonging and were also aware that their participation in these groups largely had been chosen for them by parents or teachers in their earlier years. Most students expressed a growing awareness of their ability to choose where to extend their social energy for themselves, including political participation: "I feel like because I am still so young that my role in society is minimal. I voted for the mayor . . . for the first time this winter and that has been the extent of my political involvement in my community and country for that matter." It is, at least, a beginning. While most of the students noted serious constraints regarding their time consumed by school and work, many of them identified activities they would like to cultivate when they have more time, or so they hope, as they move out of the academic environment.

The liberation of academic constraints in the reflective paper allowed students some space in which to explore their historical, current, and possible future social engagement, and most did so with unanticipated energy. By contrast, the academic research paper generated nothing in terms of social engagement; the task and its tone appear to preclude personal engagement with the topic under investigation, perhaps because of the deification of the objective voice in much academic writing. Instructors who wish to encourage social engagement and empowerment may consider crafting course assignments that allow students to engage directly and personally with the material at hand, grounding their experience in some degree of theoretical understanding and actual evidence. In the reflective papers, students were given permission to become authorities of their own experience, and to our surprise, these papers produced the clearest picture of these particular students' social engagement. Without academic research and references as part of its requirements, the reflective paper allowed space for students' emergent ideas and the possibility of social engagement.

Faculty cannot assume that social engagement will develop in response to provocative readings assessed in the same old ways. Linda Suskie contends that although courses have different categories of goals (knowledge and understanding, skills, attitudes and values, dispositions and habits of mind), assessment strategies tend to focus on the first two categories.[41] And yet faculty know that students learn what they will be assessed on. We need to provide opportunities for meaningful assessment of the attitudes and the habits of mind that critical reading as social engagement involves. And as Michael B. Smith, Rebecca S. Nowacek, and Jeffrey L. Bernstein note about citizenship education, this engagement cannot be sequestered in a specific course or discipline.[42] If we value building students' civic capacities to read critically and become part of an informed and engaged public, we need to take action.

## Lessons Learned

- Exposure to and discussion of provocative issues is not enough to generate critical reading for social engagement.
- Student responses to readings suggest a taxonomy of absence whereby students have to complete a series of actions in order to read critically for social engagement: compliance, comprehension, identification, and generalization. Students could get stuck at any one of these stages. Sometimes this inability to move forward is linked to epistemological development.
- The specific type of intervention depends on where the students seem stuck: making students accountable for reading; practicing comprehension activities; exploring assumptions; and fostering oscillation.
- For successful critical reading for social engagement to occur, students had to read and understand, be willing and able to identify an issue, and oscillate between generalization and specificity.
- Paying attention to the scope of an issue, modeling reading behaviors, and providing explicit opportunities for students to make connections in less academic forms can facilitate critical reading for social engagement.
- Explicitly encouraging application and integration of knowledge in everyday life may facilitate social engagement, or at least its possibility.

# 5  So Now What?

WE CONCLUDE WITH our own "What?" "So What?" and "Now What?" reflection on lessons learned through this inquiry into critical reading; we also consider the purposes of undergraduate education. This inquiry has challenged many of our assumptions about how students read and what we are doing in the classroom. In response we have changed many aspects of our courses. These changes range from redesigning assignments and rubrics to reconceptualizing courses. Change, however, cannot be limited to individual faculty practice if it is to be effective. We suggest strategies for increasing impact as we try to move from collaborative inquiry to individual and ultimately collective action. Collective action doesn't mean we all have to agree on everything, which is important to remember when trying to implement change in the academy.

## What (Did We Learn)?

We were reminded of how little we actually know about the learning that occurs in our classrooms; we carefully plan particular learning opportunities, but so often our vision of what should be happening does not match what is actually occurring. That is the opportunity of, indeed the imperative for, the scholarship of teaching and learning. By carefully and systematically gathering information, paying attention to the particular context, placing the inquiry in a larger context of scholarship, and reflecting upon our assumptions, we can see glimpses of what is, what works, and what might be.[1] We learned much about what our students were able to do and where, perhaps even why, they sometimes struggle.

The scholarship of teaching and learning must have as its ultimate goal changes in practice to improve student learning. Collaboration makes these changes more likely, especially when evidence of student learning challenges some of the assumptions of higher education. Faculty often assume that problems in critical reading rest with the students. What if they rest, at least in part, with faculty? As we reflected upon what our evidence seemed to be saying, we came to realize that many of the issues we complain about are of our own making. Students are comprehending the texts they read; if they are not doing more, perhaps it is because we haven't consistently asked them to do so. Or if we have asked, we have sabotaged our efforts with assessment schemes that do not reward struggle with difficult concepts over facile proficiency. Our assumptions about our own classroom practice and, in some cases, our disciplines have been challenged. Would we have been brave enough to continue this inquiry if we had been alone? Would we have trusted the results or retreated? It is difficult to realize, let alone share, that the best-laid plans with wonderful intentions are not working. It is difficult to avoid sinking into despair, blame, and cynicism. And yet we have to persist. We cannot afford to give up on critical reading in higher education, nor can anyone engaged in higher education today. Developing capabilities for critical reading, whether the primary focus is academic success or social engagement, is too important if we conceive of democratic choice as "the expression of a deliberative judgment about the overall good."[2]

Although we were all interested in critical reading before this inquiry, none of us realized how absolutely central it is to our ideals of postsecondary education but how marginal it is in our actual practice. It is difficult to imagine a student succeeding in postsecondary studies without critical reading, yet we saw evidence of just that; indeed we had colluded in it through our classroom and assessment practices. We habitually made assumptions about students' understanding of readings based on their reactions to our classes; we also assumed that just because students had found and used what looked like appropriate sources within their essays, they had read the material and presumably learned something from it. However, students did not need to read critically in order to succeed.

Through this inquiry we learned that our students appear to be able to comprehend nonfictional text in a variety of forms. What many faculty call a lack of comprehension seems to be students struggling with the evaluation of assumptions or the creation of relevant inferences, both of which are key elements of critical reading for academic purposes and social engagement. We advocate shifting the terms of the discussion from whether postsecondary students can read to whether they can, and are willing to, evaluate assumptions and make relevant inferences. This reframing situates the learning opportunity in an area where even faculty without formal training in literacy learning can see themselves making a difference; a historian or biologist may not know how to teach students to read, but he or she may have the confidence to point out assumptions in particular readings or explicitly make relevant inferences between readings. Reframing debates about whether our students can read to focus on particular elements of critical reading provides faculty with a way to move from lamentation to action.

A first step is to consider the gaps between what faculty members mean when they talk about reading and what students mean. For a faculty member, reading is likely a process by which he or she interprets the author's meaning, interrogates the text, and analyzes how the author reached conclusions. Most faculty members approach texts with a level of skepticism and critique, evaluating whether they support the same conclusion as the author. They tend to use contextual clues before the reading begins, and they tend to approach the author with some authority of their own. They tend to use transactional models of reading. For a student, reading may be about learning the particular language of the discipline and trying to understand the content surrounding an issue. They are not wrong; they are just novices at a task that faculty have been practicing for years. Students, on the other hand, may be relying on transmission models of reading or just beginning to experiment with transactional models. Recognizing and making explicit the different meanings of reading may be a first step toward helping students recognize the types of activities faculty hope they engage in.

Another step is to make students responsible for reading in ways that reinforce transactional activities. There can be no critical reading if there is no reading at all, but reading compliance by itself is not enough. Having students carry out activities in connection with the readings, even something as simple as taking part in brief small group discussions, is more effective than simply asking them to read something in preparation for a lecture. The quality of reading has to count, and students have to see it count, whether that is through carefully designed quizzes, rubrics, worksheets, or other assignments. Writing about what has been read seems particularly useful. Indeed, Richard Arum and Josipa Roksa note, "The combination of reading and writing in coursework was necessary to improve students' performance on tasks requiring critical thinking, complex reasoning, and writing skills in their first two years of college."[3] Arum and Roksa are talking specifically about those courses where students were required to read more than forty pages a week and write more than twenty pages over the semester, but faculty who are unable, or unwilling, to commit to these types of requirements can still find benefit in having students write about what they read. Writing deepens the reading experience and does not necessarily mean a lot of extra marking, depending on how the assignments are set up.

Faculty, regardless of discipline, are urged to consider and make explicit the purposes of the readings and the purposes of the assignments. Students are surprisingly willing to do what faculty ask them to do, but instructions can work against intent. If students are asked to read a chapter before class, is it enough that their eyes simply pass over the text? If students are asked to find and use five sources for a research essay, is it enough that they found and used them, or were faculty hoping that they would read them as well? In some cases it may be enough to skim a chapter before class, or practice the format of a research paper without concern for content, but in most cases such minimum involvement is insufficient. Faculty need to make their expectations clear and then follow through on those expectations, even if it makes students feel uncomfortable and even if the student evaluations of instruction make faculty feel uncomfortable. Finally, faculty need to help students recognize opportunities for critical reading within and beyond their disciplines.

The ability to recognize an opportunity is a crucial step toward action. Just because an individual can do something doesn't mean he or she will, a pattern we saw many times in our inquiry. Someone may be able to evaluate assumptions or create inferences but unwilling to spend the time or take the risk; conversely, someone may be willing to evaluate assumptions but may lack the necessary traits, abilities, and environment to do so. Martha Nussbaum's discussion of capabilities may be useful here. Nussbaum not only distinguishes between capabilities—what each individual is able to do—and functionings, which are the "active realization of one or more capabilities"; she also distinguishes between different types of capabilities.[4] Nussbaum defines "basic capabilities" as "the innate faculties of the person that make later training possible." She argues that, far from justifying a meritocracy, the concept of basic capabilities means "those who need more help to get above the threshold get more help."[5] She defines "internal capabilities" as "trained or developed traits and abilities, developed in most cases, in interaction with the social, economic, familial, and political environment." Far from being static, such internal capabilities are "fluid and dynamic."[6] Much of our educational system is geared toward developing such internal capabilities. However, Nussbaum also identifies a third type of capabilities: "combined capabilities," "not just abilities residing inside a person but also the freedoms or opportunities created by a combination of personal abilities and the political, social, and economic environment."[7]

Interventions to increase critical reading in higher education need to take into account not only issues of motivation to produce functioning but different types of support to develop different types of capabilities, from accommodations with accessibility services through targeted exercises in class to structured opportunities to engage communities beyond the classroom. Once the individual leaves the postsecondary environment, he or she may never exercise all of these capabilities; that's the price of a society that values, or claims to value, choice. However, that price doesn't mean we stop trying to help students develop capabilities for critical reading, even if we saw no developmental progression in reading skills, even if increased levels of evaluation or engagement didn't remain after prompts were removed, even if students sometimes found it more efficient not to read. Indeed, developing capabilities for critical reading becomes more important than ever given our findings. Our task as instructors in postsecondary institutions is to foster student capabilities to the best of our abilities, whether or not students eventually exercise these capabilities outside of the academy. We return, in particular, to the idea of combined capabilities—the internal capabilities and the opportunities afforded by the social, economic, and political environment—for our students and also for ourselves. Students need to be able to recognize the opportunities for critical reading if we hope they will take advantage of those opportunities in the classroom and beyond. We need to recognize opportunities as well—opportunities for change in higher education within our classrooms and beyond. Perhaps then we can realize some of our combined capabilities as functionings.

## So What (Does That Mean for Our Courses)?

If the scholarship of teaching and learning is "scholarship undertaken in the name of change," as Pat Hutchings suggests, our inquiry has succeeded.[8] It has profoundly changed how we teach, not only in these particular courses but across the curriculum as well. What follows are a few of the changes we have made since beginning this exploration of critical reading. We organize this material by principle rather than by particular course, because, as in our findings, we saw so many similar patterns across the four courses. In all of our courses, in general education and beyond, we recognize the following:

- Students need to be held accountable for reading.
- The quality of reading needs to be assessed.
- Assessment needs to be aligned with goals.
- Students need to write about what they read.
- Students need opportunities and practice to connect with one another and their communities.

### Need to Read

Before we conducted this inquiry, we thought we had been encouraging reading; after all, we assigned interesting texts, discussed pertinent features in class, modeled different techniques, and sat back to watch the critical reading happen. Faced with our findings, remarkably similar across four very different courses, we realize that what we were doing was simply not enough—perhaps because we were largely the ones doing it. All four of us now place greater responsibility for the reading onto the students. If students can succeed in a course without completing the readings, why would they read? It's not an efficient use of time; indeed, "reading the material may be an *unwise* use of valuable time if there are no adverse consequences."[9] But what should those consequences be? As Judith C. Roberts and Keith A. Roberts ask, "Will simply increasing the costs or benefits ultimately lead to *seeking meaning*?"[10] Roberts and Roberts suggest we need to provide students with practice using different comprehension strategies. They advocate giving students the choice of (1) annotating a text and then identifying the "big" questions; (2) summarizing the readings and visualizing the key ideas using a graphic organizer; or (3) keeping a reading response journal. In each case the students "*do* something with the readings."[11] In each case the activity should lead to an increase in deeper understanding.

In some types of courses and for some types of reading, quizzes might work. Quizzes tend to increase reading compliance, and students who read required texts are more likely to succeed on examinations of that material.[12] However, a quiz that focuses on keywords or memorable illustrations may not lead to critical reading; indeed, it may even lead away from critical reading if a transmission rather than transactional model of reading is reinforced. A quiz that emphasizes details pulled from the text relies on students' short-term memories, perhaps at the expense of comprehension. In Marton and Säljö's terms, some quizzes may unintentionally encourage a surface reading of the words over a deeper reading of meaning.[13] A quiz to foster critical reading needs to engage students in the activities of critical reading: comprehension, analysis, interpretation, evaluation, and inference. For example, Karen Wilken Braun and R. Drew Sellers use reading quizzes in introductory accounting classes, but the questions asked are conceptual and students are allowed to use any notes that they took on the reading.[14] The quizzes then provide an external motivation for a series of activities that should lead to a more critical engagement with text.

We did not incorporate reading quizzes into our courses because of the nature of these courses. The specific content of the readings is less important than how the students are able to interact with them. However, students will be unable to interact with the readings, critically or otherwise, if they haven't read them. So Manarin has made the conscious choice in all of her classes to minimize her offering of summaries of texts during her lectures, even though lecturing is itself a more efficient use of time when trying to "cover" material. She resists student desire to rely on the oral tradition of the class instead of reading the primary texts. She also spends more time talking with her students about how they read primary and secondary sources. She has developed worksheets to help English majors practice reading—and understanding—critical articles. She also spends more time exploring with her students how knowledge is created in a discipline like English.

Rathburn now uses structured reading groups to engage students with the readings. Adapting Heather Macpherson Parrott and Elizabeth Cherry's assignment for sociology majors,[15] Rathburn turned Controversies in Science on its head and made students accountable for their reading. She makes it a high-stakes task, as the reading discussion groups are now their main instruction on that particular topic; at the end of the unit, students are required to integrate the information from the readings into a position paper that is worth 20 percent of their grade. Rather than assigning questions to be discussed, the conversations come from student-generated questions and responses to assigned tasks. As a variation to Parrott and Cherry's assignment in which each student was assigned a particular role within the reading group, Rathburn makes each student responsible for generating discussion questions, finding particular passages in the text that were important in some way, making connections among readings and their previous knowledge, and also highlighting aspects of the text where they could play devil's advocate. This technique leverages the power of group discussion to clarify and reinforce meaning but also provides opportunities to discuss and interrogate alternative viewpoints. At the same time, this format provides a structure to help students manage the different cognitive demands of critical reading. It also reinforces the value of critical reading, as students are allowed to bring their readings and notes for the in-class essay. Parrott and Cherry designed the activity to help students read in a sociology class; Rathburn adapted it for both her general education and her biology classes, and since she began using it at Mount Royal, another five faculty from disciplines such as journalism, information design, public relations, and the library have adapted the activity for their classes. Instructors from a wide variety of disciplines are learning from one another in order to help their students read critically, and the students seem to be responding by completing the readings more carefully and more critically. Granted, in each case the motivation for careful and critical reading is extrinsic rather than intrinsic, but maybe that is all right while they are building their capabilities. Critical reading for academic purposes, in particular, can be motivated by assessment practices.

## Need to Assess

Although postsecondary students are relatively used to getting feedback on their writing, they are not used to getting feedback on their reading beyond general, usually positive, comments during a class discussion. Indeed, if some instructors do not insist that students read the material because they fear low student evaluations,[16] how will they handle a situation in which the student has read but not understood, or has read but has failed to place the information in a relevant context? Yet critical reading has to count, and students need to see it count, whether that is through graded exercises or rubrics that explain the different types of reading behaviors we are looking for. Rubrics can help. During this inquiry we made the deliberate choice not to share the VALUE rubrics with our students, because those rubrics were not designed for grading student work during an individual course; they describe faculty expectations across an undergraduate degree. However, it is possible to use the VALUE rubrics as a starting point to create a more specific rubric targeted at particular elements and levels.

For example, now that we know many of our students score at benchmark or milestone levels in comprehension, we can unpack what those descriptors might look like in the written work they produce for these particular classes. Ryland reworked his essay rubric with our Critical Reading rubrics in mind and now spends more time going over the rubric with the students. He also now uses the rubric as a tool to assess published essays and has students use it for self-assessment when writing their essays. Rathburn has also adapted her rubrics to include critical reading characteristics and has implemented peer review of essays whereby students have the option to get their completed paper assessed by another student using the rubrics. Students then have the option to revise and resubmit their papers based on this feedback. The goal underlying this new strategy is that the more the students read and use the rubric, the more they understand the descriptors and can use it for self-assessment. By adapting the rubrics and sharing them with students, we can be clearer about what we want students to learn to do. We need to provide specific feedback on elements of critical reading, even though it is sometimes difficult to distinguish reading skills from writing skills.

## Need to Write

The nature of the relationship between reading and writing provoked lively discussions in our team, from worries about how to differentiate reading ability from writing ability in written artifacts, to calls for a culture shift from a required writing course to a reading course, to arguments over whether it is possible to emphasize critical reading without writing instruction across the curriculum. Reading and writing are sometimes seen as "essentially similar processes of meaning construction"; Robert Tierney and David Pearson influentially argued that both are "acts of composing" with similar stages: planning, drafting, aligning, revising, and monitoring.[17] Others like Timothy Shanahan have argued that reading and writing offer "separate, but overlapping, ways of thinking about the world."[18] He and Jill Fitzgerald argue, "Reading and writing encourage enough different cognitive operations that they offer alternative perspectives that can give rise to new learning or appreciation. Writing about a text, for example, leads to different types of rethinking than rereading alone provides. If reading and writing were identical, this would not be the case, and if they were very separate, they may not be so mutually supportive."[19]

They suggest that "rather than separately focusing on a student's reading and writing skills, researchers and educators should focus on the critical shared thinking that underlies both reading and writing."[20] Thus, both reading and writing should be taught within a context of critical thinking. Critical thinking requires questioning of assumptions; writing about reading can provide time and space for such critical reflection.

The relationship between reading and writing means an emphasis on critical reading in frequent written assignments on the class readings. Carey advocates a multi-stage process, with rereading as a required stage. So students read the assigned texts; answer the "What?" "So What?" and "Now What?" prompts; engage in small group discussion to raise points to be brought to the whole class; and then complete another writing assignment on the same reading, this one with deeper, more targeted questions. Ryland changed the reading reflections in his class from the three open-ended questions to two specific questions per reading. The first question requires students to answer by finding specific information in the reading; the second asks students to identify the meaning they see in the reading material. Such reflection requires guidance, modeling, and reinforcement in the classroom so that students will develop their capacities for reflection in two distinct ways: to see the meaning of the reading in its context and to see how the reading shapes their own understanding or perspective on key issues.

Of course, writing about readings means that probably fewer readings will be covered, but if students are actually reading them, perhaps we can afford to assign fewer pages. This approach, however, involves students writing and instructors marking more pages. One suggestion is to ask students to identify one reading reflection out of every three or four on which they would like feedback from the instructor. This encourages students to further reflect on their reading and the insights they have made while also enabling the instructor to focus the feedback in a more manageable manner throughout the semester. Some feedback on reading can also be provided by modeling reading strategies for the entire class. Ryland now asks the students to write a reflection on the first reading, and when they bring it to class, he models the process and then gives them the opportunity to review and refine their first reflection before handing it in. Writing serves as a mechanism to deepen reading. We also recognize, however, that writing is most effective when students have some instruction and feedback in how to write about readings, whether that is in the form of guided questions or modeled reflection.

## Need to Research

What, then, do we do with our research assignments—the genre that demonstrated a lot of writing without much reading at all? We realized that asking students to find and use sources led them to do just that, not necessarily to read, understand, or synthesize them. Librarians discussing information literacy have suggested that the idea that research "has a purpose beyond the compilation of information" may be a threshold concept for many students.[21] We all circled back to the issue of purpose. Why assign a research paper in the first place? What did we hope the students would achieve? Were we primarily interested in the final product or the process? We realized we needed to align our assessment practices with our goals for the research assignment. Three of us have dramatically changed our approach to the research paper at this level. Ryland continues to adapt his textual analysis assignment, providing greater guidance on how to think about both primary and secondary sources. His assignment instructions have become more precise and concise. The class discusses examples of student writing to explore different ways for presenting analysis of a primary text using supporting secondary texts. He has learned that he cannot assume students know how to do this or even that a two-page guide will suffice. It takes classroom time.

Rathbun moved away from a research paper altogether. She argues that if she kept assigning a research paper that students wrote and then seemingly went to the library, or probably online, to find citations that supported their already developed conclusions, she was not achieving the learning outcomes for the course. The outcomes of the course she teaches are centered on themes of understanding the role of science in society and recognizing the importance of scientific knowledge. To do this, students must learn to evaluate and interpret various forms of information. Instead of a research paper, students now write an in-class position paper based on material discussed by

their reading groups. In this way, students learn not only to respect multip
but also to question, analyze, and evaluate the information they are readi
immersion into their readings will students gain an understanding of the inrormation
at a level where they have the confidence to form their own opinions on the subject.
Although the reading discussion groups sacrifice the process of research, Rathburn
believes that the final product, which forces students to evaluate the information and
arguments underlying a particular topic, is a more important skill for the students to
learn in this particular course.

Both Carey and Manarin realized that although their assessment practices
focused on the final product, their objectives for the research assignment focused on
the process—students' abilities to find, comprehend, interpret, analyze, evaluate, and
make inferences between texts and experiences. They wanted critical reading but were
rewarding format. So they have restructured research assignments in all of their classes
to foreground the process of research. Part of the process involves allowing sufficient
time for students to risk, fail, reframe, and try again. They are developing a scaffolded
approach to research that breaks the research task into smaller components, provides
opportunities for students to practice these elements, and rewards students who engage
in the process. The scaffold involves several assignments, leading students through the
steps of a research project: selecting an area of inquiry, identifying a frame, conducting
a literature review, integrating claim and evidence, and incorporating feedback from a
poster session. Students create posters that summarize what they have read and illustrate the main claim of their essays; they then stand by their posters and interact with
their classmates who circulate asking questions. When they hand in the final essays,
they are expected to describe how they have at least considered their peers' comments
about their ideas. The poster session is particularly important, because it allows students to frame their research as knowledge creation that should be presented publicly
for peer review and critique. Explicitly identifying research as knowledge creation provides a powerful justification for critical reading.

Some faculty may scoff at the idea of first-year, or even senior, undergraduates creating knowledge. We would draw their attention to the work promoted by the Council
for Undergraduate Research in America, the Research Skills Development Framework
out of Australia, and Mick Healey and Alan Jenkins's work in the United Kingdom.[22]
For Carey and Manarin, teaching in the new general education foundation course
Writing about Images, undergraduate research means students have to select an image
that has never been written about before; some students choose to create their own
images. They then learn about different ways to talk and write about their image; they
research what people have said about similar sorts of images; they apply what they are
learning to their artifacts in order to make an argument for their peers in the poster
session; and then they write about their image in the final paper, considering elements
brought up in the textual and social conversations. For example, a student who takes a
selfie might not only research the selfie phenomenon but also consider self-portraiture

traditions before articulating how he or she thinks this particular image fits into these conversations. The students cannot rely upon keyword searches and sound-bite quotations; they have to read and think as they try to apply a body of knowledge to a unique object. It may not be "an original intellectual or creative contribution to the discipline," to quote the Council for Undergraduate Research's definition, but it is a beginning, hopefully a beginning that will be built on in other courses. But even if this is the only time students will experience an approximation of the research process beyond the faux research paper, at least they did it once. Manarin tries to take the original undergraduate research idea further through the levels of English courses she teaches, until in a senior-level seminar, students are expected to make an original intellectual contribution that could be presented at a disciplinary conference; some students have even taken their work beyond the institution. All of this came about because of this investigation into critical reading at the foundation level of general education.

## Need to Connect

Before this inquiry we had not realized the extent to which explicit opportunities for engagement are required for critical reading. Exposure to provocative ideas or interesting texts is simply not enough for many students. Critical reading for academic purposes, then, is more likely to occur when students do something with that text, whether that something is creating posters, participating in reading groups, or making written responses. Critical reading for social engagement requires an additional level of engagement, because students need to make connections between texts and the worlds in which they live. This can be a serious challenge for students and teachers involved in a course like Text and Ideas—Genocide. Activities that attempt to personalize a reading from a genocide, such as a survivor account from Rwanda, can lead to trivializing the severity of the genocide. Students are sometimes at a loss for how to make connections to this theme, and their reflections tend to focus on their emotional response to the reading rather than the meaning and significance of the text. For this reason, Ryland has realized that the classroom discussion is crucial and needs to have more intention. Many students will require help from the instructor and other students to learn how to draw connections from a reading on genocide. At a number of points in the semester, Ryland begins a lecture with a five- or ten-minute look at current events related to the week's reading to help students make connections. At the end of a class he may also introduce the upcoming reading using a relevant news clip. Ryland also provides a "Genocide in the News" section on the class announcement website and usually tries to get one or two groups in each class to make a presentation on a current conflict. In the end, however, acknowledging the gap between a historical moment of extreme violence and the student's world and life may itself be an instructive discussion for the classroom. Students need to learn how to engage the unfamiliar and distant.

Students also need to learn how to engage the familiar in academic terms. Carey's reflection papers, in which students talk about what community and society mean for them, demonstrate that many students are socially engaged in different ways; however, they keep that part of their lives separate from the academy. We need to value and reward social engagement in the academy if we hope to have an impact outside of the academy. If we want students to take some of the material they are learning academically back to their lives or put some of these ideas into action, we need to help them recognize, practice, and take advantage of opportunities for social engagement. Remember Nussbaum's concept of combined capabilities: personal abilities and opportunities. Individuals might choose not to exercise this capability, but they won't have the choice if they cannot recognize the opportunity in the first place.

Of course, an obvious opportunity for structured social engagement would be in a service-learning experience. Unlike practicum requirements or internships, where the primary concern is with the individual student gaining applied experience, or volunteerism, where the community may benefit but there is usually no academic component, service-learning experiences are designed to benefit the community and the individual academically. Most service-learning experiences are embedded within course curricula. Another opportunity for social engagement might be in an international experience. Being exposed to a new culture in a study abroad or field school experience can help students recognize global differences and expose them to social issues in ways they have never before experienced even though many of those issues exist in North America. An international experience can promote engagement with the community while they are abroad, because many schools have community-service components built into the curriculum, but many students also return to campuses with a renewed desire to engage with their own community. These international experiences can highlight the importance of the contributions of a single individual and can open students' eyes to the role they can play in society. Although universities see these experiences as a valuable addition to a students' academic learning, with more than 96 percent of Canadian institutions listing internationalization as a university priority, most of our students will not take part in these structured experiences. In 2012–2013 only 3.1 percent of Canadian university students engaged in these experiences, and although the rate of US student participation is at a record high, only 1.5 percent of US students took part in some form of study abroad during that same year.[23] With such limited participation, how can we make opportunities for social engagement more visible for students in our regular classes?

One answer is to connect students with events on campus. It may be something big, such as a Holocaust symposium for high school students or a conference on environmental issues. Or it may be a regular event like a film and discussion series sponsored by the students' association or some other opportunity to connect with diverse groups across campus. Students may see posters for such events but not realize they are welcome. Many of our students come, take their classes, and leave campus. To combat this, not all opportunities need to be co-curricular or extracurricular. Another way to increase social engagement is to integrate global learning within the classroom by discussing concepts and theories from perspectives that integrate different cultural, economic, and social viewpoints. By including global learning within the curricula, students can learn the "knowledge, skills, habits, dispositions/attitudes, and actions that transcend disciplinary boundaries."[24] Elizabeth Brewer and Kiran Cunningham argue that global learning needs to be integrated within the classroom so that the knowledge, skills, and attitudes necessary for being a global citizen are reinforced within an academic setting.[25] We need to help develop citizens who are able to respond to global problems and inequities.

Another possibility for stimulating social engagement among our students is to let them know about our own areas of engagement, whether it be volunteering with a humane society, being a member of a religious congregation, or participating in campus events. We do not believe that our personal commitments should be the focus of the curricula, but if we pretend we are nothing more than disembodied intellects in the academy, why would we be surprised that students also resist merging intellectual and personal spheres? In *The Courage to Teach*, Parker Palmer talks about the fragmentation of the academic life and calls for teachers to acknowledge the interplay of intellect, emotion, and spirit in knowing.[26] Of course, any type of disclosure, on our part or theirs, involves risks—the risk of being human and the risk of making a connection with another human—but surely that is what social engagement is all about.

In our inquiry we also learned that those students who showed a greater willingness to read critically for social engagement were those who were able to oscillate between the general and the specific. We suggest that many faculty members can structure readings and activities to encourage this oscillation. An essay about sexist representations in biology textbooks could lead to students investigating their own textbooks, but it is not enough to end there, particularly in a genre that many students don't care about. Faculty need to confront directly the fragmentation that is tacitly encouraged in postsecondary systems: the academy divided from society, disciplines from one another, and objective from subjective knowledge. Palmer invites faculty to try to unite our fragmented, academic selves; faculty need to share that invitation with their students. Can faculty devise assignments that are grounded in the theory of the academy but that relate to the student as a person in this community, in this state, on this planet? If faculty could consistently imagine students both as individuals (the specific) and as citizens (the general) and oscillate between those identities in the classroom, the students' postsecondary experience might move beyond the merely academic. Faculty can both model and encourage the oscillation necessary for empowered and empowering social engagement.

Is it possible to link assigned reading in our classes to the communities students care about? The specific answers depend on the students who are engaged, and maybe that is the hardest part of encouraging critical reading for social engagement. So much of it depends on those particular students in that particular moment. It requires faculty to give up some control. If faculty cannot imagine giving students some limited agency in the classroom, how can they imagine students having agency in a larger context? And if faculty cannot imagine that possibility, why should students? Faculty need to risk not knowing and the messiness of emotions in an academic environment.

## Now What (Else Can We Do)?

As individual faculty members, we need to continue exploring how to help our students read more critically. As scholars of teaching and learning, we need to begin another cycle of inquiry. It is impossible for us to replicate this particular study, since one of the four courses has since undergone significant curricular revision, and our teaching practices have changed significantly in the other three while our thinking and our assignments continue to evolve. We never intended our classes to function as some sort of control group against which we could measure future change; learning doesn't usually work like that.[27] Rather, this inquiry provided a snapshot of where we are and an impetus toward future systematic inquiry. Each of us continues this work.

As faculty members in a community, we also need to connect with one another. We cannot do everything in our individual courses. We cannot expect that thirteen weeks will provide such profound changes in capabilities that students will be able to read critically. In our general education program, the courses we teach are described  as foundational, which implies that other courses continue to develop the intellectual and civic capabilities we value. But after these foundation courses, students move to a distributive model of general education and into disciplinary courses. Faculty never talk to one another about how to scaffold these critical capabilities across the different departments. Even among the foundation courses, instructors rarely talk to one another about how their particular approach builds common capabilities.

Our team still debates whether it is possible to teach critical reading for both academic purposes and social engagement in the same course. Carey, from a political science background, believes it is possible with careful and intentional scaffolding that encourages oscillation between transmission and transactional models of reading; Manarin, from a literature background, believes it isn't possible because of the differing assumptions about knowledge underlying the two critical reading traditions. Rathbun and Ryland try to keep the peace. Our disagreement probably has much to do with our disciplinary assumptions about the academy and society; it may have to do with the types of readings we are most likely to ask our students to do. However, we agree that it is possible to create conditions where critical reading is more likely to occur; it is possible to be more explicit with students about what critical reading entails; it is possible to model and reward behaviors that are likely to produce critical reading, whether for academic purposes or social engagement. And, we argue, instructors do not have to be literacy experts in order to create these opportunities for learning, but they do have to recognize such opportunities.

Given this situation, we need to become advocates for critical reading across our institution. This work needs to occur simultaneously, and iteratively, at different levels. Working at the institutional level, we push for language about critical reading for academic purposes and social engagement in official documents like the academic plan, and if that language exists or is used by the university administration in communications to the media, we need to hold the administration accountable. Our university claims that a student learns to be a "better citizen" or develops "civic capacities"; we need to ask what those terms mean in forums like the university senate, the board of governors, and various university committees. We cannot expect that the good citizen will just happen; we need to be willing to put some effort into building that possibility. We need to take advantage of opportunities like scheduled program and accreditation reviews to advocate for increased attention to critical reading across general education and the university as a whole. For example, we noticed that our general education documents consistently refer to "information retrieval" rather than reading; critical reading has now become a key theme in our general education review and advancement plan. Language in official documents provides a necessary framework for systematic change; however, it is easier to change a document than to change a single institutional culture, let alone an entire system.

Sometimes it is difficult to recognize opportunities for change in higher education, because the issues and obstacles seem so overwhelming. Governments in financial difficulties reduce support and demand greater accountability, often through indicators that have little to do with student learning. Tuition rises, and students take on more debt and part-time jobs and stress. Class sizes increase, and institutions turn to cheaper, and disposable, adjunct faculty. Faculty feel defensive as they take on more students and administrative duties, including measuring characteristics and abilities that they don't believe can be adequately measured, all the while trying to produce specialized scholarship. Many faculty fear outcomes and assessment as likely to threaten their autonomy in the classroom; they suggest both give a misleading picture of what happens in an undergraduate education. Governments, the media, and the larger society see this fear as reluctance to be accountable to society's needs. As David M. Scobey notes, "Budget cuts, tuition hikes, and debt burdens make manifest (and to some extent obscure) a crisis of legitimacy: a growing sense that, as the 'official' undergraduate paradigm has frayed, the academy has betrayed its commitments to, and turned away from, the larger society."[28] Undergraduate education seems to cost a lot and, its critics say, to deliver very little. How, then, can individuals improve a system that so many claim is broken?

Perhaps, as with our experience with the research papers, we need to circle back to the purpose—or, rather, purposes—of an undergraduate education. Is undergraduate education intended to create specialists in a specific discipline or generally educated citizens who are able to read everyday texts critically and able to respond to their world with curiosity, resilience, and compassion? The default position is to say that higher education needs to do both, but it seems to be doing neither well right now. Perhaps we can extrapolate a lesson for ourselves from this inquiry into critical reading. We learned that those students who are most likely to read critically for social engagement were those who were able to oscillate between the specific and the general. Perhaps we too can oscillate between the specific and the general, between our classrooms and higher education more broadly. Perhaps that is what the scholarship of teaching and learning does. Insights from individual classrooms are brought together for conversation, though not necessarily consensus, in the hope of creating change.

We need conversation among different stakeholders, including faculty, administrators, governments, students, parents, and communities. We need to recognize that there are many different, and often conflicting, mandates at a postsecondary institution, and not all of them are about student learning. Institutions try to improve enrollment, as measured through application rate and entering averages, retention rates, average time to complete a degree, graduation rates, job placement rates, and external reputation as measured by various rankings. Those factors that can be easily measured are more likely to be given attention, whether or not they are the most important aspects in terms of student learning and development. Everyone is trying to do their best to foster student success, but our definitions of success differ dramatically. Is it better for a student to complete as fast as possible or to learn as much as possible? Is the most important thing the product, a credential, or the process, education?

As we four talked about what we thought the purpose of higher education at the undergraduate level should be, we were struck by how rarely we discuss the purpose of higher education with colleagues and by how much easier it is to say what higher education should *not* be. We all agree that the purpose is not to replicate our disciplines, as only a few of our undergraduate students will continue on to graduate studies. Yet many undergraduate majors are set up primarily to provide a background to graduate studies in that discipline. General education, whether distributive or prescriptive, is intended to broaden the student experience beyond the specific discipline but is often marginalized in the quotidian life of postsecondary institutions, faculty, and students. At the same time, it is obsessively debated in curricular reviews to the exclusion of other parts of the curricula. As Derek Bok writes, "Eventually general education programs take on so many responsibilities that they cannot possibly do justice to them all."[29] It is telling, for example, that a senior administrator at our institution referred to our official aims of an undergraduate education, based on the AAC&U's Essential Learning Outcomes,[30] as "General Education Outcomes," as if general education can fulfill all the aims of an undergraduate education in 25–30 percent of the course load (or indeed much less if disciplinary courses that are taken to meet general education requirements don't look beyond discipline-specific content).

We all agreed that the purpose of higher education is much more than job training or a credential for a good job, although well-paying employment is important, especially in an era of increasing student debt. Even though job placement, expected salaries, and employer satisfaction are important, success must be measured in more than economic terms for students in all majors. Some majors claim to provide clearer career paths than others: the nursing or engineering student expects to practice a profession at the end of his or her undergraduate degree. Lee Shulman described this "presumed tension between the *liberal* and the *pragmatic*," a tension he sought to negotiate by positioning the liberal arts as professional learning that shares with other professions the characteristics of service, understanding, practice, judgment, learning, and community.[31] These characteristics perhaps offer a glimpse into the purpose of an undergraduate education regardless of the major.

We all agreed that *what* is studied is less important than *how* it is studied. We believe each discipline involves finding information, assessing its value, solving problems, and communicating. Each discipline has developed its own frame of reference and methodological approaches, so their similarities may be difficult for students shuttling from class to class to discern. However, the heart of all of it is critical thinking in order to do something.[32] As Carol Geary Schneider notes, "Every major should be infused with those larger values of rigorous inquiry, evidence-based reasoning, and deep engagement with ethical and social responsibilities that characterize liberal learning at its best."[33] Few faculty or administrators engaged in higher education would disagree; neither, apparently, would many employers.[34]

The AAC&U's Essential Learning Outcomes and the Lumina Foundation's Degree Qualifications Profile are two well-recognized attempts to describe an undergraduate education.[35] Such attempts typically seek to balance knowledge acquisition and skill development, but as Derek Bok, former president of Harvard University, notes, faculty are likely to have a different view of knowledge than many other stakeholders in higher education. For many faculty, "knowledge is not a means to other ends; it is an end in itself—indeed, the principal end of academic life. . . . Professors who value knowledge for its own sake are not likely to attach the same importance to skills as undergraduates who have come to college seeking instruction that will help them succeed in their careers."[36] Faculty rely on reading, analysis, problem solving, and communication all the time, but often they do not think to make these skills an explicit part of the curricula, or perhaps they believe that students should have learned the skills elsewhere. Foregrounding knowledge, rather than the process by which that knowledge was constructed, faculty are dismayed that students cannot deduce what the process looks like in that particular discipline. The Decoding the Discipline movement out of Indiana University seeks to encourage faculty to reflect upon their own processes of knowledge creation in the hopes of helping students overcome difficulties with understanding disciplines.[37] However, even if students are trained to engage in critical thinking in a particular discipline, they may not be able to recognize opportunities elsewhere, because the process may look different. So faculty need to make more explicit the commonalities between disciplines so that the undergraduate experience might feel less random as students come to appreciate that they are being asked to do similar tasks in different courses.

We all agreed that higher education has a moral purpose, although we wouldn't necessarily all call it that. We disagreed over whether higher education needs to return to an earlier monastic model where individuals withdraw from the world in order to reflect upon their place in it, or whether higher education is the place where students are thrust into the world and given the chance to discover who they are or who they might become. We argued over whether it is the only place, or even the best place, for such self-realization to occur. We argued over whether we should spend more time providing additional tools and developing skills for students to succeed, or if students are unlikely to use those tools and skills until they have something to say that matters to them. We all want to expose students to ideas that are unfamiliar to them, but we know exposure by itself makes little difference. We want students to become uncomfortable in a relatively safe environment—hardly a slogan that a university can pop onto its website. However, we want this discomfort to produce something good. We want "to confront the passivity of the pupil, challenging the mind to take charge of its own thought."[38] How can we achieve this lofty, indeed Socratic, goal given limited resources, large classes, conflicting mandates, faculty and student resistance, and systemic barriers both within and outside the institution? Where can we start? One place, though certainly not the only one, is a radical rethinking of the purpose of undergraduate education to foreground the intellectual and ethical components of critical reading throughout the curricula.

Foregrounding the intellectual and ethical components of critical reading allows for both knowledge acquisition and skill development, yet critical reading is absent from many of the lists about undergraduate education, probably because it is so ubiquitous in assumptions about higher education. If, as Derek Bok suggests, faculty reluctance to teach skills can be traced back to how faculty view knowledge,[39] reading needs to be framed not as a basic skill, but as a complex process worthy of study and reflection in itself before we will see large numbers of faculty taking up our call to pay attention to critical reading in their classrooms and their disciplines. Faculty often assume that critical reading, like writing, is taught in English courses; however, each faculty member must be responsible for showing students how to approach a particular text from their perspective—whether disciplinary, interdisciplinary, or pre-disciplinary— whether or not the faculty member has any training in literacy instruction.

We need to start multiple conversations across the institution in what Parker Palmer calls "a conversational strategy of change."[40] We need to form communities of like-minded individuals who are interested in critical reading: faculty, administrators, students, and staff. Such communities will not spontaneously occur. We know we need to invite people into the conversation with a variety of forums. For example, we have presented our findings to the university community in a well-attended critical reading forum; we want to partner with Mount Royal's Student Learning Services to develop strategies to assist students in critical reading; we are pursuing opportunities to participate in k–12 discussions about curricula; we are engaged in critical reading circles for faculty teaching in general education; and we would like to involve students as change agents in our curricula. We need to develop champions of critical reading who can continue to move this work forward at our institution and beyond. Of course, merely getting people together to talk doesn't mean the conversation will be transformative, any more than merely getting someone to read something means he or she will read it critically, but it is a first step in an environment often described in terms of disciplinary silos and credit hours.

In *The Heart of Higher Education: A Call to Renewal,* Parker Palmer offers some guidance on how to create transformative conversations on campus. He notes that too often what we call a conversation is actually several people speaking in parallel, never intersecting:[41] one tells a story about a student who "can't" read; another complains about students who "won't" read; yet another has all the answers. As Palmer notes, "Those of us who want to host conversations that are generative for ourselves and our institutions must be intentional about creating spaces that are hospitable to the human spirit as we make ourselves vulnerable to honest exchanges, new ideas, and hopes for change."[42] Palmer's recommendations—careful listening and open questions—are nothing new; as he points out, "They are rooted in principles of inquiry at the heart of the academic tradition, principles we tend to honor more in the breach than the observance as we relate to each other,"[43] and as we relate to our students. If we bring honest inquiry to our classrooms and to our institutions, perhaps we can move from lamentation to action about critical reading. We know it will be difficult to integrate critical reading for academic purposes and social engagement across the curriculum and beyond the institution. We understand our own resistance to change, with both the effort involved in creating something new and the grief of letting go what has been. We are very aware of the curricular space and time that foundational skill development requires, yet we cannot afford to continue the status quo. We need to work for change together. We have begun.

# Introduction to the Appendixes

THESE THREE APPENDIXES offer more details about the collaborative scholarship of teaching and learning project explored in this book.

Appendix 1 contains the two rubrics we used when examining our students' writing: Critical Reading for Academic Purposes and Critical Reading for Social Engagement. We built the rubrics by using elements from the Association for American Colleges and Universities' VALUE rubrics for reading, information literacy, civic engagement, and integrative learning. We thank the Association for American Colleges and Universities for permission to reproduce those elements here. For others who might be interested in doing this sort of collaborative study, we also include the worksheets we used when examining our students' work. We found it very useful to record our interpretive judgments in a similar form.

Appendix 2 contains material about the "taxonomy of absence" discussed in chapter 4. We present a list of different actions that students appeared to be doing in their responses when they were not reading for social engagement. We experimented with various organizational patterns before finding one that seemed to account for most of the responses.

Appendix 3 is our "Coda on Collaboration." A coda can be variously described as a concluding piece, something beyond the regular structure of a work, or a tail. In it we describe the tale of our specific collaboration and lessons we have learned about collaboration.

# Appendix 1: Rubrics and Worksheets

Because this inquiry involved complex qualitative judgments about oblique measures of critical reading, it was important for us to articulate our expectations and to have some common vocabulary when discussing our findings. The rubrics and worksheets were useful, even though we remain aware that they could not capture everything that was going on in our students', and our own, readings.

## Hybridized Rubric: Critical Reading for Academic Purposes

For Critical Reading for Academic Purposes, we examined the following abilities:

- Comprehension—the ability to summarize text and recognize its implications
- Analysis—the ability to recognize and use features of a text to support understanding
- Interpretation—the ability to construe meaning from a text and recognize different ways of reading
- Evaluation—the ability to identify and analyze one's own and others' assumptions
- Recognition of Genres—the ability to adjust reading strategies to genre
- Connection to Discipline—the ability to make connections among texts or perspectives

We used the following categories from the Association of American Colleges and Universities' VALUE rubrics.

## COMPREHENSION (FROM VALUE READING RUBRIC)

| | | |
|---|---|---|
| Capstone | 4 | Recognizes possible implications of the text for contexts, perspectives, or issues beyond the assigned task within the classroom or beyond the author's explicit message (e.g., might recognize broader issues at play, or might pose challenges to the author's message and presentation). |
| Milestone | 3 | Uses the text, general background knowledge, and/or specific knowledge of the author's context to draw more complex inferences about the author's message and attitude. |
| | 2 | Evaluates how textual features (e.g., sentence and paragraph structure or tone) contribute to the author's message; draws basic inferences about context and purpose of text. |
| Benchmark | 1 | Apprehends vocabulary appropriately to paraphrase or summarize the information the text communicates. |
| Failure | 0 | Does not meet benchmark but appears to have tried. |
| Absence | N/A | No attempt to meet benchmark. |

## ANALYSIS (FROM VALUE READING RUBRIC).
*Interacting with texts in parts and as wholes*

| | | |
|---|---|---|
| Capstone | 4 | Evaluates strategies for relating ideas, text structure, or other textual features in order to build knowledge or insight within and across texts and disciplines. |
| Milestone | 3 | Identifies relations among ideas, text structure, or other textual features, to evaluate how they support an advanced understanding of the text as a whole. |
| | 2 | Recognizes relations among parts or aspects of a text, such as effective or ineffective arguments or literary features, in considering how these contribute to a basic understanding of the text as a whole. |
| Benchmark | 1 | Identifies aspects of a text (e.g., content, structure, or relations among ideas) as needed to respond to questions posed in assigned tasks. |
| Failure | 0 | Does not meet benchmark but appears to have tried. |
| Absence | N/A | No attempt to meet benchmark. |

## INTERPRETATION (FROM VALUE READING RUBRIC).
*Making sense with texts as blueprints for meaning*

| | | |
|---|---|---|
| Capstone | 4 | Provides evidence not only that s/he can read by using an appropriate epistemological lens but that s/he can also engage in reading as part of a continuing dialogue within and beyond a discipline or a community of readers. |
| Milestone | 3 | Articulates an understanding of the multiple ways of reading and the range of interpretive strategies particular to one's discipline(s) or in a given community of readers. |
| | 2 | Demonstrates that s/he can read purposefully, choosing among interpretive strategies depending on the purpose of the reading. |
| Benchmark | 1 | Can identify purpose(s) for reading, relying on an external authority such as an instructor for clarification of the task. |
| Failure | 0 | Does not meet benchmark but appears to have tried. |
| Absence | N/A | No attempt to meet benchmark. |

## EVALUATE INFORMATION AND ITS SOURCES CRITICALLY (FROM VALUE INFORMATION LITERACY RUBRIC)

| | | |
|---|---|---|
| Capstone | 4 | Thoroughly (systematically and methodically) analyzes own and others' assumptions and carefully evaluates the relevance of contexts when presenting a position. |
| Milestone | 3 | Identifies own and others' assumptions and several relevant contexts when presenting a position. |
| | 2 | Questions some assumptions. Identifies several relevant contexts when presenting a position. May be more aware of others' assumptions than one's own (or vice versa). |
| Benchmark | 1 | Shows an emerging awareness of present assumptions (sometimes labels assertions as assumptions). Begins to identify some contexts when presenting a position. |
| Failure | 0 | Does not meet benchmark but appears to have tried. |
| Absence | N/A | No attempt to meet benchmark. |

**GENRES (FROM VALUE READING RUBRIC)**

| | | |
|---|---|---|
| Capstone | 4 | Uses ability to identify texts within and across genres, monitoring and adjusting reading strategies and expectations based on generic nuances of particular texts. |
| Milestone | 3 | Articulates distinctions among genres and their characteristic conventions. |
| | 2 | Reflects on reading experiences across a variety of genres, reading both with and against the grain experimentally and intentionally. |
| Benchmark | 1 | Applies tacit genre knowledge to a variety of classroom reading assignments in productive, if unreflective, ways. |
| Failure | 0 | Does not meet benchmark but appears to have tried. |
| Absence | N/A | No attempt to meet benchmark. |

**CONNECTIONS TO DISCIPLINE (FROM VALUE INTEGRATIVE LEARNING RUBRIC).**
*Sees (makes) connections across disciplines, perspectives*

| | | |
|---|---|---|
| Capstone | 4 | Independently creates wholes out of multiple parts (synthesizes) or draws conclusions by combining examples, facts, or theories from more than one field of study or perspective. |
| Milestone | 3 | Independently connects examples, facts, or theories from more than one field of study or perspective. |
| | 2 | When prompted, connects examples, facts, or theories from more than one field of study or perspective. |
| Benchmark | 1 | When prompted, presents examples, facts, or theories from more than one field of study or perspective. |
| Failure | 0 | Does not meet benchmark but appears to have tried. |
| Absence | N/A | No attempt to meet benchmark. |

*Source:* Reprinted with permission from "VALUE: Valid Assessment of Learning in Undergraduate Education." Copyright 2014 by the Association of American Colleges and Universities. http://www.aacu.org/value.

## Hybridized Rubric: Critical Reading for Social Engagement

For Critical Reading for Social Engagement, we examined the following factors:

- Comprehension—the ability to summarize text and recognize its implications
- Analysis—the ability to recognize and use features of a text to support understanding
- Interpretation—the ability to construe meaning from a text and recognize different ways of reading
- Evaluation—the ability to identify and analyse own and others' assumptions
- Analysis of Knowledge—the ability to connect knowledge from a discipline to a social or civic context
- Connection to Experience—the ability to make connections between personal experience and academic texts

We used the following categories from the Association of American Colleges and Universities' VALUE rubrics.

### COMPREHENSION (FROM VALUE READING RUBRIC)

| | | |
|---|---|---|
| Capstone | 4 | Recognizes possible implications of the text for contexts, perspectives, or issues beyond the assigned task within the classroom or beyond the author's explicit message (e.g., might recognize broader issues at play, or might pose challenges to the author's message and presentation). |
| Milestone | 3 | Uses the text, general background knowledge, and/or specific knowledge of the author's context to draw more complex inferences about the author's message and attitude. |
| | 2 | Evaluates how textual features (e.g., sentence and paragraph structure or tone) contribute to the author's message; draws basic inferences about context and purpose of text. |
| Benchmark | 1 | Apprehends vocabulary appropriately to paraphrase or summarize the information the text communicates. |
| Failure | 0 | Does not meet benchmark but appears to have tried. |
| Absence | N/A | No attempt to meet benchmark. |

ANALYSIS (FROM VALUE READING RUBRIC).
*Interacting with texts in parts and as wholes*

| | | |
|---|---|---|
| Capstone | 4 | Evaluates strategies for relating ideas, text structure, or other textual features in order to build knowledge or insight within and across texts and disciplines. |
| Milestone | 3 | Identifies relations among ideas, text structure, or other textual features, to evaluate how they support an advanced understanding of the text as a whole. |
| | 2 | Recognizes relations among parts or aspects of a text, such as effective or ineffective arguments or literary features, in considering how these contribute to a basic understanding of the text as a whole. |
| Benchmark | 1 | Identifies aspects of a text (e.g., content, structure, or relations among ideas) as needed to respond to questions posed in assigned tasks. |
| Failure | 0 | Does not meet benchmark but appears to have tried. |
| Absence | N/A | No attempt to meet benchmark. |

INTERPRETATION (FROM VALUE READING RUBRIC).
*Making sense with texts as blueprints for meaning*

| | | |
|---|---|---|
| Capstone | 4 | Provides evidence not only that s/he can read by using an appropriate epistemological lens but that s/he can also engage in reading as part of a continuing dialogue within and beyond a discipline or a community of readers. |
| Milestone | 3 | Articulates an understanding of the multiple ways of reading and the range of interpretive strategies particular to one's discipline(s) or in a given community of readers. |
| | 2 | Demonstrates that s/he can read purposefully, choosing among interpretive strategies depending on the purpose of the reading. |
| Benchmark | 1 | Can identify purpose(s) for reading, relying on an external authority such as an instructor for clarification of the task. |
| Failure | 0 | Does not meet benchmark but appears to have tried. |
| Absence | N/A | No attempt to meet benchmark. |

## EVALUATE INFORMATION AND ITS SOURCES CRITICALLY
## (FROM VALUE INFORMATION LITERACY RUBRIC)

| | | |
|---|---|---|
| Capstone | 4 | Thoroughly (systematically and methodically) analyzes own and others' assumptions and carefully evaluates the relevance of contexts when presenting a position. |
| Milestone | 3 | Identifies own and others' assumptions and several relevant contexts when presenting a position. |
| | 2 | Questions some assumptions. Identifies several relevant contexts when presenting a position. May be more aware of others' assumptions than one's own (or vice versa). |
| Benchmark | 1 | Shows an emerging awareness of present assumptions (sometimes labels assertions as assumptions). Begins to identify some contexts when presenting a position. |
| Failure | 0 | Does not meet benchmark but appears to have tried. |
| Absence | N/A | No attempt to meet benchmark. |


## ANALYSIS OF KNOWLEDGE (FROM VALUE CIVIC ENGAGEMENT RUBRIC)

| | | |
|---|---|---|
| Capstone | 4 | Connects and extends knowledge (facts, theories, etc.) from one's own academic study/field/discipline to civic engagement and to one's own participation in civic life, politics, and government. |
| Milestone | 3 | Analyzes knowledge (facts, theories, etc.) from one's own academic study/field/discipline making relevant connections to civic engagement and to one's own participation in civic life, politics, and government. |
| | 2 | Begins to connect knowledge (facts, theories, etc.) from one's own academic study/field/discipline to civic engagement and to one's own participation in civic life, politics, and government. |
| Benchmark | 1 | Begins to identify knowledge (facts, theories, etc.) from one's own academic study/field/discipline that is relevant to civic engagement and to one's own participation in civic life, politics, and government. |
| Failure | 0 | Does not meet benchmark but appears to have tried. |
| Absence | N/A | No attempt to meet benchmark. |

**CONNECTIONS TO EXPERIENCE (FROM VALUE INTEGRATIVE LEARNING RUBRIC).** *Connects relevant experience and academic knowledge*[a]

| | | |
|---|---|---|
| Capstone | 4 | Meaningfully synthesizes connections among experiences outside of the formal classroom (including life experiences and academic experiences such as internships and travel abroad) to deepen understanding of fields of study and to broaden own points of view. |
| Milestone | 3 | Effectively selects and develops examples of life experiences, drawn from a variety of contexts (e.g., family life, artistic participation, civic involvement, work experience), to illuminate concepts/theories/frameworks of fields of study. |
| | 2 | Compares life experiences and academic knowledge to infer differences, as well as similarities, and acknowledge perspectives other than own. |
| Benchmark | 1 | Identifies connections between life experiences and those academic texts and ideas perceived as similar and related to own interests. |
| Failure | 0 | Does not meet benchmark but appears to have tried. |
| Absence | N/A | No attempt to meet benchmark. |

*Source:* Reprinted with permission from "VALUE: Valid Assessment of Learning in Undergraduate Education." Copyright 2014 by the Association of American Colleges and Universities. http://www.aacu.org/value.

[a] Emphasis removed.

## Worksheets

We recorded the rubric scores on worksheets, which allowed us to identify patterns in the responses more easily. We examined reading log scores by specific reading and by specific student. Examining the same information in multiple ways highlighted different aspects of critical reading. We also took a closer look at the sources our students used for the research paper. Here we include examples of all three worksheets.

*Reading for Academic Purposes and Social Engagement Reading Logs: Rubric Scores Arranged by Participant*

### READING FOR ACADEMIC PURPOSES READING LOG

| Student: | 1 | 2 | 3 | 4 | 5 | 6 | 7 | 8 | 9 | 10 |
|---|---|---|---|---|---|---|---|---|---|---|
| Comprehension (from VALUE reading) | | | | | | | | | | |
| Analysis (from VALUE reading) *Interacting with texts in parts and as wholes* | | | | | | | | | | |
| Interpretation (from VALUE reading) *Making sense with texts as blueprints for meaning* | | | | | | | | | | |
| Evaluate Information and Its Sources Critically (from VALUE information literacy) | | | | | | | | | | |
| Genres (from VALUE reading) | | | | | | | | | | |
| Connections to Discipline (from VALUE integrative learning) *Sees (makes) connections across disciplines, perspectives* | | | | | | | | | | |

**READING FOR SOCIAL ENGAGEMENT READING LOG**
**RUBRIC SCORES BY PARTICIPANT**

| Student: | 1 | 2 | 3 | 4 | 5 | 6 | 7 | 8 | 9 | 10 |
|---|---|---|---|---|---|---|---|---|---|---|
| Comprehension (from VALUE reading) | | | | | | | | | | |
| Analysis (from VALUE reading) *Interacting with texts in parts and as wholes* | | | | | | | | | | |
| Interpretation (from VALUE reading) *Making sense with texts as blueprints for meaning* | | | | | | | | | | |
| Evaluate Information and Its Sources Critically (from VALUE information literacy) | | | | | | | | | | |
| Analysis of Knowledge (from VALUE civic engagement) | | | | | | | | | | |
| Connections to Experience (from VALUE integrative learning) *Connects relevant experience and academic knowledge* | | | | | | | | | | |

## Reading for Academic Purposes and Social Engagement Reading Logs: Rubric Scores Arranged by Reading

READING FOR ACADEMIC PURPOSES READING LOG RUBRIC SCORES BY READING

| Title of Reading: | 1 | 2 | 3 | 4 | 5 | 6 | 7 | 8 | 9 | 10 | 11 | 12 | 13 | 14 | 15 | 16 | 17 | 18 |
|---|---|---|---|---|---|---|---|---|---|---|---|---|---|---|---|---|---|---|
| Comprehension (from VALUE reading) | | | | | | | | | | | | | | | | | | |
| Analysis (from VALUE reading) *Interacting with texts in parts and as wholes* | | | | | | | | | | | | | | | | | | |
| Interpretation (from VALUE reading) *Making sense with texts as blueprints for meaning* | | | | | | | | | | | | | | | | | | |
| Evaluate Information and Its Sources Critically (from VALUE information literacy) | | | | | | | | | | | | | | | | | | |
| Genres (from VALUE Reading) | | | | | | | | | | | | | | | | | | |
| Connections to Discipline (from VALUE integrative learning) *Sees (makes) connections across disciplines, perspectives* | | | | | | | | | | | | | | | | | | |

**READING FOR SOCIAL ENGAGEMENT READING LOG RUBRIC SCORES BY READING**

| Title: | 1 | 2 | 3 | 4 | 5 | 6 | 7 | 8 | 9 | 10 | 11 | 12 | 13 | 14 | 15 | 16 | 17 | 18 |
|---|---|---|---|---|---|---|---|---|---|---|---|---|---|---|---|---|---|---|
| Comprehension (from VALUE reading) | | | | | | | | | | | | | | | | | | |
| Analysis (from VALUE reading) *Interacting with texts in parts and as wholes* | | | | | | | | | | | | | | | | | | |
| Interpretation (from VALUE reading) *Making sense with texts as blueprints for meaning* | | | | | | | | | | | | | | | | | | |
| Evaluate Information and Its Sources Critically (from VALUE information literacy) | | | | | | | | | | | | | | | | | | |
| Analysis of Knowledge (from VALUE civic engagement) | | | | | | | | | | | | | | | | | | |
| Connections to Experience (from VALUE integrative learning) *Connects relevant experience and academic knowledge* | | | | | | | | | | | | | | | | | | |

*Worksheet for Reading for the Research Paper (RP)*

Reading for the research paper for Student _____

Title of paper _____

Source #1_____

| When in RP source was used (give page number of RP) | How the source was used: Summary of main ideas (S); Paraphrase of sentence or sentences (P); Quotation (Q); Copy w/o quotation (C); Detail taken from source (D); Other (O)— describe. | What part of the source was used: abstract, intro, lit review, method, findings, discussion. Other—describe Also give page or paragraph #. | Evidence of comprehension? How was source used? |
|---|---|---|---|

Source #2_____

| When in RP source was used (give page number of RP) | How the source was used: Summary of main ideas (S); Paraphrase of sentence or sentences (P); Quotation (Q); Copy w/o quotation (C); Detail taken from source (D); Other (O)— describe. | What part of the source was used: abstract, intro, lit review, method, findings, discussion. Other—describe Also give page or paragraph #. | Evidence of comprehension? How was source used? |
|---|---|---|---|

# Appendix 2: Taxonomy of Absence Regarding Social Engagement

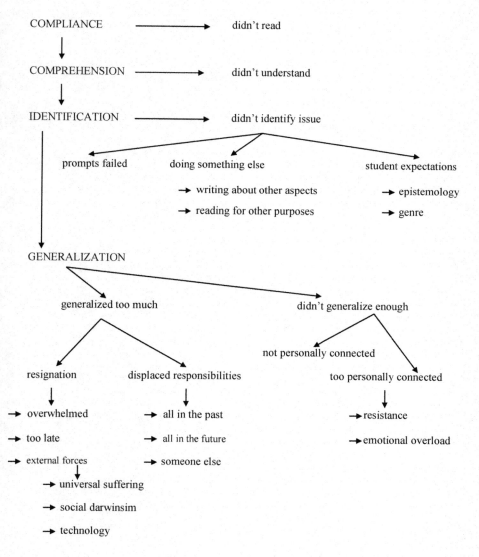

# Appendix 3: Coda on Collaboration

In THIS BOOK we explore critical reading in higher education through a collaborative scholarship of teaching and learning inquiry involving four general education classes. We discuss our findings with reference to current research on reading from a variety of perspectives, including composition studies, cognitive psychology, and educational research. We end with a call for transformative conversations across the academy and beyond, because critical reading is too important for us all to be satisfied with status quo. But critical reading is not the only issue in higher education that requires urgent, and collaborative, attention. In this coda we offer some suggestions for others who may want to engage in collaborative scholarship of teaching and learning inquiries. Collaboration offers tremendous possibilities for transformative change in our individual classrooms and in our institutions. We realize, however, that collaborative scholarship is more common in some disciplines than in others, so we begin with some reflections on collaboration more broadly before turning to our lessons learned.

In an increasingly competitive postsecondary environment marked by scarce resources, governments, institutions, community stakeholders, and funding agencies talk about the value of collaboration in research. While the natural sciences have a longer tradition of collaboration and co-authorship, driven in part by increasing specialization, external funding opportunities, and equipment needs,[1] the humanities and social sciences have been slower to move away from what Judith Davidson Wasser and Liora Bresler call "the myth of the lone researcher."[2] Part of this reluctance comes from the way collaborative work is sometimes judged in the academy. Annual performance reviews sometimes require each author to specify a percentage of credit for the work; this division of labor model includes "the assumption that when the value of an academic is equal to one unit, a single author can assume 100% of the effort, responsibility and credit. When two or more researchers work together on a project, each one of the collaborators can claim only partial credit, the total of which should be equal to one. This practice seems to assume that each one of the collaborators has spent proportionally less time and effort in a collaborative work than in a single-authored work."[3] Yet most members of productive collaborations will challenge these assumptions. Collaborative work often takes more time and effort (and luck), but can lead to enhanced insight, particularly, we suggest, for the scholarship of teaching and learning.

Most will agree that teaching and learning are fundamentally social processes, but so is scholarship, especially when done collaboratively. As Lorraine Walsh and Peter Kahn note,

- Teaching primarily involves a social process, where the aim is to catalyse the interest and engagement of the student, rather than to download information into their minds.
- Research is not just designed to lead to outputs that collect dust in a library or languish "un-clicked-upon" in cyberspace; the aim is that others build on this work and learn from it. And such wider learning is more likely to occur if one's research involved a collaborative process.

Collaboration provides a way to realize these goals for learning, forming as it does a key aspect of academic work for teachers and researchers.[4]

Collaboration as an approach focusing on individuals learning from each other and co-constructing meaning is particularly congruent with the scholarship of teaching and learning, as evident in Lee Shulman's call to treat teaching as community property as well as Mary Taylor Huber and Pat Hutchings's vision of a teaching commons.[5] Jane Mackenzie and Renee Meyers note the synergy between recent theories of collaboration "where conversation is at the center of the collaborative endeavor" and the scholarship of teaching and learning.[6] Although anchored in the rich context of the specific classroom, the scholarship of teaching and learning has to generate insights that are significant beyond that context. Scholarship of teaching and learning can have greater impact through collaborative and collective inquiry.[7]

Seeking to move the scholarship of teaching and learning beyond the individual classroom, we designed this collaborative study to examine how undergraduates read in our four different general education courses. During the process, we had several structural advantages, particularly in the initial stages; we also encountered serious challenges to the entire project. In retrospect, we wish we had thought through some of the inevitable issues of collaborative work so that we could have been more prepared when encountering them.

## Designing a Collaborative Study

Planning began for the inquiry in February 2010 when Richard Gale, then director of Mount Royal's Institute for Scholarship of Teaching and Learning, and Miriam Carey discussed the possibility of conducting a scholarship of teaching and learning inquiry across our general education program. Karen Manarin and Melanie Rathburn were invited to join. Carey, Manarin, and Rathburn had already participated in a teaching and learning scholars program and shared a common language for scholarship of teaching and learning. They had all taught in the general education program before, and during the study each served as a coordinator for these courses, which contributed to a systems perspective on general education within the university. Carey, Gale, Manarin, and Rathburn wanted to examine a question that was relevant across the undergraduate experience and decided on critical reading, in part because of expertise Manarin brought to the inquiry. Senior administration supported the initiative and funded our participation in the AAC&U Engaging Departments Initiative, an opportunity for the team to learn more about the rubrics and to build relationships with one another.

Adriana Kezar's study of collaboration within higher education institutions identifies relationships as the key lever for collaboration within such institutions.[8] Noting that the majority of collaborations fail, she proposes a three-stage model for fostering collaboration at the institutional level, stressing the importance of a campus network, initial conditions, and formal processes. In our collaborative inquiry we were fortunate to have in place many of the elements Kezar identifies, particularly in the first phase. She identifies values, external pressure, and learning as key elements in building commitment. Our institution, like those in her study, would describe itself as "being student centered, innovative, and egalitarian."[9] The institution had recently shifted from a two-year college to a four-year baccalaureate-granting university with a new general education program, so there were significant internal and external pressures for change. As part of the transition, Mount Royal formally endorsed the scholarship of teaching and learning, creating a research institute that served as what Walsh and Kahn call a "collaboration broker."[10] Our institution created a larger campus network, and its Department of General Education served as a social vehicle, a location with stable patterns of interactions, something Walsh and Kahn emphasize in their model of collaboration in higher education.[11]

However, if relationships are the key driver in academic collaboration, they are also the key risk. Relationships change as circumstances change. Gale had to withdraw from the research team shortly before we began gathering data, and Glen Ryland, another teaching and learning scholar who taught a general education course, generously agreed to step in, even though he was already busy with other research projects. Ryland had not been part of the design process, and although we tried to provide information and support, we had no plan for what to do when personnel change. We should have had both exit and entrance strategies in place before we needed them. We should have discussed issues like time commitments, intellectual property, and roles within the collaboration.

We also should have paid more attention to our individual and collective academic identities. As Brenda Leibowitz, Clever Ndebele, and Christine Winberg note, "Collective identities depend on how individuals perceive themselves, as well as how they are perceived and positioned by others. Academic identity influences, and is influenced by, participation, and in turn has an influence on deep learning."[12] Academic identity may "change over time, as participants position and reposition themselves."[13] This repositioning can impact organizational structures. While organizational structures in certain types of collaboration are well defined, we were a group of faculty who came together over a common interest. We did not have and, as relatively autonomous faculty members, are not used to a formal reporting structure. But neither were we completely egalitarian, as some members had greater experience and greater confidence in this field. The organizational structure of a collaboration falls on a spectrum, from hierarchical through egalitarian; indeed, it may move along the spectrum during the life span of the collaboration. Our collaboration benefited from an informal leader who shepherded the project along and who was able to make space in her regular workload for the additional demands of this project. It is challenging to get work done together; it is probably impossible if you expect everyone to do things equally at the same time all the time. For the four of us, different roles in the collaboration were essential. However, we should have talked about how to evaluate whether the collaboration was working for all members and how to support members' development and participation. Walsh and Kahn suggest formalizing the initial agreement to collaborate, with attention to planned and emergent working, professional dialogues, strategies for engagement, and social vehicles.[14]

In retrospect, we should have explicitly addressed all of these elements long before gathering data instead of muddling along, even though we recognize that it is impossible to foresee everything that might happen. And sometimes the unexpected is a gift. Some things we got right, like making the decision to record analysis on worksheets, which allowed for easier comparison among courses later on. Some things we got wrong, like losing the opportunity to conduct interviews with students across the four classes because we could not all afford the time after classes were done. Many things we would do slightly differently now, but that's part of the inevitable learning process of collaborative inquiry.

## Disseminating Findings and Recognizing Impact

Many of these findings have been shared at various national and international conferences over the past few years. We deliberately used conference presentations as a way to keep forward momentum in the analysis, to make the task manageable, and to sustain commitment to the collaboration. We addressed different aspects of the project in different presentations—for example, focusing on the two categories that are unique to critical reading for social engagement in one presentation or describing our supplemental analysis of the research papers in another. If we had not divided the inquiry into these smaller pieces, the analysis would have been overwhelming. The presentations also allowed us to develop different members' capacities as we varied responsibilities. Finally, the presentations kept us connected. Over time other scholarship projects have arisen; members have taken on different responsibilities at the institution; teaching assignments have changed; and roles within this collaboration have changed, particularly as we have moved toward the writing stage. Such changes are probably an inevitable part of any longer-term collaboration. The presentations helped us sustain commitment to the collaboration; however, the analysis does not end there. Writing involves yet another layer of analysis and reflection. Bringing the disparate pieces together, reexamining the literature on reading, and reflecting on our experiences has made a significant impact on us as individual instructors and collaborative researchers. Writing this book provided an opportunity for structured critical reflection, for greater learning and for change.

## Lessons Learned

- Since relationships are fundamental to academic collaboration, they need to be nurtured.
- Roles within the collaboration will likely change over time and may be asymmetrical.
- It is important to formalize aspects of a collaboration, including entrance and exit strategies, expectations, intellectual property, collaborative protocols, and evaluation.
- Recording analysis of data in a consistent way—for example, by using worksheets—can make later comparison much easier.
- Collaborations need to balance planned work with openness toward emergent possibilities, especially since the possibility of things going wrong is greater in collaborative inquiry.
- Collaborations may be more successful if work is broken into smaller segments, for example, by subtopic. However, it is necessary to synthesize those disparate pieces at some point, or the potential of collaborative inquiry may be lost.

# Notes

## Introduction

1. National Endowment for the Arts, *To Read or Not to Read: A Question of National Consequence* (Washington, DC: National Endowment for the Arts, 2007), 5.

2. David A. Joliffe and Allison Harl, "Studying the 'Reading Transition' from High School to College: What Our Students are Reading and Why?" *College English* 70, no. 6 (2008): 599–617.

3. Alvin Sanoff, "What Professors and Teachers Think: A Perception Gap over Students' Preparation," *Chronicle of Higher Education* 52, no. 27 (2006), http://chronicle.com/articl/A-Perception-Gap-Over/31426.

4. Richard Arum and Josipa Roksa, *Academically Adrift: Limited Learning on College Campuses* (Chicago: University of Chicago Press, 2011), 94–95.

5. National Endowment for the Arts, *To Read or Not to Read*, 12.

6. Stanislas Dehaene, *Reading in the Brain: The Science and Evolution of a Human Invention* (New York: Viking, 2009), 1.

7. Ibid., 210.

8. Maryanne Wolf, *Proust and the Squid: The Story and Science of the Reading Brain* (New York: Harper Collins, 2007), 216.

9. Ibid., 221, 225.

10. Nicholas Carr, *The Shallows: How the Internet Is Changing the Way We Think, Read, and Remember* (London: Atlantic Books, 2010); Gary Small and Gigi Vorgan, *iBrain: Surviving the Technological Alteration of the Modern Mind* (New York: Harper Collins, 2008).

11. Barry Cull, "Reading Revolutions: Online Digital Text and Implications for Reading in Academe," *First Monday* 16, no. 6 (2011), http://www.firstmonday.org.

12. Ziming Liu, "Reading Behavior in the Digital Environment: Changes in Reading Behavior over the Past Ten Years," *Journal of Documentation* 61, no. 6 (2005): 700–712.

13. Wolfgang Iser, *The Act of Reading: A Theory of Aesthetic Response* (Baltimore: Johns Hopkins University Press, 1978), ix.

14. Ibid., 34–35.

15. Ibid., 34.

16. See, for example, David Bleich, *Readings and Feelings: An Introduction to Subjective Criticism* (Urbana, IL: National Council of Teachers of English, 1975), and Norman Holland, *Five Readers Reading* (New Haven, CT: Yale University Press, 1975).

17. See, for example, many of the essays in Patricia Waugh, ed., *Literary Theory and Criticism: An Oxford Guide* (Oxford: Oxford University Press, 2006).

18. Patricia Harkin, "The Reception of Reader-Response Theory," *College Composition and Communication* 56, no. 3 (2005): 421.

19. Mariolina Rizzi Salvatori and Patricia Donahue, "What Is College English? Stories about Reading: Appearance, Disappearance, Morphing and Revival," *College English* 75, no. 2 (2012): 199–217.

20. Kathleen McCormick, *The Culture of Reading and the Teaching of English* (Manchester, UK: Manchester University Press, 1994).

21. Robert Scholes, "The Transition to College Reading," *Pedagogy: Critical Approaches to Teaching Literature, Language, Composition, and Culture* 2, no. 2 (2002): 165.

22. Louise M. Rosenblatt, "The Aesthetic Transaction," *Journal of Aesthetic Education* 20, no. 4 (1986): 124.

23. Louise M. Rosenblatt, *The Reader, the Text, the Poem: The Transactional Theory of the Literary Work* (Carbondale: Southern Illinois University Press, 1994), 20.

24. Ibid., 23.

25. John Guillory, "How Scholars Read," *Association of the Departments of English Bulletin* 146 (2008): 13.

26. Kathleen McWhorter and Brette M. Sember, *Essential Reading Skills: Preparing for College Reading*, 4th ed. (New York: Pearson, 2012); Kathleen McWhorter, *Guide to College Reading*, 10th ed. (New York: Pearson, 2015); Kathleen McWhorter, *Efficient and Flexible Reading*, 10th ed. (New York: Pearson, 2014); Kathleen McWhorter, *Reading across the Disciplines*, 6th ed. (New York: Pearson, 2015); Kathleen McWhorter, *Academic Reading: College Major and Career Applications*, 8th ed. (New York: Pearson, 2014).

27. David Bartholomae and Anthony Petrosky, *Ways of Reading: An Anthology for Writers*, 8th ed. (Boston: Bedford-St. Martin's, 2008); Joseph Harris, *Rewriting: How to Do Things with Texts* (Logan: Utah State University Press, 2006); Mariolina Rizzi Salvatori and Patricia Donahue, *The Elements (and Pleasures) of Difficulty* (New York: Pearson, 2005).

28. David Bartholomae, "Inventing the University," *Journal of Basic Writing* 5, no. 1 (1986): 4–5.

29. Ibid., 9.

30. Joseph Harris, *A Teaching Subject: Composition since 1966* (Logan: Utah State University Press, 2012), 28.

31. Joseph Harris, "Revision as a Critical Practice," *College English* 65, no. 6 (2003): 577–592.

32. Ibid., 578; emphasis in original.

33. Cheryl Dozier, Peter Johnston, and Rebecca Rogers, *Critical Literacy/Critical Teaching: Tools for Preparing Responsive Teachers* (New York: Teachers College Press, 2006), 18.

34. Joe L. Kincheloe, *Critical Pedagogy Primer*, 2nd ed. (New York: Peter Lang, 2008).

35. Patricia Bizzell, *Academic Discourse and Critical Consciousness* (Pittsburgh: University of Pittsburgh Press, 1992); Ira Shor, *When Students Have Power: Negotiating Authority in a Critical Pedagogy* (Chicago: University of Chicago Press, 1996).

36. Association of American Colleges and Universities (hereafter, AAC&U), "Essential Learning Outcomes." https://www.aacu.org/leap/essential-learning-outcomes.

37. Terrel L. Rhodes, ed. *Assessing Outcomes and Improving Achievement: Tips and Tools for Using Rubrics* (Washington, DC: AAC&U, 2010), 32.

38. Paulo Freire, *Teachers as Cultural Workers: Letters to Those Who Dare to Teach*, trans. Donald Macedo, Dale Koike, and Alexandre Oliveira (Boulder, CO: Westview Press, 2005), 46.

39. Lisa Patel Stevens and Thomas W. Bean, *Critical Literacy: Context Research and Practice in the K–12 Classroom* (Thousand Oaks, CA: Sage, 2007), 6, 5.

40. Ibid., 7.

41. Ira James Allen, "Reprivileging Reading: The Negotiations of Uncertainty," *Pedagogy: Critical Approaches to Teaching Literature, Language, Composition, and Culture* 12, no. 1 (2011): 101.

42. Ibid., 113.

43. Gina Cervetti, Michael J. Pardales, and James S. Damico, "A Tale of Differences: Comparing the Traditions, Perspectives, and Educational Goals of Critical Reading and Critical Literacy," *Reading Online* (2001), htpp://www.readingonline.org/articles/cervetti/index.html.

44. Allan Luke, "Critical Literacy: Foundational Notes," *Theory into Practice* 51, no. 1 (2012): 6.

45. Cervetti, Pardales, and Damico, "Tale of Differences."

46. Luke, "Critical Literacy," 6.

47. Peter Roberts, *Education, Literacy, and Humanization: Exploring the Work of Paulo Freire* (Westport, CT: Bergin and Garvey, 2000), 94; emphasis in original.

48. Allen, "Reprivileging Reading," 117.

49. Hart Research Associates, *Raising the Bar: Employers' Views on College Learning in the Wake of the Economic Downturn* (Washington, DC: AAC&U, 2010), 2.

50. Conference Board of Canada, "Employability Skills 2000+," http://www.conference-board.ca/topics/education/learning-tools/employability-skills.aspx.

51. Jennifer Cheeseman Day and Eric C. Newburger, *The Big Payoff: Educational Attainment and Synthetic Estimates of Work-Life Earnings* (US Census Bureau 2002), http://www.eric.ed.gov/PDFS/ED467533.pdf.

52. Eric J. Anctil, "Market Driven versus Mission Driven," *ASHE Higher Education Report* 34, no. 2 (2008): 1–8.

53. Colin Harrison, *Understanding Reading Development* (London: Sage, 2004), 5.

54. Ibid., 3.

55. Ibid., 155.

56. Alice S. Horning, "Reading across the Curriculum as the Key to Student Success," *Across the Disciplines* 4 (May 14, 2007), http://wac.colostate.edu/atd/articles/horning2007.cfm.

57. See, for example, Mark Sadoski, Allan Paivio, and Ernest T. Goetz, "A Critique of Schema Theory in Reading and a Dual Coding Alternative," *Reading Research Quarterly* 26, no. 4 (1991): 463–484, and Mary B. McVee, Kailonnie Dunsmore, and James R. Gavelek, "Schema Theory Revisited," *Review of Educational Research* 75 (2005): 531–566.

58. James Collins and Richard K. Blot, *Literacy and Literacies: Texts, Power, and Identity* (Cambridge, UK: Cambridge University Press, 2003); Mary Jo Fresch, ed., *An Essential History of Current Reading Practices* (Newark, NJ: International Reading Association, 2008); Colin Lankshear and Michele Knobel, *New Literacies: Changing Knowledge and Classroom Learning* (Maidenhead, Berkshire, UK: Open University Press, 2003).

59. Michael Pressley, "What Should Comprehension Instruction Be the Instruction Of?" in *Handbook of Reading Research,* ed. Michael L. Kamil et al. (Mahwah, NJ: Lawrence Erlbaum, 2000), 3: 545–561.

60. Susan E. Israel et al., eds., *Metacognition in Literacy Learning: Theory, Assessment, Instruction, and Professional Development* (Mahwah, NJ: Lawrence Erlbaum, 2005); Cathy Collins Block and Sheri R. Parris, ed. *Comprehension Instruction: Research-Based Best Practices,* 2nd ed. (New York: Guilford, 2008).

61. See, for example, Donna Qualley, ed., "Disciplinary Ways of Teaching Reading in English," Introduction to a special issue of *Reader: Essays in Reader-Oriented Theory, Criticism, and Pedagogy* 60 (Fall 2010): 4–18.

62. Debrah Huffman, "Towards Modes of Reading in Composition," *Reader: Essays in Reader-Oriented Theory, Criticism, and Pedagogy* 60 (2010): 162–188; Arlene Wilner, "Asking for It: The Role of Assignment Design in Critical Literacy," *Reader: Essays in Reader-Oriented Theory, Criticism, and Pedagogy* 52 (2005): 56–90; Salvatori and Donahue, *Elements (and Pleasures) of Difficulty.*

63. M. Anne Britt and Jodie Sommer, "Facilitating Textual Integration with Macro-Structure Focusing Tasks," *Reading Psychology* 25, no. 4 (2004): 332.

64. Carnegie Corporation of New York's Council on Advancing Adolescent Literacy, *Time to Act: An Agenda for Advancing Adolescent Literacy for College and Career Success* (New York: Carnegie, 2010), 56.

65. Martha Maxwell, *The Dismal Status of Required Developmental Reading Programs: Roots, Causes, and Solutions,* Educational Resource Education Center (ERIC), No ED 415 501, 1997, http://files.eric.ed.gov/fulltext/ED415501.pdf.

66. Eric J. Paulson and Sonya L. Armstrong, "Postsecondary Literacy: Coherence in Theory, Terminology, and Teacher Preparation," *Journal of Developmental Education* 33, no. 3 (2010): 3.

67. Greg Mannion, Kate Miller, Ian Gibb, and Ronnie Goodman, "Reading, Writing, Resonating: Striking Chords across the Contexts of Students' Everyday and College Lives," *Pedagogy, Culture, and Society* 17, no. 3 (2009): 323–339.

68. Scholes, "Transition to College Reading," 166.

69. Pat Hutchings, ed. *Opening Lines: Approaches to the Scholarship of Teaching and Learning* (Menlo Park, CA: Carnegie Foundation for the Advancement of Teaching, 2000), 8.

## 1. Different Courses, Common Concern

1. Liz Grauerholz and Eric Main, "Fallacies of SoTL: Rethinking How We Conduct Our Research," in *The Scholarship of Teaching and Learning in and across the Disciplines,* ed. Kathleen McKinney (Bloomington: Indiana University Press, 2013), 158.

2. Cheryl Albers, "Growing our Own Understanding of Teaching and Learning: Planting the Seeds and Reaping the Harvest," in McKinney, *Scholarship of Teaching and Learning,* 233–234.

3. Ibid., 234.

4. Ibid., 235.

5. Celia Popovic and David A. Green, *Understanding Undergraduates: Challenging Our Preconceptions of Student Success* (New York: Routledge, 2012), 40.

6. In 2011/2012 tuition for Canadian students at Mount Royal University was $2,544 for five courses in a thirteen-week semester; tuition for international students was $5,725. For 2011/2012 government grants made up 45 percent of Mount Royal's operating budget. Statistics about Mount Royal are taken from Mount Royal's website: www.mtroyal.ca/AboutMount Royal/FastFacts/index.

7. Ibid.

8. Terrel L. Rhodes, introduction to *General Education and Liberal Learning: Principles of Effective Practice,* ed. Paul L. Gaston (Washington, DC: AAC&U, 2010), 5; Ann S. Ferren, "Intentionality," in Gaston, *General Education and Liberal Learning,* 29.

9. The general education provision has since been reduced to 25 percent of a degree, and some Mount Royal University professional programs, such as nursing, have a further modified general education component because of accreditation restrictions.

10. Paul Hanstedt, *General Education Essentials: A Guide for College Faculty* (San Francisco: Jossey-Bass, 2012), 4–5.

11. Ferren, "Intentionality," 28.

12. Robert Shoenberg, "Greater Expectations for Student Transfer: Seeking Intentionality and the Coherent Curriculum," in *General Education and Student Transfer: Fostering Intentionality and Coherence in State Systems* (Washington, DC: AAC&U, 2005), 8–9.

13. The requirement is now ten courses across the four clusters, but students still have to take a foundation-level course in each cluster.

14. Much of the language in the descriptions and goals of study for each cluster comes from the official General Education Policy at Mount Royal.

15. Eboo Patel, *Acts of Faith: The Story of an American Muslim, the Struggle for the Soul of a Generation* (Boston: Beacon Press, 2007); John Paul Lederach, *The Moral Imagination: The Art and Soul of Building Peace* (New York: Oxford University Press, 2010).

16. Roberta Birks, Tomi Eng, and Julie Walchli, eds., *Landmarks: A Process Reader,* 2nd ed. (Toronto: Pearson, 2004); Gerald Graff and Cathy Birkenstein, *They Say/I Say: The Moves That Matter in Academic Writing* (New York: Norton, 2006).

17. Richard Gale, former director of the Mount Royal Institute for Scholarship of Teaching and Learning, participated in this design process. More details about our collaborative process are available in appendix 3.

18. Unlike America, where federal policy allows possible exemption for scholarship conducted on normal educational practices in educational settings, scholarship of teaching and learning studies in Canada must go through an ethical review process at the institutional level.

19. Pat Hutchings, "Ethics and Aspiration in the Scholarship of Teaching and Learning," in *Ethics of Inquiry: Issues in the Scholarship of Teaching and Learning* (Menlo Park, CA: Carnegie Foundation for the Advancement of Teaching, 2002), 8.

20. Examining critical reading of film would be a fascinating but difficult project.

21. See appendix 1 for images of the hybridized rubrics and worksheets that we used.

22. Lorraine Walsh and Peter Kahn, *Collaborative Working in Higher Education: The Social Academy* (New York: Routledge, 2010), 30.

23. Judith Davidson Wasser and Liora Bresler, "Working in the Interpretive Zone: Conceptualizing Collaboration in Qualitative Research Teams," *Educational Researcher* 25 (1996): 6.

24. Popovic and Green, *Understanding Undergraduates,* 60.

25. For a brief summary of several techniques, see Maryellen Weimer, ed., *11 Strategies for Getting Students to Read What's Assigned,* Faculty Focus Special Report (Madison, WI: Magna, 2010).

26. Brian D. Brost and Karen A. Bradley, "Student Compliance with Assigned Reading: A Case Study," *Journal of Scholarship of Teaching and Learning* 6, no. 2 (2006): 101–111.

27. Ibid., 103.

28. Mary E. Hoeft, "Why University Students Don't Read: What Professors Can Do to Increase Compliance," *International Journal of Scholarship of Teaching and Learning* 6, no. 2 (2012), http://digitalcommons.georgiasouthern.edu/ij-sotl/vol6/iss2/12. In the K–12 classroom many strategies have been proposed to increase student engagement in reading; far fewer seem to increase comprehension. See Cathy Collins Block and Gerald D. Duffy, "Research on Teaching Comprehension: Where We've Been and Where We're Going," in *Comprehension Instruction: Research-Based Best Practices,* 2nd ed., ed. Cathy Collins Block and Sheri R. Parris, 19–37 (New York: Guilford, 2008).

29. See, for example, Douglas Buehl, *Developing Readers in the Academic Disciplines* (Newark, NJ: International Reading Association, 2011), and David Pace and Joan Middendorf, eds. *Decoding the Disciplines: Helping Students Learn Disciplinary Ways of Thinking.* New Directions for Teaching and Learning series 98 (San Francisco: Jossey-Bass, 2004).

30. Wasser and Bresler, "Working in the Interpretive Zone," 12.

## 2. Can Students Read?

1. See Fresch, *Essential History of Current Reading Practices.*

2. Wolf, *Proust and the Squid*; Carr, *Shallows*; Mark Bauerlein, *The Dumbest Generation: How the Digital Age Stupefies Young Americans and Jeopardizes Our Future; or, Don't Trust Anyone under 30* (New York: Penguin, 2009).

3. Complaints about the "current" generation's reading abilities stretch back through the twentieth century; see, for example, Frederick Rudolph, *Curriculum: A History of the American Undergraduate Course of Study since 1636* (San Francisco: Jossey-Bass, 1977); Claudia Goldin and Lawrence F. Katz, *The Shaping of Higher Education: The Formative Years in the United States, 1890 to 1940* (Cambridge, MA: National Bureau of Economic Research, 1998).

4. Stephen D. Brookfield, *Teaching for Critical Thinking: Tools and Techniques to Help Students Question Their Assumptions* (San Francisco: Jossey-Bass, 2012), 24.

5. James Paul Gee, "Reflections on Reading Cope and Kalatzis' 'Multiliteracies': New Literacies, New Learning," *Pedagogies: An International Journal* 4 (2009): 196. See also Lankshear and Knobel, *New Literacies.*

6. Sadoski, Paivio, and Goetz, "Critique of Schema Theory."

7. McVee, Dunsmore, and Gavelek, "Schema Theory Revisited," 534.

8. Ibid., 546.

9. Ibid., 551.

10. Gregory Schraw and Roger Bruning, "How Implicit Models of Reading Affect Motivation to Read and Reading Engagement," *Scientific Studies of Reading* 3 (1999): 282.

11. David Yun Dai and Xiaolei Wang, "The Role of Need for Cognition and Reader Beliefs in Text Comprehension and Interest Development," *Contemporary Educational Psychology* 32 (2007): 333–334.

12. Ibid., 344.

13. See William G. Perry Jr., *Forms of Ethical and Intellectual Development in the College Years: A Scheme* (San Francisco: Jossey-Bass, 1999), and Marcia B. Baxter Magolda, *Knowing and Reasoning in College: Gender-Related Patterns in Students' Intellectual Development* (San Francisco: Jossey-Bass, 1992).

14. Paul van den Broek, David N. Rapp, and Panyiota Kendeou argue that any naturalistic reading includes memory-based and constructionist processes that "dynamically interact, borrowing from, supporting, and, possibly, conflicting with each other." See their "Integrating Memory-Based and Constructionist Processes in Accounts of Reading Comprehension," *Discourse Processes* 39 (2005): 301.

15. Tracy Linderholm, "Reading with Purpose," *Journal of College Reading and Learning* 36 (2006): 74.

16. AAC&U, *Assessing Outcomes and Improving Achievement: Tips and Tools for Using Rubrics*, ed. Terrel L. Rhodes (Washington, DC: AAC&U, 2009), 33.

17. Ibid., 37.

18. Bartholomae and Petrosky, *Ways of Reading*, 12.

19. Salvatori and Donahue, *Elements (and Pleasures)*, xxv.

20. Ibid., 136.

21. Guillory, "How Scholars Read," 13.

22. Bartholomae and Petrosky, *Ways of Reading*, 12.

23. Paul van den Broek, Robert F. Lorch Jr., Tracy Linderholm, and Mary Gustafson, "The Effects of Readers' Goals on Inference Generation and Memory for Texts," *Memory and Cognition* 29 (2001): 1,085.

24. Linderholm, "Reading with Purpose," 75.

25. Mariolina Rizzi Salvatori and Patricia Donahue, "Tracing the Moves: How Students Read," *Reader: Essays in Reader-Oriented Theory, Criticism, and Pedagogy* 62 (2012): 81.

26. Steve Graham and Michael Hebert, *Writing to Read: Evidence for How Writing Can Improve Reading* (Washington, DC: Alliance for Excellent Education, 2010), 14.

27. AAC&U, *Assessing Outcomes*, 32.

28. Emily Martin, "The Egg and the Sperm: How Science Has Constructed a Romance Based on Stereotypical Male-Female Roles," in Birks et al., *Landmarks*, 169–184.

29. Anthony Garrison, Dirk Remley, Patrick Thomas, and Emily Wierszewski complicate this dismissive view of emoticons in "Conventional Faces: Emoticons in Instant Messaging Discourse," *Computers and Composition* 28 (2011): 112–125.

30. The student used the words "Frightening thought!" to comment on how easy it is to indoctrinate someone.

31. Nicholas Carr, "Is Google Making Us Stupid? What the Internet Is Doing to Our Brains," *Atlantic* (July 1, 2008), http://www.theatlantic.com/magazine/archive/2008/07/is -google-making-us-stupid/306868.

32. Alex Haley, "*Playboy* Interview: Malcolm X," The Malcolm X Project at Columbia University, May 6, 1963, http://www.columbia.edu/cu/ccbh/mxp/pdf/050063playboy.pdf.

33. Kenneth A. Myers, "Cigarette Smoking: An Underused Tool in High-Performance Endurance Training," *Canadian Medical Association Journal* 182, no. 18 (2010): 867–869.

34. Brookfield, *Teaching for Critical Thinking*, 27–52.

35. Ibid., 28.

36. Ibid., 135–141.

37. Gary Genosko, "Hockey and Culture," in Birks et al, *Landmarks*, 231–243.

38. Brookfield, *Teaching for Critical Thinking*, 135.

39. See, for example, Israel et al., *Metacognition in Literacy Learning*.

40. Bartholomae and Petrosky, *Ways of Reading*; Harris, *Rewriting*; Salvatori and Donahue, *Elements (and Pleasures)*.

41. Although transfer is often seen as rare, Daniel L. Schwartz, Catherine C. Chase, and John D. Bransford argue, "Transfer is ubiquitous. There is no situation, no matter how novel, where people do not transfer in prior experiences to make some sense of that situation." As instructors, we need to help people avoid negative transfer or overzealous transfer. See "Resisting Overzealous Transfer: Coordinating Previously Successful Routines with Needs for New Learning," *Educational Psychologist* 47, no. 3 (2012): 212.

42. Daniel M. Belenky and Timothy J. Nokes-Malach, "Motivation and Transfer: The Role of Mastery-Approach Goals in Preparation for Future Learning," *Journal of the Learning Sciences* 21 (2012): 402.

43. Ibid., 426.

44. Mark Bauerlein, for example, claims many youth see reading as counterproductive. *Dumbest Generation*, 42.

45. Karen Manarin, "Reading Value: Student Choice in Reading Strategies," *Pedagogy: Critical Approaches to Teaching Literature, Language, Composition, and Culture* 12, no. 2 (2012): 281–282.

46. See, for example, Block and Parris, *Comprehension Instruction.*

47. Tracy Linderholm and Adam Wilde, "College Students' Beliefs about Comprehension When Reading for Different Purposes," *Journal of College Reading and Learning* 40 (2010): 15.

## 3. Critical Reading for Academic Purposes

1. Ference Marton and Roger Säljö, "Approaches to Learning," in *The Experience of Learning,* ed. Ference Marton, Dai Hounsell, and Noel Entwhistle (Edinburgh: Scottish Academic Press, 1984), 39.

2. Tamsin Haggis, "Constructing Images of Ourselves? A Critical Investigation into 'Approaches of Learning' Research in Higher Education," *British Educational Research Journal* 29, no. 1 (2003): 89–104; Graham Webb, "Deconstructing Deep and Surface: Towards a Critique of Phenomenography," *Higher Education* 33 (1997): 199.

3. John C. Bean, *Engaging Ideas: The Professor's Guide to Integrating Writing, Critical Thinking, and Active Learning in the Classroom* (San Francisco: Jossey-Bass, 2001), 137.

4. Huffman, "Towards Modes of Reading," 169.

5. Ibid., 179.

6. Eric Henderson, *The Active Reader: Strategies for Academic Reading and Writing,* 2nd ed. (Don Mills, ON: Oxford University Press, 2012), 26.

7. Bean, *Engaging Ideas,* 136.

8. Manarin, "Reading Value," 294.

9. Saranne Weller's "New Lecturers' Accounts of Reading Higher Education Research," *Studies in Continuing Education* 33, no. 1 (2011): 93–106, identifies several areas of discomfort beyond linguistic problems and generic conventions. Weller argues that being positioned as an outsider undermines the reader's sense of agency and identity (99–100).

10. Latricia Trites and Mary McGroarty, "Reading to Learn and Reading to Integrate: New Tasks for Reading Comprehension Tests?" *Language Testing* 22, no. 2 (2005): 174–210.

11. Ibid., 175.

12. Teun A. van Dijk and Walter Kintsch theorize models of text processing in *Strategies of Discourse Comprehension* (New York: Academic Press, 1983), while Rolf Zwaan has explored how readers construct and monitor the situation model in naturalistic reading tasks; see for example, Rolf A. Zwaan, Joseph P. Magliano, and Arthur C. Graesser, "Dimensions of Situation Model Construction in Narrative Comprehension," *Journal of Experimental Psychology: Learning, Memory, and Cognition* 21, no. 2 (1995): 386–397.

13. Charles A. Perfetti, "Sentences, Individual Differences, and Multiple Texts: Three Issues in Text Comprehension," *Discourse Processes* 23, no. 3 (1997): 337–355.

14. Trites and McGroarty, "Reading to Learn," 177.

15. Britt and Sommer, "Facilitating Textual Integration."

16. Ivar Bråten and Helge I. Strømsø, "Effects of Personal Epistemology on the Understanding of Multiple Texts," *Reading Psychology* 27, no. 5 (2006): 457–484.

17. See, for example, Walter Kintsch, *Comprehension: A Paradigm for Cognition* (New York: Cambridge University Press, 1998).

18. Bråten and Strømsø, "Effects of Personal Epistemology," 476.

19. Ibid.

20. Perry, *Forms of Intellectual and Ethical Development.*

21. Laura Gil, Ivar Bråten, Eduardo Vidal-Abarca, and Helge I. Strømsø, "Summary versus Argument Tasks When Working with Multiple Documents: Which Is Better for Whom?" *Contemporary Educational Psychology* 35, no. 3 (2010): 157–173.

22. Betty Samraj, "Discourse Features of the Student-Produced Academic Research Paper: Variations across Disciplinary Courses," *Journal of English for Academic Purposes* 3, no. 1 (2004): 19.

23. Ibid., 6.

24. AAC&U, *Assessing Outcomes.*

25. Ibid., 33.

26. Ibid., 51.

27. Graham and Hebert, *Writing to Read.*

28. Richard Larson, "The 'Research Paper' in the Writing Course: A Non-Form of Writing," *College English* 44, no. 8 (1982): 811–816.

29. Samraj, "Discourse Features," 5–22.

30. Carra Leah Hood, "Ways of Research: The Status of the Traditional Research Paper Assignment in First-Year Writing/Composition Courses," *Composition Forum* 22 (2010), http://compositionforum.com/issue/22/ways-of-research.php.

31. Carlton Clark, "The Mock Research Paper," *Teaching English in the Two-Year College* 36, no. 1 (2008): 47–49.

32. Alison J. Head and Michael B. Eisenberg, "Assigning Inquiry: How Handouts for Research Assignments Guide Today's College Students," *Project Information Literacy Progress Report,* The Information School, University of Washington, July 12, 2010, http://projectinfolit .org/images/pdfs/pil_handout_study_finalvjuly_2010.pdf, 26.

33. Ibid., 26–27.

34. Robert A. Schwegler and Linda K. Shamoon, "The Aims and Process of the Research Paper," *College English* 44, no. 8 (1982): 820.

35. Sherry Lee Linkon, *Literary Learning: Teaching the English Major* (Bloomington: Indiana University Press, 2011), 86.

36. Sandra Jamieson and Rebecca Moore Howard, "Unraveling the Citation Trail," *Project Information Literacy Smart Talks,* no. 8, The Citation Project (August 15, 2011), Project Information Literacy, http://projectinfolit.org/smart-talks/item/110-sandra-jamieson-rebecca-moore-howard.

37. Rebecca Moore Howard, "A Plagiarism Pentimento," *Journal of Teaching Writing* 11, no. 2 (1992): 233.

38. Miguel Roig, "Plagiarism and Paraphrasing Criteria of College and University Professors," *Ethics and Behavior* 11, no. 3 (2001): 307–323.

39. Rebecca Moore Howard, Tricia Serviss, and Tanya K. Rodrigue, "Writing from Sources, Writing from Sentences," *Writing and Pedagogy* 2 (2010): 182.

40. A cautionary note: it is worth remembering that only nine students from Texts and Ideas—Genocide agreed to have their class work included in this study, and those students who struggled with reading are less likely to have consented.

41. Mark Emmons, Wanda Martin, Carroll Botts, and Cassandra Amundson, "Engaging Sources: Information Literacy and the Freshman Research Paper," *LOEX Quarterly* 36, no. 4 (2010): 8–9, 12; 37, no. 2 (2010): 8–10.

42. Howard, Serviss, and Rodrigue, "Writing from Sources," 187; emphasis in original.

43. Ibid., 186.

44. Interestingly, there is a lot of variation in the scores for evaluation of sources in the reading logs for this student.

45. Rebecca Moore Howard, "Why This Humanist Codes," *Research in the Teaching of English* 49, no. 1 (2014): 78.

46. Henderson, *Active Reader*, 26.

47. The "backward design" movement in curriculum development suggests beginning with the desired results, considering potential evidence, and only then planning instruction. See, for example, Grant Wiggins and Jay McTighe, *Understanding by Design*, 2nd ed. (Alexandria, VA: Association for Supervision and Curriculum Development, 2005).

## 4. Critical Reading for Social Engagement

1. Ira Shor and Paulo Freire, *A Pedagogy for Liberation: Dialogues on Transforming Education* (South Hadley, MA: Bergin & Garvey, 1987), 137.

2. Andrew Furco, "Service-Learning: A Balanced Approach to Experiential Education," *Expanding Boundaries: Service and Learning* (Washington, DC: Corporation for National Service, 1996), 2–6.

3. The National Task Force on Civic Learning and Democratic Engagement, *A Crucible Moment: College Learning and Democracy's Future* (Washington, DC: AAC&U, 2012), 30.

4. David Scobey, "Why Now? Because This Is the Copernican Moment," in *Civic Provocations*, ed. Donald W. Harward (Washington, DC: Bringing Theory to Practice, 2012), 5.

5. George G. Kuh, *High-Impact Educational Practices: What They Are, Who Has Access to Them, and Why They Matter* (Washington, DC: AAC&U, 2008), 16–17.

6. Ashley Finley, *Making Progress? What We Know about the Achievement of Liberal Education Outcomes* (Washington, DC: AAC&U, 2012), 23–25.

7. Association of Universities and Colleges in Canada, *The Revitalization of Undergraduate Education in Canada* (AUCC, 2011), 3, http://www.aucc.ca/wp-content/uploads/2011/09/the-revitalization-of-undergraduate-education-in-canada-2011.pdf.

8. Freire, *Teachers as Cultural Workers*, 46.

9. AAC&U, *Assessing Outcomes*, 43.

10. Miriam Carey, "In the Valley of the Giants: Cultivating Intentionality and Integration," *International Journal of the Scholarship of Teaching and Learning* 6, no. 1 (2012), http://academics.georgiasouthern.edu/ijsotl/v6n1.html.

11. AAC&U, *Assessing Outcomes*, 51; emphasis removed.

12. We have reproduced a graphic representation of this taxonomy of absence in appendix 2.

13. Shor and Freire, *Pedagogy for Liberation*, 121–141.

14. Ibid., 137.

15. Brost and Bradley, "Student Compliance."

16. Wolf, *Proust and the Squid*, 160.

17. Shor and Freire, *Pedagogy for Liberation*, 10.

18. Sadoski, Paivio, and Goetz, "Critique of Schema Theory," 468–472.

19. Heather Menzies, "When Roots Grow Back into Earth," in Birks et al., *Landmarks*, 118.

20. Perry, *Forms of Ethical and Intellectual Development*; L. Lee Knefelkamp, Introduction to Perry, *Forms of Ethical and Intellectual Development*, xi–xxviii; Patricia M. King and Karen Strohm Kitchener, *Developing Reflective Judgment: Understanding and Promoting Intellectual Growth and Critical Thinking in Adolescents and Adults* (San Francisco: Jossey-Bass, 1994).

21. King and Kitchener, *Developing Reflective Judgment,* 18.

22. Ibid., 250–254.

23. Bråten and Strømsø, "Effects of Personal Epistemology," 476.

24. See, for example, John Sweller, "Cognitive Load Theory, Learning Difficulty, and Instructional Design," *Learning and Instruction* 4, no. 4 (1994): 295–312.

25. Jeffrey D. Sachs, *Common Wealth: Economics for a Crowded Planet* (New York: Penguin Books, 2008), 3–15.

26. Stephen Lewis, "AIDS in Africa," in Birks et al., *Landmarks,* 302–314.

27. Shor and Freire, *Pedagogy for Liberation,* 132.

28. Martha C. Nussbaum, *Creating Capabilities: The Human Development Approach* (Cambridge, MA: Harvard University Press, 2011).

29. Perry, *Forms of Ethical and Intellectual Development,* 11.

30. Dave Meslin, "The Antidote to Apathy," TEDxToronto, October 2010, http://www.ted.com/talks/dave_meslin_the_antidote_to_apathy.html.

31. John Docker, "Are Settler-Colonies Inherently Genocidal? Re-reading Lemkin," in *Empire, Colony, Genocide: Conquest, Occupation, and Subaltern Resistance in World History,* ed. Dirk Moses (New York: Berghahn Books, 2010), 81–101.

32. Martin Luther King Jr., "Loving Your Enemies," sermon given at Dexter Avenue Baptist Church, Montgomery, Alabama, November 17, 1957, http://www.mlkonline.net/enemies.html.

33. AAC&U, *Assessing Outcomes,* 43.

34. Freire, *Teachers as Cultural Workers,* 35.

35. Ibid., 42.

36. Sean Murray, "Investigating College Campus Conflicts: Possibilities for Tapping into Genuine Student Interest," *Pedagogy: Critical Approaches to Teaching Literature, Language, Composition, and Culture* 12, no. 1 (2012): 161–167.

37. Shor and Freire, *Pedagogy for Liberation,* 11.

38. David Weiss Halivni, *The Book and the Sword: A Life of Learning in the Shadow of Destruction* (Boulder, CO: Westview Press, 1996).

39. Mariolina Rizzi Salvatori, "Difficulty: The Great Educational Divide," in *Opening Lines: Approaches to the Scholarship of Teaching and Learning,* ed. Pat Hutchings (Menlo Park, CA: Carnegie Foundation for the Advancement of Teaching, 2000), 81.

40. Margaret Atwood, "The Female Body," in Birks et al., *Landmarks,* 211–213.

41. Linda Suskie, "Engaging Students in Demonstrating and Understanding their Learning," presentation, Mount Royal University, Calgary, Alberta, April 18, 2012.

42. Michael B. Smith, Rebecca S. Nowacek, and Jeffrey L. Bernstein, "Ending the Solitude of Citizenship Education," *Citizenship across the Curriculum* (Bloomington: Indiana University Press), 9.

## 5. So Now What?

1. See Pat Hutchings's taxonomy of questions in the introduction to *Opening Lines,* 4–6.

2. Martha C. Nussbaum, *Cultivating Humanity: A Classical Defense of Reform in Liberal Education* (Cambridge, MA: Harvard University Press, 1997), 27.

3. Arum and Roksa, *Academically Adrift,* 94.

4. Nussbaum, *Creating Capabilities,* 24–25.

5. Ibid., 24.

6. Ibid., 21.

7. Ibid., 20.

8. Hutchings, *Opening Lines*, 8.

9. Judith C. Roberts and Keith A. Roberts, "Deep Reading, Cost/Benefit, and the Construction of Meaning: Enhancing Reading Comprehension and Deep Learning in Sociology Courses," *Teaching Sociology* 36, no. 2 (2008): 129; emphasis in original.

10. Ibid., 130; emphasis in original.

11. Ibid., 132–133; emphasis in original.

12. John Sappington, Kimberly Kinsey, and Kirk Munsayac, "Two Studies of Reading Compliance among College Students," *Teaching of Psychology* 29, no. 4 (2002): 272–274.

13. Marton and Säljö, "Approaches to Learning."

14. Karen Wilken Braun and R. Drew Sellers, "Using a 'Daily Motivational Quiz' to Increase Student Preparation, Attendance, and Participation," *Issues in Accounting Education* 27, no. 1 (2012): 267–279.

15. Heather Macpherson Parrott and Elizabeth Cherry, "Using Structured Reading Groups to Facilitate Deep Learning," *Teaching Sociology* 39, no. 4 (2011): 354–370.

16. Simon A. Lei, Kerry A. Bartlett, Suzanne E. Gorney, and Tamra R. Herschbach, "Resistance to Reading Compliance among College Students: Instructors' Perspectives," *College Student Journal* 44, no. 2 (2010): 219–229.

17. Robert J. Tierney and P. David Pearson, *Toward a Composing Model of Reading*, Reading Education Report no. 43, Center for the Study of Reading, University of Illinois Urbana-Champaign, August 1983, https://www.ideals.illinois.edu/bitstream/handle/2142 /17470/ctrstreadeducrepv01983i00043_opt.pdf?sequence=1, 1.

18. Timothy Shanahan, "Reading-Writing Relationships, Thematic Units, Inquiry Learning . . . In Pursuit of Effective Integrated Literacy Instruction," *Reading Teacher* 51 (1997): 14.

19. Jill Fitzgerald and Timothy Shanahan, "Reading and Writing Relations and Their Development," *Educational Psychologist* 35, no. 1 (2000): 43.

20. Ibid., 47.

21. Amy R. Hofer, Lori Townsend, and Korey Brunetti, "Troublesome Concepts and Information Literacy: Investigating Threshold Concepts for IL Instruction," *Portal: Libraries and the Academy* 12, no. 4 (2012): 403.

22. Council for Undergraduate Research, www.cur.org; Research Skills Development Framework, www.adelaide.edu.au/rsd; Mick Healey and Alan Jenkins, *Developing Undergraduate Research and Inquiry* (York, UK: Higher Education Academy, 2009), www.heacademy .ac.uk/node/3146.

23. Association of Universities and Colleges of Canada, *Canada's Universities in the World*, AUCC *Internationalization Survey*, 2014, http://www.aucc.ca/wp-content/uploads /2014/12/internationalization-survey-2014.pdf; Institute of International Education, *Open Doors 2014 Report on International Educational Exchange* (Sewickley, PA: Institute of International Education Books, 2014), http://www.iie.org/Research-and-Publications/Open-Doors /Data/US-Study-Abroad.

24. Nina Namaste, *Current Trends in Global Learning*, Elon University Center for Engaged Learning, October 28, 2014, http://www.centerforengagedlearning.org/current-trends -in-global-learning.

25. Elizabeth Brewer and Kiran Cunningham, eds. *Integrating Study Abroad into the Curriculum: Theory and Practice across the Disciplines* (Sterling, VA: Stylus Publishing, 2010).

26. Parker J. Palmer, *The Courage to Teach* (San Francisco: Jossey-Bass, 2007).

27. Grauerholz and Main, "Fallacies of SOTL."

28. David M. Scobey, "A Copernican Moment: On the Revolutions in Higher Education," in *Transforming Undergraduate Education: Theory That Compels and Practices That Succeed,* ed. Donald W. Harward (Lanham, MD: Rowman and Littlefield, 2012), 41.

29. Derek Bok, *Our Underachieving Colleges: A Candid Look at How Much Students Learn and Why They Should Be Learning More* (Princeton, NJ: Princeton University Press, 2006), 46.

30. The AAC&U promotes the following Essential Learning Outcomes: Knowledge of Human Cultures, and the Physical and Natural World; Intellectual and Practical Skills; Personal and Social Responsibility; and Integrative and Applied Learning. See Finley, *Making Progress?* for information about whether these outcomes are being achieved in undergraduate education.

31. Lee Shulman, "Professing the Liberal Arts," in *Teaching as Community Property: Essays on Higher Education,* ed. Pat Hutchings (San Francisco, CA: Jossey-Bass, 2004), 12–31; emphasis in original.

32. Brookfield, *Teaching for Critical Thinking,* 24.

33. Carol Geary Schneider, "Losing Our Way on the Meanings of Student Success," *Liberal Education* 99, no. 2 (2013), https://www.aacu.org/publications-research/periodicals/losing-our -way-meanings-student-success.

34. Hart Research Associates, *It Takes More Than a Major: Employer Priorities for College Learning and Student Success* (Washington, DC: Hart Research Associates for AAC&U, 2013).

35. Lumina Foundation, *The Degree Qualifications Profile: Defining Degrees: A New Direction for American Higher Education to Be Tested and Developed in Partnership with Faculty, Students, Leaders, and Stakeholders* (Indianapolis: Lumina Foundation, 2011).

36. Bok, *Our Underachieving Colleges,* 35.

37. See, for example, Pace and Middendorf, *Decoding the Disciplines.*

38. Nussbaum, *Cultivating Humanity,* 28.

39. Bok, *Our Underachieving Colleges,* 35.

40. Parker J. Palmer and Arthur Zajonc, *The Heart of Higher Education: A Call to Renewal* (San Francisco: Jossey-Bass, 2010), 125.

41. Ibid., 131.

42. Ibid., 137–138.

43. Ibid., 142.

## Appendix 3

1. Timothy L. O'Brien, "Change in Academic Coauthorship, 1953–2003," *Science, Technology, and Human Values* 37 (2012): 210–234.

2. Judith Davidson Wasser and Liora Bresler, "Working in the Interpretive Zone: Conceptualizing Collaboration in Qualitative Research Teams," *Educational Researcher* 25 (1996): 5.

3. Wai-ming Yu, Chun-kwok Lau, and John Chi-kin Lee, "Into Collaborative Research and Co-authorship: Experiences and Reflections," *Reflective Practice: International and Multidisciplinary Perspectives* 14 (2013): 31–42.

4. Lorraine Walsh and Peter Kahn, *Collaborative Working in Higher Education: The Social Academy* (New York: Routledge, 2010), 6.

5. Lee S. Shulman, "Teaching as Community Property: Putting an End to Pedagogical Solitude," *Change* 25, no. 6 (1993): 6–7; Mary Taylor Huber and Pat Hutchings, *The Advancement of Learning: Building the Teaching Commons* (San Francisco: Jossey-Bass, 2005).

6. Jane MacKenzie and Renee A. Meyers, "International Collaboration in SOTL: Current Status and Future Direction," *International Journal of Scholarship of Teaching and Learning* 6, no. 1 (2012), article 4.

7. Richard Gale, "Points without Limits: Individual Inquiry, Collaborative Investigation, and Collective Scholarship," in *To Improve the Academy: Resources for Faculty, Instructional, and Organizational Development*, ed. Douglas Reimondo Robinson and Linda B. Nilson (San Francisco: Jossey-Bass, 2008), 39–52.

8. Adrianna Kezar, "Redesigning for Collaboration within Higher Education Institutions: An Exploration into the Developmental Process," *Research in Higher Education* 46, no. 7 (2005): 857.

9. Ibid., 846.

10. Walsh and Kahn, *Collaborative Working*, 81.

11. Ibid., 16.

12. Brenda Leibowitz, Clever Ndebele, and Christine Winberg, "'It's an Amazing Learning Curve to Be Part of a Project': Exploring Academic Identity in Collaborative Research," *Studies in Higher Education* 37, no. 7 (2014): 1,266.

13. Ibid.

14. Walsh and Kahn, *Collaborative Working*, 64.

# Bibliography

Albers, Cheryl. "Growing Our Own Understanding of Teaching and Learning: Planting the Seeds and Reaping the Harvest." In *The Scholarship of Teaching and Learning in and across the Disciplines,* edited by Kathleen McKinney, 221–239. Bloomington: Indiana University Press, 2013.

Allen, Ira James. "Reprivileging Reading: The Negotiations of Uncertainty." *Pedagogy: Critical Approaches to Teaching Literature, Language, Composition, and Culture* 12, no. 1 (2011): 97–120.

Anctil, Eric J. "Market Driven versus Mission Driven." *ASHE Higher Education Report* 34, no. 2 (2008): 1–8.

Arum, Richard, and Josipa Roksa. *Academically Adrift: Limited Learning on College Campuses.* Chicago: University of Chicago Press, 2011.

Association of American Colleges and Universities (hereafter, AAC&U). *Assessing Outcomes and Improving Achievement: Tips and Tools for Using Rubrics.* Edited by Terrel L. Rhodes. Washington, DC: AAC&U, 2009.

———. "Essential Learning Outcomes." Washington, DC: AAC&U, 2010. https://www.aacu.org/leap/essential-learning-outcomes.

Association of Universities and Colleges of Canada. *Canada's Universities in the World. AUCC Internationalization Survey,* 2014. http://www.aucc.ca/wp-content/uploads/2014/12/internationalization-survey-2014.pdf.

———. *The Revitalization of Undergraduate Education in Canada.* Association of Universities and Colleges in Canada, 2011. http://www.aucc.ca/wp-content/uploads/2011/09/the-revitalization-of-undergraduate-education-in-canada-2011.pdf.

Atwood, Margaret. "The Female Body." In Birks et al., *Landmarks,* 211–213.

Bartholomae, David. "Inventing the University." *Journal of Basic Writing* 5, no. 1 (1986): 4–23.

Bartholomae, David, and Anthony Petrosky. *Ways of Reading: An Anthology for Writers.* 8th ed. Boston: Bedford-St. Martin's, 2008.

Bauerlein, Mark. *The Dumbest Generation: How the Digital Age Stupefies Young Americans and Jeopardizes Our Future; or, Don't Trust Anyone under 30.* New York: Penguin, 2009.

Bean, John C. *Engaging Ideas: The Professor's Guide to Integrating Writing, Critical Thinking, and Active Learning in the Classroom.* San Francisco: Jossey-Bass, 2001.

Belenky, Daniel M., and Timothy J. Nokes-Malach. "Motivation and Transfer: The Role of Mastery-Approach Goals in Preparation for Future Learning." *Journal of the Learning Sciences* 21 (2012): 399–432.

Birks, Roberta, Tomi Eng, and Julie Walchli, eds. *Landmarks: A Process Reader.* 2nd ed. Toronto: Pearson, 2004.

Bizzell, Patricia. *Academic Discourse and Critical Consciousness.* Pittsburgh: University of Pittsburgh Press, 1992.

Bleich, David. *Readings and Feelings: An Introduction to Subjective Criticism*. Urbana, IL: National Council of Teachers of English, 1975.

Block, Cathy Collins, and Gerald D. Duffy. "Research on Teaching Comprehension: Where We've Been and Where We're Going." In *Comprehension Instruction: Research-Based Best Practices*, 2nd ed., edited by Cathy Collins Block and Sheri R. Parris, 19–37. New York: Guilford, 2008.

Block, Cathy Collins, and Sheri R. Parris, eds. *Comprehension Instruction: Research-Based Best Practices*. 2nd ed. New York: Guilford, 2008.

Bok, Derek. *Our Underachieving Colleges: A Candid Look at How Much Students Learn and Why They Should Be Learning More*. Princeton, NJ: Princeton University Press, 2006.

Bråten, Ivar, and Helge I. Strømsø. "Effects of Personal Epistemology on the Understanding of Multiple Texts." *Reading Psychology* 27, no. 5 (2006): 457–484.

Braun, Karen Wilken, and R. Drew Sellers. "Using a 'Daily Motivational Quiz' to Increase Student Preparation, Attendance, and Participation." *Issues in Accounting Education* 27, no. 1 (2012): 267–279.

Brewer, Elizabeth, and Kiran Cunningham, eds. *Integrating Study Abroad into the Curriculum: Theory and Practice across the Disciplines*. Sterling, VA: Stylus Publishing, 2010.

Britt, M. Anne, and Jodie Sommer. "Facilitating Textual Integration with Macro-Structure Focusing Tasks." *Reading Psychology* 25, no. 4 (2004): 313–339.

Brookfield, Stephen D. *Teaching for Critical Thinking: Tools and Techniques to Help Students Question Their Assumptions*. San Francisco: Jossey-Bass, 2012.

Brost, Brian D., and Karen A. Bradley. "Student Compliance with Assigned Reading: A Case Study." *Journal of Scholarship of Teaching and Learning* 6, no. 2 (2006): 101–111.

Buehl, Douglas. *Developing Readers in the Academic Disciplines*. Newark, NJ: International Reading Association, 2011.

Carey, Miriam. "In the Valley of the Giants: Cultivating Intentionality and Integration." *International Journal of the Scholarship of Teaching and Learning* 6, no. 1 (2012). http://academics.georgiasouthern.edu/ijsotl/v6n1.html.

Carnegie Corporation of New York's Council on Advancing Adolescent Literacy. *Time to Act: An Agenda for Advancing Adolescent Literacy for College and Career Success*. New York: Carnegie, 2010.

Carr, Nicholas. "Is Google Making Us Stupid? What the Internet Is Doing to Our Brains." *Atlantic* (July 1, 2008). http://www.theatlantic.com/magazine/archive/2008/07/is-google-making-us-stupid/306868.

———. *The Shallows: How the Internet Is Changing the Way We Think, Read, and Remember*. London: Atlantic Books, 2010.

Cervetti, Gina, Michael J. Pardales, and James S. Damico. "A Tale of Differences: Comparing the Traditions, Perspectives, and Educational Goals of Critical Reading and Critical Literacy." *Reading Online* (2001). http://www.readingonline.org/articles/cervetti/index.html.

Clark, Carlton. "The Mock Research Paper." *Teaching English in the Two-Year College* 36, no. 1 (2008): 47–49.

Collins, James, and Richard K. Blot. *Literacy and Literacies: Texts, Power, and Identity*. Cambridge, UK: Cambridge University Press, 2003.

Conference Board of Canada. "Employability Skills 2000+." http://www.conferenceboard.ca/topics/education/learning-tools/employability-skills.aspx.

Council for Undergraduate Research. http:// www.cur.org.

Cull, Barry. "Reading Revolutions: Online Digital Text and Implications for Reading in Academe." *First Monday* 16, no. 6 (2011). http://www.firstmonday.org.

Dai, David Yun, and Xiaolei Wang. "The Role of Need for Cognition and Reader Beliefs in Text Comprehension and Interest Development." *Contemporary Educational Psychology* 32 (2007): 332–347.

Day, Jennifer Cheeseman, and Eric C. Newburger. *The Big Payoff: Educational Attainment and Synthetic Estimates of Work-Life Earnings*. US Census Bureau, 2002. http://www.eric .ed.gov/PDFS/ED467533.pdf.

Dehaene, Stanislas. *Reading in the Brain: The Science and Evolution of a Human Invention*. New York: Viking, 2009.

Docker, John. "Are Settler-Colonies Inherently Genocidal? Re-reading Lemkin." In *Empire, Colony, Genocide: Conquest, Occupation, and Subaltern Resistance in World History*, edited by Dirk Moses, 81–101. New York: Berghahn Books, 2008.

Dozier, Cheryl, Peter Johnston, and Rebecca Rogers. *Critical Literacy/Critical Teaching: Tools for Preparing Responsive Teachers*. New York: Teachers College Press, 2006.

Emmons, Mark, Wanda Martin, Carroll Botts, and Cassandra Amundson. "Engaging Sources: Information Literacy and the Freshman Research Paper." *LOEX Quarterly* 36, no. 4 (2010): 8–9, 12; *LOEX Quarterly* 37, no. 2 (2010): 8–10.

Ferren, Ann, S. "Intentionality." In *General Education and Liberal Learning: Principles of Effective Practice*, edited by Paul L. Gaston, 25–32. Washington, DC: Association of American Colleges and Universities, 2010.

Finley, Ashley. *Making Progress? What We Know about the Achievement of Liberal Education Outcomes*. Washington, DC: AAC&U, 2012.

Fitzgerald, Jill, and Timothy Shanahan. "Reading and Writing Relations and Their Development." *Educational Psychologist* 35, no. 1 (2000): 39–50.

Freire, Paulo. *Teachers as Cultural Workers: Letters to Those Who Dare to Teach*. Translated by Donald Macedo, Dale Koike, and Alexandre Oliveira. Boulder, CO: Westview Press, 2005.

Fresch, Mary Jo, ed. *An Essential History of Current Reading Practices*. Newark, NJ: International Reading Association, 2008.

Furco, Andrew. "Service-Learning: A Balanced Approach to Experiential Education." In *Expanding Boundaries: Service and Learning*, 2–6. Washington, DC: Corporation for National Service, 1996.

Gale, Richard. "Points without Limits: Individual Inquiry, Collaborative Investigation, and Collective Scholarship." In *To Improve the Academy: Resources for Faculty, Instructional, and Organizational Development*, edited by Douglas Reimondo Robinson and Linda B. Nilson, 39–52. San Francisco: Jossey-Bass, 2008.

Garrison, Anthony, Dirk Remley, Patrick Thomas, and Emily Wierszewski. "Conventional Faces: Emoticons in Instant Messaging Discourse." *Computers and Composition* 28 (2011): 112–125.

Gee, James Paul. "Reflections on Reading Cope and Kalatzis' 'Multiliteracies': New Literacies, New Learning." *Pedagogies: An International Journal* 4 (2009): 196–204.

Genosko, Gary. "Hockey and Culture." In Birks et al., *Landmarks*, 231–243.

Gil, Laura, Ivar Bråten, Eduardo Vidal-Abarca, and Helge I. Strømsø. "Summary versus Argument Tasks When Working with Multiple Documents: Which Is Better for Whom?" *Contemporary Educational Psychology* 35, no. 3 (2010): 157–173.

Goldin, Claudia, and Lawrence F. Katz. *The Shaping of Higher Education: The Formative Years in the United States, 1890 to 1940*. Cambridge, MA: National Bureau of Economic Research, 1998.

Graff, Gerald, and Cathy Birkenstein. *They Say/I Say: The Moves That Matter in Academic Writing*. New York: Norton, 2006.

Graham, Steve, and Michael Hebert. *Writing to Read: Evidence for How Writing Can Improve Reading*. Washington, DC: Alliance for Excellent Education, 2010.

Grauerholz, Liz, and Eric Main. "Fallacies of SOTL: Rethinking How We Conduct Our Research." In *The Scholarship of Teaching and Learning in and across the Disciplines*, edited by Kathleen McKinney, 152–168. Bloomington: Indiana University Press, 2013.

Guillory, John. "How Scholars Read." *Association of the Departments of English Bulletin* 146 (2008): 8–17.

Haggis, Tamsin. "Constructing Images of Ourselves? A Critical Investigation into 'Approaches of Learning' Research in Higher Education." *British Educational Research Journal* 29, no. 1 (2003): 89–104.

Haley, Alex. "*Playboy* Interview: Malcolm X." The Malcolm X Project at Columbia University. May 6, 1963. http://www.columbia.edu/cu/ccbh/mxp/pdf/050063playboy.pdf.

Halivni, David Weiss. *The Book and the Sword: A Life of Learning in the Shadow of Destruction*. Boulder, CO: Westview Press, 1996.

Hanstedt, Paul. *General Education Essentials: A Guide for College Faculty*. San Francisco: Jossey-Bass, 2012.

Harkin, Patricia. "The Reception of Reader-Response Theory." *College Composition and Communication* 56, no. 3 (2005): 410–425.

Harris, Joseph. "Revision as a Critical Practice." *College English* 65, no. 6 (2003): 577–592.

———. *Rewriting: How to Do Things with Texts*. Logan: Utah State University Press, 2006.

———. *A Teaching Subject: Composition since 1966*. Logan: Utah State University Press, 2012.

Harrison, Colin. *Understanding Reading Development*. London: Sage, 2004.

Hart Research Associates. *It Takes More Than a Major: Employer Priorities for College Learning and Student Success*. Washington, DC: Hart Research Associates for AAC&U, 2013.

———. *Raising the Bar: Employers' Views on College Learning in the Wake of the Economic Downturn*. Washington, DC: AAC&U, 2010.

Head, Alison J., and Michael B. Eisenberg. "Assigning Inquiry: How Handouts for Research Assignments Guide Today's College Students." *Project Information Literacy Progress Report*. The Information School, University of Washington, July 12, 2010. http://project infolit.org/images/pdfs/pil_handout_study_finaljuly_2010.pdf.

Healey, Mick, and Alan Jenkins. *Developing Undergraduate Research and Inquiry*. York, UK: Higher Education Academy, 2009. www.heacademy.ac.uk/node/3146.

Henderson, Eric. *The Active Reader: Strategies for Academic Reading and Writing*. 2nd ed. Don Mills, ON: Oxford University Press, 2012.

Hoeft, Mary E. "Why University Students Don't Read: What Professors Can Do to Increase Compliance." *International Journal of Scholarship of Teaching and Learning* 6, no. 2 (2012). http://digitalcommons.georgiasouthern.edu/ij-sotl/vol6/iss2/12.

Hofer, Amy R., Lori Townsend, and Korey Brunetti. "Troublesome Concepts and Information Literacy: Investigating Threshold Concepts for IL Instruction." *Portal: Libraries and the Academy* 12, no. 4 (2012): 387–405.

Holland, Norman. *Five Readers Reading*. New Haven, CT: Yale University Press, 1975.

Hood, Carra Leah. "Ways of Research: The Status of the Traditional Research Paper Assignment in First-Year Writing/Composition Courses." *Composition Forum* 22 (2010). http://compositionforum.com/issue/22/ways-of-research.php.

Horning, Alice S. "Reading across the Curriculum as the Key to Student Success." *Across the Disciplines* 4 (May 14, 2007). http://wac.colostate.edu/atd/articles/horning2007.cfm.

Howard, Rebecca Moore. "A Plagiarism Pentimento." *Journal of Teaching Writing* 11, no. 2 (1993): 233–245.

———. "Why This Humanist Codes." *Research in the Teaching of English* 49, no. 1 (2014): 75–81.

Howard, Rebecca Moore, Tricia Serviss, and Tanya K. Rodrigue. "Writing from Sources, Writing from Sentences." *Writing and Pedagogy* 2 (2010): 177–192.

Huber, Mary Taylor, and Pat Hutchings. *The Advancement of Learning: Building the Teaching Commons*. San Francisco: Jossey-Bass, 2005.

Huffman, Debrah. "Towards Modes of Reading in Composition." *Reader: Essays in Reader-Oriented Theory, Criticism, and Pedagogy* 60 (2010): 162–188.

Hutchings, Pat. "Ethics and Aspiration in the Scholarship of Teaching and Learning." In *Ethics of Inquiry: Issues in the Scholarship of Teaching and Learning*, edited by Pat Hutchings, 1–17. Menlo Park, CA: Carnegie Foundation for the Advancement of Teaching, 2002.

———, ed. *Opening Lines: Approaches to the Scholarship of Teaching and Learning*. Menlo Park, CA: Carnegie Foundation for the Advancement of Teaching, 2000.

Hutchings, Pat, Mary Taylor Huber, and Anthony Ciccone. *The Scholarship of Teaching and Learning Reconsidered: Institutional Integration and Impact*. San Francisco: Jossey-Bass, 2011.

Institute of International Education. *Open Doors 2014 Report on International Educational Exchange*. Sewickley, PA: Institute of International Education Books, 2014. http://www.iie.org/Research-and-Publications/Open-Doors/Data/US-Study-Abroad.

Iser, Wolfgang. *The Act of Reading: A Theory of Aesthetic Response*. Baltimore: Johns Hopkins University Press, 1978.

Israel, Susan E., Cathy Collins Block, Kathryn L. Bauserman, and Kathryn Kinnucan-Welsch, eds. *Metacognition in Literacy Learning: Theory, Assessment, Instruction, and Professional Development*. Mahwah, NJ: Lawrence Erlbaum, 2005.

Jamieson, Sandra, and Rebecca Moore Howard. "Unraveling the Citation Trail." *Project Information Literacy Smart Talks*, no. 8, The Citation Project, 2011. Project Information Literacy. http://projectinfolit.org/smart-talks/item/110-sandra-jamieson-rebecca-moore-howard.

Joliffe, David A., and Allison Harl. "Studying the 'Reading Transition' from High School to College: What Our Students Are Reading and Why?" *College English* 70, no. 6 (2008): 599–617.

Kezar, Adrianna. "Redesigning for Collaboration within Higher Education Institutions: An Exploration into the Developmental Process." *Research in Higher Education* 46, no. 7 (2005): 831–860.

Kincheloe, Joe L. *Critical Pedagogy Primer*. 2nd ed. New York: Peter Lang, 2008.

King, Martin Luther, Jr. "Loving Your Enemies." Dexter Avenue Baptist Church, Montgomery, Alabama. November 17, 1957. http://www.mlkonline.net/enemies.html.

King, Patricia M., and Karen Strohm Kitchener. *Developing Reflective Judgment: Understanding and Promoting Intellectual Growth and Critical Thinking in Adolescents and Adults*. San Francisco: Jossey-Bass, 1994.

Kintsch, Walter. *Comprehension: A Paradigm for Cognition.* New York: Cambridge University Press, 1998.

Knefelkamp, L. Lee. Introduction to *Forms of Ethical and Intellectual Development in the College Years: A Scheme.* By William G. Perry Jr. San Francisco: Jossey-Bass, 1999.

Kuh, George G. *High-Impact Educational Practices: What They Are, Who Has Access to Them, and Why They Matter.* Washington, DC: AAC&U, 2008.

Lankshear, Colin, and Michele Knobel. *New Literacies: Changing Knowledge and Classroom Learning.* Maidenhead, Berkshire, UK: Open University Press, 2003.

Larson, Richard. "The 'Research Paper' in the Writing Course: A Non-Form of Writing." *College English* 44, no. 8 (1982): 811–816.

Lederach, John Paul. *The Moral Imagination: The Art and Soul of Building Peace.* New York: Oxford University Press, 2010.

Lei, Simon A., Kerry A. Bartlett, Suzanne E. Gorney, and Tamra R. Herschbach. "Resistance to Reading Compliance among College Students: Instructors' Perspectives." *College Student Journal* 44, no. 2 (2010): 219–229.

Leibowitz, Brenda, Clever Ndebele, and Christine Winberg. "'It's an Amazing Learning Curve to Be Part of a Project': Exploring Academic Identity in Collaborative Research." *Studies in Higher Education* 37, no. 7 (2014): 1,256–1,269.

Lewis, Stephen. "AIDS in Africa." In Birks et al., *Landmarks,* 302–314.

Linderholm, Tracy. "Reading with Purpose." *Journal of College Reading and Learning* 36 (2006): 70–80.

Linderholm, Tracy, and Adam Wilde. "College Students' Beliefs about Comprehension When Reading for Different Purposes." *Journal of College Reading and Learning* 40 (2010): 7–19.

Linkon, Sherry Lee. *Literary Learning: Teaching the English Major.* Bloomington: Indiana University Press, 2011.

Liu, Ziming. "Reading Behavior in the Digital Environment: Changes in Reading Behavior over the Past Ten Years." *Journal of Documentation* 61, no. 6 (2005): 700–712.

Luke, Allen. "Critical Literacy: Foundational Notes." *Theory into Practice* 51, no. 1 (2012): 4–11.

Lumina Foundation. *The Degree Qualifications Profile: Defining Degrees: A New Direction for American Higher Education to Be Tested and Developed in Partnership with Faculty, Students, Leaders, and Stakeholders.* Indianapolis: Lumina Foundation, 2011.

MacKenzie, Jane, and Renee A. Meyers. "International Collaboration in SoTL: Current Status and Future Direction." *International Journal of Scholarship of Teaching and Learning* 6, no. 1 (2012): Article 4.

Magolda, Marcia B. Baxter. *Knowing and Reasoning in College: Gender-Related Patterns in Students' Intellectual Development.* San Francisco: Jossey-Bass, 1992.

Manarin, Karen. "Reading Value: Student Choice in Reading Strategies." *Pedagogy: Critical Approaches to Teaching Literature, Language, Composition, and Culture* 12, no. 2 (2012): 281–297.

Mannion, Greg, Kate Miller, Ian Gibb, and Ronnie Goodman. "Reading, Writing, Resonating: Striking Chords across the Contexts of Students' Everyday and College Lives." *Pedagogy, Culture, and Society* 17, no. 3 (2009): 323–339.

Martin, Emily. "The Egg and the Sperm: How Science Has Constructed a Romance Based on Stereotypical Male-Female Roles." In Birks et al., *Landmarks,* 169–184.

Marton, Ference, and Roger Säljö. "Approaches to Learning." In *The Experience of Learning*, edited by Ference Marton, Dai Hounsell, and Noel Entwhistle, 36–55. Edinburgh, UK: Scottish Academic Press, 1984.

Maxwell, Martha. *The Dismal Status of Required Developmental Reading Programs: Roots, Causes and Solutions*. Educational Resource Education Center (ERIC), No. ED 415 501, 1997. http://files.eric.ed.gov/fulltext/ED415501.pdf.

McCormick, Kathleen. *The Culture of Reading and the Teaching of English*. Manchester, UK: Manchester University Press, 1994.

McWhorter, Kathleen. *Academic Reading: College Major and Career Applications*, 8th ed. New York: Pearson, 2014.

——. *Efficient and Flexible Reading*, 10th ed. New York: Pearson, 2014.

——. *Guide to College Reading*, 10th ed. New York: Pearson, 2015.

——. *Reading across the Disciplines*, 6th ed. New York: Pearson, 2015.

McWhorter, Kathleen, and Brette M. Sember. *Essential Reading Skills: Preparing for College Reading*, 4th ed. New York: Pearson, 2012.

McVee, Mary B., Kailonnie Dunsmore, and James R. Gavelek. "Schema Theory Revisited." *Review of Educational Research* 75 (2005): 531–566.

Menzies, Heather. "When Roots Grow Back into Earth." In Birks et al., *Landmarks*, 115–119.

Meslin, Dave. "The Antidote to Apathy." TEDxToronto, 2010. http://www.ted.com/talks/dave_meslin_the_antidote_to_apathy.html.

Murray, Sean. "Investigating College Campus Conflicts: Possibilities for Tapping into Genuine Student Interest." *Pedagogy: Critical Approaches to Teaching Literature, Language, Composition, and Culture* 12, no. 1 (2011): 161–167.

Myers, Kenneth A. "Cigarette Smoking: An Underused Tool in High-Performance Endurance Training." *Canadian Medical Association Journal* 182, no. 18 (2010): 867–869.

Namaste, Nina. Current Trends in Global Learning. Elon University Center for Engaged Learning. October 28, 2014. http://www.centerforengagedlearning.org/current-trends-in-global-learning.

National Endowment for the Arts. *To Read or Not to Read: A Question of National Consequence*. Washington, DC: National Endowment for the Arts, 2007.

National Task Force on Civic Learning and Democratic Engagement. *A Crucible Moment: College Learning and Democracy's Future*. Washington, DC: AAC&U, 2012.

Nussbaum, Martha C. *Creating Capabilities: The Human Development Approach*. Cambridge, MA: Harvard University Press, 2011.

——. *Cultivating Humanity: A Classical Defense of Reform in Liberal Education*. Cambridge, MA: Harvard University Press, 1997.

O'Brien, Timothy L. "Change in Academic Coauthorship, 1953–2003." *Science, Technology, and Human Values* 37 (2012): 210–234.

Pace, David, and Joan Middendorf, eds. *Decoding the Disciplines: Helping Students Learn Disciplinary Ways of Thinking*. New Directions for Teaching and Learning Series 98. San Francisco: Jossey-Bass, 2004.

Palmer, Parker J. *The Courage to Teach*. San Francisco: Jossey-Bass, 2007.

Palmer, Parker J., and Arthur Zajonc. *The Heart of Higher Education: A Call to Renewal*. San Francisco: Jossey-Bass, 2010.

Parrott, Heather Macpherson, and Elizabeth Cherry. "Using Structured Reading Groups to Facilitate Deep Learning." *Teaching Sociology* 39, no. 4 (2011): 354–370.

Patel, Eboo. *Acts of Faith: The Story of an American Muslim, the Struggle for the Soul of a Generation*. Boston: Beacon Press, 2007.

Paulson, Eric J., and Sonya L. Armstrong. "Postsecondary Literacy: Coherence in Theory, Terminology, and Teacher Preparation." *Journal of Developmental Education* 33, no. 3 (2010): 2–13.

Perfetti, Charles A. "Sentences, Individual Differences, and Multiple Texts: Three Issues in Text Comprehension." *Discourse Processes* 23, no. 3 (1997): 337–355.

Perry, William G., Jr. *Forms of Ethical and Intellectual Development in the College Years: A Scheme*. San Francisco: Jossey-Bass, 1999.

Popovic, Celia, and David A. Green. *Understanding Undergraduates: Challenging Our Preconceptions of Student Success*. New York: Routledge, 2012.

Pressley, Michael. "What Should Comprehension Instruction Be the Instruction Of?" In *Handbook of Reading Research*, vol. 3, edited by Michael L. Kamil, P. David Pearson, Elizabeth Birr Moje, and Peter P. Afflerbach, 545–561. Mahwah, NJ: Lawrence Erlbaum, 2000.

Qualley, Donna. "Disciplinary Ways of Teaching Reading in English." Introduction to special issue. *Reader: Essays in Reader-Oriented Theory, Criticism, and Pedagogy* 60 (Fall 2010): 4–18.

Research Skills Development Framework, University of Adelaide. www.adelaide.edu.au/rsd.

Rhodes, Terrel L., ed. *Assessing Outcomes and Improving Achievement: Tips and Tools for Using Rubrics*. Washington, DC: AAC&U, 2010.

———. Introduction to *General Education and Liberal Learning: Principles of Effective Practice*, edited by Paul L. Gaston, 1–6. Washington, DC: AAC&U, 2010.

Roberts, Judith C., and Keith A. Roberts. "Deep Reading, Cost/Benefit, and the Construction of Meaning: Enhancing Reading Comprehension and Deep Learning in Sociology Courses." *Teaching Sociology* 36, no. 2 (2008): 125–140.

Roberts, Peter. *Education, Literacy, and Humanization: Exploring the Work of Paulo Freire*. Westport, CT: Bergin and Garvey, 2000.

Roig, Miguel. "Plagiarism and Paraphrasing Criteria of College and University Professors." *Ethics and Behavior* 11, no. 3 (2001): 307–323.

Rosenblatt, Louise M. "The Aesthetic Transaction." *Journal of Aesthetic Education* 20, no. 4 (1986): 122–128.

———. *The Reader, the Text, the Poem: The Transactional Theory of the Literary Work*. Carbondale: Southern Illinois University Press, 1994.

Rudolph, Frederick. *Curriculum: A History of the American Undergraduate Course of Study since 1636*. San Francisco: Jossey-Bass, 1977.

Sachs, Jeffrey D. *Common Wealth: Economics for a Crowded Planet*. New York: Penguin Books, 2008.

Sadoski, Mark, Allan Paivio, and Ernest T. Goetz. "A Critique of Schema Theory in Reading and a Dual Coding Alternative." *Reading Research Quarterly* 26, no. 4 (1991): 463–484.

Salvatori, Mariolina Rizzi. "Difficulty: The Great Educational Divide." In *Opening Lines: Approaches to the Scholarship of Teaching and Learning*, edited by Pat Hutchings, 81–93. Menlo Park, CA: Carnegie Foundation for the Advancement of Teaching, 2000.

Salvatori, Mariolina Rizzi, and Patricia Donahue. *The Elements (and Pleasures) of Difficulty*. New York: Pearson, 2005.

———. "Tracing the Moves: How Students Read." *Reader: Essays in Reader-Oriented Theory, Criticism, and Pedagogy* 62 (2012): 80–88.

———. "What Is College English? Stories about Reading: Appearance, Disappearance, Morphing, and Revival." *College English* 75, no. 2 (2012): 199–217.

Samraj, Betty. "Discourse Features of the Student-Produced Academic Research Paper: Variations across Disciplinary Courses." *Journal of English for Academic Purposes* 3, no. 1 (2004): 5–22.

Sanoff, Alvin. "What Professors and Teachers Think: A Perception Gap over Students' Preparation." *Chronicle of Higher Education* 52, no. 27 (2006). http://chronicle.com/articl/A-Perception-Gap-Over/31426.

Sappington, John, Kimberly Kinsey, and Kirk Munsayac. "Two Studies of Reading Compliance among College Students." *Teaching of Psychology* 29, no. 4 (2002): 272–274.

Schneider, Carol Geary. "Losing Our Way on the Meanings of Student Success." *Liberal Education* 99, no. 2 (2013). https://www.aacu.org/publications-research/periodicals/losing-our-way-meanings-student-success.

Scholes, Robert. "The Transition to College Reading." *Pedagogy: Critical Approaches to Teaching Literature, Language, Composition, and Culture* 2, no. 2 (2002): 165–172.

Schraw, Gregory, and Roger Bruning. "How Implicit Models of Reading Affect Motivation to Read and Reading Engagement." *Scientific Studies of Reading* 3 (1999): 281–302.

Schwartz, Daniel L., Catherine C. Chase, and John D. Bransford. "Resisting Overzealous Transfer: Coordinating Previously Successful Routines with Needs for New Learning." *Educational Psychologist* 47, no. 3 (2012): 204–214.

Schwegler, Robert A., and Linda K. Shamoon. "The Aims and Process of the Research Paper." *College English* 44, no. 8 (1982): 817–824.

Scobey, David M. "A Copernican Moment: On the Revolutions in Higher Education." In *Transforming Undergraduate Education: Theory That Compels and Practices That Succeed,* edited by Donald W. Harward, 37–50. Lanham, MD: Rowman and Littlefield, 2012.

———. "Why Now? Because This Is the Copernican Moment." In *Civic Provocations,* edited by Donald W. Harward, 3–6. Washington, DC: Bringing Theory to Practice, 2012.

Shanahan, Timothy. "Reading-Writing Relationships, Thematic Units, Inquiry Learning . . . In Pursuit of Effective Integrated Literacy Instruction." *Reading Teacher* 51 (1997): 12–19.

Shoenberg, Robert. "Greater Expectations for Student Transfer: Seeking Intentionality and the Coherent Curriculum." In *General Education and Student Transfer: Fostering Intentionality and Coherence in State Systems,* edited by Robert Schoenberg, 1–23. Washington, DC: AAC&U, 2005.

Shor, Ira. *When Students Have Power: Negotiating Authority in a Critical Pedagogy.* Chicago: University of Chicago Press, 1996.

Shor, Ira, and Paulo Freire. *A Pedagogy for Liberation: Dialogues on Transforming Education.* South Hadley, MA: Bergin & Garvey, 1987.

Shulman, Lee S. "Professing the Liberal Arts." In *Teaching as Community Property: Essays on Higher Education,* edited by Pat Hutchings, 12–31. San Francisco: Jossey-Bass, 2004.

———. "Situated Studies in Teaching and Learning: The New Mainstream." Plenary address at the annual conference of the International Society for the Scholarship of Teaching and Learning. Raleigh, North Carolina, October 3, 2013. http://www.centerforengaged learning.org/situated-studies-of-teaching-and-learning-the-new-mainstream.

———. "Teaching as Community Property: Putting an End to Pedagogical Solitude." *Change* 25, no. 6 (1993): 6–7.

Small, Gary, and Gigi Vorgan. *iBrain: Surviving the Technological Alteration of the Modern Mind.* New York: Harper Collins, 2008.

Smith, Michael B., Rebecca S. Nowacek, and Jeffrey L. Bernstein. "Ending the Solitude of Citizenship Education." In *Citizenship across the Curriculum.* Edited by Michael B. Smith, Rebecca S. Nowacek, and Jeffrey L. Bernstein, 7–12. Bloomington: Indiana University Press, 2010.

Stevens, Lisa Patel, and Thomas W. Bean. *Critical Literacy: Context Research and Practice in the K–12 Classroom.* Thousand Oaks, CA: Sage, 2007.

Suskie, Linda. "Engaging Students in Demonstrating and Understanding Their Learning." Presentation, Mount Royal University, Calgary, AB, April 18, 2012.

Sweller, John. "Cognitive Load Theory, Learning Difficulty, and Instructional Design." *Learning and Instruction* 4, no. 4 (1994): 295–312.

Tierney, Robert J., and P. David Pearson. *Toward a Composing Model of Reading.* Reading Education Report No. 43. Center for the Study of Reading, University of Illinois Urbana-Champaign. August 1983, 1. https://www.ideals.illinois.edu/bitstream/handle/2142/17470/ctrstreadeducrepv01983i00043_opt.pdf?sequence=1.

Trites, Latricia, and Mary McGroarty. "Reading to Learn and Reading to Integrate: New Tasks for Reading Comprehension Tests?" *Language Testing* 22, no. 2 (2005): 174–210.

van den Broek, Paul, Robert F. Lorch Jr., Tracy Linderholm, and Mary Gustafson. "The Effects of Readers' Goals on Inference Generation and Memory for Texts." *Memory and Cognition* 29 (2001): 1,081–1,087.

van den Broek, Paul, David N. Rapp, and Panyiota Kendeou. "Integrating Memory-Based and Constructionist Processes in Accounts of Reading Comprehension." *Discourse Processes* 39 (2005): 299–316.

van Dijk, Teun A., and Walter Kintsch. *Strategies of Discourse Comprehension.* New York: Academic Press, 1983.

Walsh, Lorraine, and Peter Kahn. *Collaborative Working in Higher Education: The Social Academy.* New York: Routledge, 2010.

Wasser, Judith Davidson, and Liora Bresler. "Working in the Interpretive Zone: Conceptualizing Collaboration in Qualitative Research Teams." *Educational Researcher* 25 (1996): 5–15.

Waugh, Patricia, ed. *Literary Theory and Criticism: An Oxford Guide.* Oxford: Oxford University Press, 2006.

Webb, Graham. "Deconstructing Deep and Surface: Towards a Critique of Phenomenography." *Higher Education* 33 (1997): 195–212.

Weimer, Maryellen, ed. *11 Strategies for Getting Students to Read What's Assigned.* Faculty Focus Special Report. Madison, WI: Magna, 2010.

Weller, Saranne. "New Lecturers' Accounts of Reading Higher Education Research." *Studies in Continuing Education* 33, no. 1 (2011): 93–106.

Wiggins, Grant, and Jay McTighe. *Understanding by Design.* 2nd ed. Alexandria, VA: Association for Supervision and Curriculum Development, 2005.

Wilner, Arlene. "Asking for It: The Role of Assignment Design in Critical Literacy." *Reader: Essays in Reader-Oriented Theory, Criticism, and Pedagogy* 52 (2005): 56–90.

Wolf, Maryanne. *Proust and the Squid: The Story and Science of the Reading Brain.* New York: Harper Collins, 2007.

Yu, Wai-ming, Chun-kwok Lau, and John Chi-kin Lee. "Into Collaborative Research and Co-authorship: Experiences and Reflections." *Reflective Practice: International and Multidisciplinary Perspectives* 14 (2013): 31–42.

Zwaan, Rolf A., Joseph P. Magliano, and Arthur C. Graesser. "Dimensions of Situation Model Construction in Narrative Comprehension." *Journal of Experimental Psychology: Learning, Memory, and Cognition* 21, no. 2 (1995): 386–397.

# Index

Note: Page numbers in *italics* indicate charts and illustrations.

absence of social engagement: and generalization, 76; and lessons learned through research, 105; and structure of collaborative research, 25, 28; and study design, 13; taxonomy of non-engagement, 13, 70, 85, 105, *121*

"absence" scores: and Analysis of Knowledge, *68*; and assessment of student reading skills, *33, 36, 37,* 40, *41*; and Connections to Disciplines, *54*; and Connections to Experience, *69*; and genre recognition, *52*; hybrid rubrics for critical reading, 108–110, 111–114; and reading logs, 70; and structure of collaborative research, 25, 27–28

academic implications of reading declines, 1

academic prose, 48

academic purposes, critical reading for: and assessment of student reading skills, 43; and critical reading for social engagement, 65; and definition of critical reading, 4–7; described, 47–51; fostering, 63–64; hybrid rubric for, 107–110; key elements of, 66–67; and lessons learned through research, 87, 92, 96, 100, 104, 105; and reading logs, 51–54; and research papers, 55–63; and structure of collaborative research, xii–xiii, 24–25; and study design, 12–13; worksheets for, 115

academic purposes, reading for, xiii, 47

*Academic Reading* (McWhorter), 5

academic reading, 4–8, 12–13

academic services, 87

academic writing, 5–6, 42

*Academically Adrift* (Arum and Roksa), 1

accessibility services, 89

accountability, 90–92, *91,* 100

ACT exams, 16

*Act of Reading, The* (Iser), 3

*Active Reader, The* (Henderson), 48

*Acts of Faith* (Patel), 20

adjunct faculty, 100

Aesthetic Experience and Ideas (course), 20

aesthetic reading, 4

agency, 81–82

Ahmad, Arshad, vii

AIDS/HIV, 74–75

Albers, Cheryl, 15

Alberta, 16

allegory, 82

Allen, Ira James, 7

ambiguity, 34

American higher education, xii, 16

Amundson, Cassandra, 60

Analysis of Knowledge rubric, 25, 67–70, *68,* 111, 113, 116, 118

analysis skills: and accountability schemes, 91; and assessment of student reading skills, 30–32, 35, 37–39, *37*; and critical reading for academic purposes, 47; hybrid rubrics for critical reading, 107, 108; and reading for academic purpose, 66–67; and research papers, 58; and structure of collaborative research, 24; and study design, 12

analytic philosophy, 42

annotation, 90

arts and sciences requirements, 16

Arum, Richard, 1, 88

assessment schemes, 87, 90, 92

Association of American Colleges and Universities (AAC&U), xii, 6, 24, 141n30

Atwood, Margaret, 82
automaticity, 45
autonomy, 50

bachelor degrees, 16
Bartholomae, David, 5–6, 33
basic capabilities, 89
Bauerlein, Mark, 29
Bean, John, 48
Bean, Thomas W., 7
behaviors of reading, 2
Belenky, Daniel M., 45
"benchmark" proficiency: and Analysis of
    Knowledge, 68; and assessment of student
    reading skills, 31–32, 33, 36–37, 36, 37,
    39–40, 41, 44, 46; and Connections to Dis-
    ciplines, 54; and Connections to Experi-
    ence, 69; and critical reading for academic
    purposes, 51; and critical reading for social
    engagement, 67–69; and generalization,
    77; and genre recognition, 52; and hybrid
    rubrics for critical reading, 108–110,
    111–114; and identification with reading
    topics, 74–75; and lessons learned through
    research, 92; and reading comprehension,
    71; and reading logs, 54; and research
    papers, 62; and structure of collaborative
    research, 25, 27–28; and student perfor-
    mance levels, 47; and study design, 12
Bernstein, Jeffrey L., 85
bias, 73
bibliographies, 19, 22
biology classes, 92
Birkenstein, Cathy, 22
Bizzell, Patricia, 6
Bleich, David, 3
blogs, 61
Bok, Derek, 101–103
Botts, Carroll, 60
Bradley, Karen A., 27
Bråten, Ivar, 49–50
Braun, Karen Wilken, 91
Bresler, Liora, 26, 123
Brewer, Elizabeth, 98
Bringing Theory to Practice project, 65
Britt, M. Anne, 49

Brookfield, Stephen, 30, 42–43
Brost, Bryan D., 27, 71
Bruning, Roger, 31

Campus Compact, 65–66
Canadian Alliance for Community Service-
    Learning, 66
Canadian higher education, xii, 16
Canadian Institute of Health Research, 59
Canadian Medical Association Journal, 42
"capstone" proficiency: and Analysis of
    Knowledge, 68; and assessment of student
    reading skills, 32, 33, 36, 37, 41; and Con-
    nections to Disciplines, 54; and Con-
    nections to Experience, 69; and critical
    reading for academic purposes, 51; and
    critical reading for social engagement, 67;
    and genre recognition, 52; hybrid rubrics
    for critical reading, 108–110, 111–114; and
    structure of collaborative research, 25,
    27–28; and study design, 17
Carey, Miriam: and assessment of student
    reading skills, 44; background, 21; and
    collaborative scholarship, 124–125; contri-
    bution to research, vii; and genre recogni-
    tion, 53; and lessons learned through
    research, 93, 95, 97, 99
Carnegie Corporation, 10
Carr, Nicholas, 29, 40
Cervetti, Gina, 7
Chernobyl nuclear disaster, 78
Cherry, Elizabeth, 91, 92
Christian Church, 57–58
Chronic Cerebrospinal Venous Insufficiency
    (CCSVI), 58
Chronicle of Higher Education, 1
Ciccone, Anthony, viii
"Cigarette Smoking: An Underused Tool in
    High-Performance Endurance Training"
    (Myers), 41–42
Citation Project, 56
civic engagement: and advocacy for criti-
    cal reading, 100–101; and Analysis of
    Knowledge rubric, 67; and Communica-
    tions cluster, 22; and Community and
    Society cluster, 21; and critical reading for

social engagement, 83–84; and definition of critical reading, 4; and study design, 13. *See also* social engagement, critical reading for

civic implications of reading declines, 1

*Civic Provocations,* 65

civic responsibility, 68–69

class discussion, 33–34, 81, 88, 95

class size, 16

climate change, 81

close reading, 3

co-curricular activities, 98

cognition behaviors, 2, 30

cognitive demands of critical reading, 92

cognitive load theory, 74

cognitive processes, 45

cognitive psychology, xi

cognitive time, 2

collaborative scholarship: designing collaborative studies, 124–126; disseminating findings, 126–127; and fostering critical reading, ix; and lessons learned through research, 86–87, 123–124, 127; and structure of collaborative research, 23–28; and study design, 12

collective action, 86

colleges, 16

Collegiate Learning Assessment, 1

combined capabilities, 76, 89, 97

communal approach to critical reading, 103–104

Communication (thematic cluster), 17, 21–22

Communities and Societies (thematic cluster): and analysis criteria, 37; and background of researchers, viii, 11; and compliance with reading assignments, 71; and Connections to Disciplines, 54; and Connections to Experience, 68; and critical reading for academic purposes, 50; and critical reading for social engagement, 68, 81, 83; described, 20–21; and evaluation criteria, 41; and generalization, 77, 79; and genre recognition, 52; and identification with reading topics, 73–74; and interpretation criteria, 36; and reading logs, 51–53; and research papers, 57, 60–61; and structure

of collaborative research, 23; and study design, 17

community engagement, 77, 99. *See also* social engagement, critical reading for

community-based learning, 66

competition in class, 64

compliance with reading tasks, 13, 26–27, 65, 70–72, 85, 88, 91, *121*

composition studies, 3

composition theorists, 35

comprehension skills: and accountability schemes, 91; and assessment of student reading skills, 30, 39; criteria, 12, 24, 31–32; and critical reading described, 4–5; and critical reading for academic purposes, 47; and critical reading for social engagement, 71–72; decline in, 1; effect of writing on, 13; factors affecting, 10; hybrid rubrics for critical reading, 107, 108; and reading for academic purpose, 66–67; and research papers, 58; and writing about texts, 35

Conference Board of Canada, 8

connections to discipline skills: and critical reading for academic purposes, 48, 50–51; and definition of critical reading, 7; and hybrid rubrics for critical reading, 107, 110; and reading logs, 53; and research papers, 55; and rubric score worksheets, 115, 117; and structure of collaborative research, 25; student proficiency levels, *54*

Connections to Experience rubric, 25, 67, 69–70, *69*, 114, 116, 118

constructivist epistemologies, 73

Controversies in Science (course): and analysis criteria, 37; and Analysis of Knowledge, 68; and background of researchers, viii, 11; and Connections to Disciplines, *54*; and Connections to Experience, *69*; and critical reading for academic purposes, 50–53; and critical reading for social engagement, 68; and evaluation criteria, 40, 41–42, *41*; and generalization, 77; and genre recognition, *52*; and identification with reading topics, 73–74; and interpretation criteria, *36*; and lessons learned through research,

91; and Numeracy and Scientific Literacy cluster, 18; and research papers, 50, 57–60; and structure of collaborative research, 23, 27–28
Cooperative Institute Research Project, 66
core-distributional model, 17
Council for Undergraduate Research, 95, 96
Courage to Teach, The (Palmer), 98
Critical Literacy (Stevens and Bean), 7
Critical Pedagogy Primer (Kincheloe), 6
Critical Reading for Social Engagement rubric, 25, 67–68
critical theory, 42–43
Critical Writing and Reading (course): and analysis criteria, 37; and Analysis of Knowledge, 68; and assessment of student reading skills, 35; and background of researchers, 11; and Communication cluster, 22; and Connections to Disciplines, 54; and critical reading for academic purposes, 50; and critical reading for social engagement, 68, 82; and evaluation criteria, 41; and genre recognition, 52; and identification with reading topics, 73–75; and interpretation criteria, 36; and reading comprehension, 71; and reading logs, 51–52; and research papers, 57, 60; and structure of collaborative research, 23
Crucible Moment, A (National Task Force on Civic Learning and Democratic Engagement), 65
cultural codes of text, 48–49
cultural genocide, 79
cultural implications of reading declines, 1
Cultural Perspectives on Science (course), 20
cultural traditions, 19–20
Cunningham, Kiran, 98
curricula design, 14, 90, 138n47

Dai, David Yun, 31
Damico, James S., 7
data analysis, 27
"Decoding the Disciplines" movement, viii, 27, 29, 102–103
deductive methods, 42
deep reading, 3

deflection strategy, 42, 76, 78–80
Degree Qualifications Profile, 102
Dehaene, Stanislas, 2
descriptive summary, 57
developmental English classes, 11
disciplinary literacy, 27, 88, 99
distributive model of general education, 99
Docker, John, 79
documentation, 22
documents model, 49
Donahue, Patricia, 3, 5, 10, 33–35
Dozier, Cheryl, 6
Dumbest Generation, The (Bauerlein), 29
Dunsmore, Kailonnie, 30

economic implications of reading declines, 1
efferent reading, 4
Efficient and Flexible Reading, 5
Eisenberg, Michael B., 55
electronic interfaces, 29–30
Elements (and Pleasures) of Difficulty, The (Salvatori and Donahue), 5, 45
emergent literacy, 26, 29
Emmons, Mark, 60
emoticons, 38
emotional investment in topics, 34, 76, 96
emotionally charged readings, 23, 30, 79
empiricism, 7, 43
empowerment, 81–82
Encyclopedia Britannica, 57
English as a Foreign Language learners, xi
English composition, 21
enrollment trends, 101
environmental issues, 77–78
epistemology, 46, 49, 50, 73
Essential Learning Outcomes, 6, 101–102, 141n30
Essential Reading Skills (McWhorter and Sember), 5
ethical component of critical reading, 23, 103
evaluation skills: and accountability schemes, 91; and assessment of student reading skills, 30, 40–44, 41; and critical reading for academic purposes, 47; and hybrid rubrics for critical reading, 107, 109; and lessons learned through research, 88–89; and reading for academic purpose, 66–67;

and research assignments, 94–95; and structure of collaborative research, 25; and study design, 12

extensive reading, 4

extracurricular activities, 98

Facebook, 61–62

Fanghanel, Joelle, vii

fatalism, 79

feedback, 92, 94

Felton, Peter, vii

"Female Body, The" (Atwood), 82

Ferren, Ann S., 16

film subtitles, 23–24

First Nations people, 79

Fitzgerald, Jill, 93

foundational courses, 17

fragmentation of academic life, 98

Freire, Paulo: and compliance with reading assignments, 70; and critical reading for social engagement, 67, 76, 80–81, 82; and definition of critical reading, 7; and forms of critical reading, 65; and fostering critical reading, ix

Fukushima nuclear disaster, 78

Gadamer, Hans-Georg, 7

Gale, Richard, vii, viii, 124–125

Galen, Clemens van, 57

Gavelek, James R., 30

Gee, James Paul, 30

gender issues, 37, 61, 68–69

general education: and lessons learned through research, 99, 101; and scope of research, xii; and study design, 11–12, 16–18; and writing courses, 22

*General Education Essentials* (Hanstedt), 17

General Education Outcomes, 101

generalization and generalizability: and assessment of student reading skills, 37; and critical reading for social engagement, 70, 76–80, 81–82, 85; and identification with reading topics, 72; and research papers, 60, 62; and study design, 11, 13, 15; and taxonomy of non-engagement, *121*

genocide, 37–38, 79

Genosko, Gary, 43

genre recognition skills: and assessment of student reading skills, 31; and Community and Society cluster, 21; and critical reading for academic purposes, 48, 50–51, 64; and definition of critical reading, 7; and hybrid rubrics for critical reading, 107, 110; and reading logs, 51–53; and research papers, 55, 58; and structure of collaborative research, 25; student proficiency levels, 52; and study design, 12–13

Gibb, Ian, 11

Gil, Laura, 50

global aid, 81

globalization, 21

Goetz, Ernest T., 30

Goodman, Ronnie, 11

grades, 24, 75–76

Graff, Gerald, 22

Graham, Steve, 35

grammar, 22

Grauerholz, Liz, 15

Green, David A., 26

group discussion, 33–34, 81, 88, 91–93

*Guide to College Reading*, 5

Guillory, John, 4, 34

Haggis, Tamsin, 47

Halivni, David Weiss, 82

Hanstedt, Paul, 17

Harkin, Patricia, 3

Harris, Joseph, 5, 6

Harrison, Colin, 8–9

Harvard University, 102

Head, Alison J., 55

Healey, Mick, 95

*Heart of Higher Education, The* (Palmer), 104

Hebert, Michael, 35

Henderson, Eric, 48, 63

hermeneutics, 7

high school education, 16

Holland, Norman, 3

Hood, Carra Leah, 55

Horning, Alice, 9

Howard, Rebecca Moore, 56–57, 60, 62

Huber, Mary Taylor, viii, 124

Huffman, Deborah, 10, 48

humanities, 22

Hutchings, Pat, 11, 23, 90, 124
hybridized rubrics: and assessment of student reading skills, 32; and critical reading for academic purposes, 107–110; and critical reading for social engagement, 111–114; and reading logs, 52; and structure of collaborative research, 24–25, 28; and study design, 12–13, 16

*iBrain* (Small and Vorgan), 2
identification, 72–76, 85
identity, 49
illiteracy, 9
implicit model of reading, 12, 31–32, 47
implied reader, 3
Indiana University, 102
individual agency, 64
inference, 25, 87, 91
information literacy, 4, 94
information processing theories, 9–10
informed consent, 23
"inoculation approach" to general education, 16
institutional review boards, 23
instrumental reading, 7
integrative model of general education, 10, 17
intellectual engagement, 56, 103
intensive reading, 4
interdisciplinary approaches, xii, 21, 53–54
internal capabilities, 89
international experience, 97
International Society for the Scholarship of Teaching and Learning, vii
Internet, 2, 29, 61–62
interpretation skills: and accountability schemes, 91; and assessment of student reading skills, 30–32, 36, 37–39; and critical reading for academic purposes, 47, 66–67; and hybrid rubrics for critical reading, 107, 109; "interpretive zone," 26; and research papers, 58; and structure of collaborative research, 24; and study design, 12
inter-rater reliability issues, 12, 26
intertext model, 49
"Inventing the University" (Bartholomae), 5

"Is Google Making us Stupid?" (Carr), 40
Iser, Wolfgang, 3

Jamieson, Sandra, 56
Jenkins, Alan, 95
job placement, 102
Johnston, Peter, 6
journals, 27

Kahn, Peter, 26, 124, 125
keyword searches, 59–60
Kezar, Adriana, 125
Kincheloe, Joe, 6
King, Martin Luther, Jr., 41, 80, 81
King, Patricia M., 72
Kitchener, Karen Strohn, 72
Knefelkamp, Lee, 72
knowledge creation, 64, 95, 102–103

*Landmarks* anthology, 22
Larson, Richard, 55
learning disabilities, xi, 29
Lederach, John Paul, 20
Leibowitz, Brenda, 125
Lemkin, Raphael, 38, 79
Lewis, Stephen, 75
liberal-humanist tradition, xii, 7–8, 43
Linderholm, Tracy, 31, 45
linguistics, xi
Linkon, Sherry Lee, 56
literary studies, 3
Liu, Ziming, 3
Luke, Allan, 7–8
Lumina Foundation, 102

Machiavelli, Niccolò, 78
Mackenzie, Jane, 124
Magolda, Marcia B. Baxter, 31
Main, Eric, 15
Manarin, Karen: and assessment of student reading skills, 44; and collaborative scholarship, 124–125; and Communication cluster, 22; contribution to research, vii; and critical reading for social engagement, 82; and lessons learned through research, 91, 95, 99; and research paper assignments, 62–63

Mannion, Greg, 11
Martin, Emily, 35–36
Martin, Wanda, 60
Marton, Ference, 47, 90
mathematical skills, 18–19
McCormick, Kathleen, 3–4
McGroarty, Mary, 49
McVee, Mary B., 30
McWhorter, Kathleen, 5
memory, 2, 10
Menzies, Heather, 34, 71
meritocracy, 89
Meslin, Dave, 77
metacognitive processes, 45
metaphor, 82
Meyers, Renee, 124
"milestone" proficiency: and Analysis of Knowledge, *68*; and assessment of student reading skills, 32, *33, 36, 37, 41,* 44; and Connections to Disciplines, *54*; and Connections to Experience, *69*; and critical reading for social engagement, *67*; and genre recognition, *52*; and hybrid rubrics for critical reading, 108–110, 111–114; and lessons learned through research, 92; and research papers, 58, 63; and structure of collaborative research, 25, 27–28
Millennial generation, 76–77
Miller, Kate, 11
modeling, 63, 99
monastic model of higher education, 103
*Moral Imagination, The* (Lederach), 20
Mount Royal University, vii, xii, 16
multidisciplinary courses, 12, 53–54

National Endowment for the Arts, 1
*National Geographic,* 39
National Hockey League (NHL), 43
National Survey of Student Engagement, 66
National Task Force on Civic Learning and Democratic Engagement, 65
Ndebele, Clever, 125
neo-Marxist philosophy, xii, 8–9, 43
neuronal recycling, 2
New Critics, 3
New York Council on Advancing Adolescent Literacy, 10–11

Nokes-Malach, Timothy J., 45
nonfiction texts, 87
"Now What?" prompt: and assessment of student reading skills, 32, 35; and generalization, 76; and identification with reading topics, 72; and lessons learned through research, 86, 93; and reading logs, 50, 54; and study design, 12–13
Nowacek, Rebecca S., 85
nuclear power, 78
numeracy, 18–19
Numeracy and Scientific Literacy (thematic cluster), 17–19
Nussbaum, Martha, 76, 89, 97

oil sands development, 18, 39, 68, 76
online resources, 61

Paivio, Allan, 30
Palmer, Parker, 98, 103
paraphrases, 56, 60
Pardales, Michael J., 7
Parrott, Heather Macpherson, 91, 92
patchwriting, 56–57
Patel, Eboo, 20
Pearson, David, 93
*Pedagogy for Liberation, A* (Shor and Freire), 65
Perfetti, Charles A., 49
Perry, William G., 31, 50, 72, 73, 76
personal resonance with readings. *See* emotional investment in topics
Petrosky, Anthony, 5, 33
plagiarism, 56
planned working, 26
poetic language, 33
Popovic, Celia, 26
position papers, 22, 62, 91, 94–95
positions of deflection, 76
postsecondary education, 10–11, 16, 87
poverty, 81
pragmatism, 42
preconceptions, 59
print-related disabilities, 29
*Proust and the Squid* (Wolf), 29
psychoanalytical theory, 42
purpose of higher education, 101–102

qualitative analysis, 12, 25
quality of readings, 90
quizzes, 26, 88, 91
quotes, 60

Rathburn, Melanie: academic background, viii; and collaborative scholarship, 124–125; contribution to research, vii; lessons learned through research, 91–92, 94–95, 99; and Numeracy and Scientific Literacy cluster, 18–19; and research papers, 58–59
reader-response movements, 3
*Reading across the Disciplines,* 5
reading logs: and assessment of student reading skills, 32–35, 37–39; and compliance with reading assignments, 70–72; and Connections to Experience, 69; and critical reading for academic purposes, 50, 51–54, 55; and critical reading for social engagement, 68–69; and evaluation criteria, 40, 43–44; and generalization, 76; and identification with reading topics, 74–75; and research papers, 62; and rubric score worksheets, 115–118; and score variations, 138n44; and structure of collaborative research, 23–24, 26–28, 27–28; and study design, 12
reading proficiency declines, 1–2
reading skills, 44
reading to integrate, 49–50, 53, 55–56, 63
reading to learn, 49–50, 53, 55, 56, 63
Reading-to-Write (course), 3–4
"real" reading, 7
reflective papers, 84
relevance of readings, 77. *See also* emotional investment in topics
research assignments: and Communication cluster, 22; and Community and Society cluster, 21; and critical reading for academic purposes, 50; and lessons learned through research, 94–96, 100–101; and Numeracy and Scientific Literacy cluster, 19; and research paper worksheet, 119; and study design, 13
research design, 11–14
Research Skills Development Framework, 95
rewarding reading skills, 99

*Rewriting: How to Do Things with Texts* (Harris), 5, 45
rhetoric and rhetorical analysis, 22, 49
Rhodes, Terrel L., 16
rich description, 15, 33
Roberts, Judith C., 90
Roberts, Keith A., 90
Roberts, Peter, 8
Rodrigue, Tanya K., 57, 60
Rogers, Rebecca, 6
Roig, Miguel, 57
Roksa, Josipa, 1, 88
Rosenblatt, Louise, 4
Rwandan genocide, 57–58
Ryland, Glen, 125; academic background, viii; and assessment of student reading skills, 38; contribution to research, vii; and critical reading for social engagement, 82; and genre recognition, 53; and lessons learned through research, 92, 94, 96, 99; and Values, Beliefs, and Identities cluster, 20

Sachs, Jeffrey D., 74
Sadoski, Mark, 30
Säljö, Roger, 47, 91
Salvatori, Mariolina Rizzi, 3, 5, 10, 33–35, 82
Samraj, Betty, 50, 55
SAT exams, 4–5, 16
satire, 41–42
scaffolding: and assessment of student reading skills, 34; and critical reading for academic purposes, 50; and critical reading for social engagement, 81; and fostering critical reading, ix; and goals of ongoing research, 95; and interdisciplinary approaches, 99; and research on critical reading, 10; and transactional reading, 45
scanning, 3
schema theory, 9–10, 30
Schneider, Carol Geary, 102
scholarly articles, 19
Scholarship of Teaching and Learning (SoTL): contributions of, vii–ix; and ethical review process, 133n18; and lessons learned through research, 86, 90, 101, 123–125; and structure of collaborative research, xii–xiii,

11–13, 15, 23–28, 105; and synergistic effects of collaboration, 124

*Scholarship of Teaching and Learning Reconsidered, The* (Hutchings, Huber, and Ciccone), viii

Scholes, Robert, 3–4, 11

Schraw, Gregory, 31

Schwegler, Robert A., 55

Scientific and Mathematical Literacy for the Modern World (course), 18

scientific literacy, 18–19, 22

scientific research, 42, 58

Scobey, David M., 65–66, 100

self-reflection, 71

Sellers, R. Drew, 91

Sember, Brette M., 5

service-learning, 13, 55, 97. *See also* social engagement, critical reading for

Serviss, Tricia, 57, 60

sexism, 68–69

*Shallows, The* (Carr), 2, 29

Shamoon, Linda K., 55

Shanahan, Timothy, 93

Shoenberg, Robert, 17

Shor, Ira, 6, 65, 70, 76

Shulman, Lee, viii, 102, 124

situated cognition, 30

situation model of reading, 31, 49–50, 52–53, 55, 63

skepticism, 88

Smith, Michael B., 85

"So What?" prompt: and assessment of student reading skills, 32, 35; and critical reading for social engagement, 68; and identification with reading topics, 72; and lessons learned through research, 86, 93; and reading logs, 50, 54; and study design, 12–13

social capital, 83–84

social contract, 84

social Darwinism, 78

social engagement, critical reading for: and assessment of student reading skills, 42; and audience of research, xii–xiii; and Community and Society cluster, 21; and comprehension skills, 71–72; and definition of critical reading, 4; fostering, ix,

64, 80–85; and generalization, 78; hybrid rubric for, 111–114; and identification with reading topics, 74–75; and importance of critical reading, 9; and lessons learned through research, 96–99, 100–101; and reading logs, 27–28; and structure of collaborative research, 25, 27–28; and study design, 13; worksheets for, 116

sociology classes, 92

Sommer, Jodie, 49

source citations, 56

specialization, 100–101

standard of coherence, 35

statistical analysis, 58–59

STEM fields, 17

Stevens, Lisa Patel, 7

Strømsø, Helge I., 49–50

student debt, 102

Student Learning Services (Mount Royal University), 103–104

study abroad, 97

style, reading for, 75

summaries, 56, 90

Suskie, Linda, 84–85

synthesizing knowledge, 64

technology, 18, 68–69

text messaging, 29, 38

text model of rhetorical features, 49–50, 53, 63

Texts and Ideas—Genocide (course): and analysis criteria, 37; and Analysis of Knowledge, 68; and assessment of student reading skills, 37–41; and background of researchers, viii, 11; and Connections to Experience, 69; and critical reading for academic purposes, 50; and critical reading for social engagement, 67; and evaluation criteria, 41; and generalization, 78–79; and genre recognition, 52; and hybridized rubrics, 114; and interpretation criteria, 36; and reading logs, 53–54; and research papers, 51, 57–58, 60; and social engagement, 96; and structure of collaborative research, 23; and study participation rates, 137n40; and Values, Beliefs, and Identities cluster, 20

textual analysis, 94

*They Say/I Say* (Graff and Birkenstein), 22

Three Mile Island nuclear disaster, 78

Thucydides, 78

Tierney, Robert, 93

*Time to Act* (Council on Advancing Adolescent Literacy), 10

*To Read or Not to Read* (National Endowment for the Arts), 1

transactional model of reading: and accountability for readings, 90; and assessment of student reading skills, 31–32, 46; and critical reading, 45; described, 4; and evaluation criteria, 40; and identification with reading topics, 73; and lessons learned through research, 88, 99; and personal epistemology, 49–50; and study design, 12

transmission model of reading: and accountability for readings, 90; and assessment of student reading skills, 31–32, 34, 46; and importance of critical reading, 11; and lessons learned through research, 99; and study design, 12

Trites, Latricia, 49

true conversation, 7

types of reading, 30. *See also* academic purposes, critical reading for; social engagement, critical reading for

universities, 16

Valid Assessment of Learning in Undergraduate Education (VALUE) rubrics: and assessment of student reading skills, 32, 39–40; and critical reading for academic purposes, 48, 50; and critical reading for social engagement, 111–114; and definition of critical reading, 6; and generalization, 80; and hybridized rubrics, 107–110; information literacy rubric, 32; and lessons learned through research, 92, 105, 125; reading rubric, 30, 31–32; and structure of collaborative research, xii, 12, 24

Values, Beliefs, and Identities (thematic cluster), 17, 19–20

van den Broek, Paul, 35

Vida-Abarca, Eduardo, 50

vocabulary, 4–5

Walsh, Lorraine, 26, 124, 125

Wang, Xiaolei, 31

Wasser, Judith Davidson, 26, 123

*Ways of Reading* (Bartholomae), 5, 45

Webb, Graham, 47

website sources, 61

"What?" prompt: and assessment of student reading skills, 32–34, 38; and critical reading for social engagement, 68; and identification with reading topics, 72; and lessons learned through research, 86, 93; and reading logs, 50, 54; and study design, 12–13

Wilde, Adam, 45

Wilner, Arlene, 10

Winberg, Christine, 125

Wolf, Maryanne, 2, 29

worksheets, 91, 115–119

Writing about Images (course), 95–96

Writing for the Professions (course), 22

Writing in a Digital Context (course), 22

writing requirements, 13, 22, 35, 88

X, Malcolm, 41

DRS. KAREN MANARIN, MIRIAM CAREY, MELANIE RATHBURN, and GLEN RYLAND teach at Mount Royal University, a public undergraduate university in western Canada. Trained as a nineteenth-century British literature scholar, Manarin teaches English and general education courses. Carey, with a background in political science, teaches policy studies and general education; she has also worked as a faculty developer. As a behavioral ecologist, Rathburn teaches biology and general education courses. Ryland, a historian with a particular interest in genocide, teaches in general education, history, and undergraduate studies. All are interested in how their students read and learn.

CPSIA information can be obtained
at www.ICGtesting.com
Printed in the USA
BVOW03s1406300817
493519BV00004B/225/P